A NUMBER OF THINGS

Margaret Drake Elliott

# A NUMBER OF THINGS

by
Margaret Drake Elliott

Illustrations by Earl Wolf

The world is so full of a number of things, I'm sure we should all be as happy as kings.

Robert Louis Stevenson

ISBN: 0-9620788-0-8

©Margaret Drake Elliott 1984

Printed in U.S.A.

Dana Printing Corporation, Muskegon, Michigan

DEDICATED
TO
ALL THOSE WHO MADE
THIS BOOK POSSIBLE

# CONTENTS

# SUMMER

## June

# FOREWORD

## MARGARET DRAKE ELLIOTT (AG-KAA-NOO-MA-GAA-QUA)
"Friendly Teacher Lady"

How does one tell about the author of this collection of nature writings? To talk about them alone is barely to touch on the accomplishments and interests of a many-gifted woman — organizer and leader, teacher, writer, poet, herb-grower, and, above all, naturalist.

I've known Margaret since college days and through the years have again and again been surprised when some new facet of her many-talented life crops up. At Albion, where she doubtless was the youngest student in her class and from which she graduated as the outstanding senior woman, she was the born organizer and leader. But the trait which impressed me most in those early days was her ability to do two things at once. I remember, over and over again, a roomful of girls, giggling, chatting, minds on everything except the serious business of studies. Margaret would be holding her own in all the chit-chat, but simultaneously she would be studying her German, reading a Lit assignment, leafing a book, yet throwing out comments in the general gay play, while memorizing, drilling, growing on her own. She will have her lessons at class time, the rest of us will be unprepared. Where is that quote about Caesar being able to dictate to seven secretaries at once?

Another time when the dual activity of her mind impressed me was a 1940 week we spent together at an Easter vacation field course in Death Valley. I brought back the choice memory of two snow geese, on Easter Sunday, landing on the desert and gabbling their way on foot to the water hole. But Margaret also returned with her lovely poem, "Holy Week." Again, the page margins of my Western Flower Guide were annotated for the flowers we had identified with the help of our patient botanist guide, Emily Smith, of San Jose Teachers' College, but Margaret also returned with sixteen verses in "A Bouquet of Western Wild Flowers." (See her "Poppy Petals, Poems of Southern California," 1977.)

The organizer and leader: Is there any organization with which she has been associated that has not known her quiet leadership ability as president or working board member? She has been a member of the Board of Directors of the Muskegon County Museum since its inception in 1937. She has served as president of the Poetry Society of Michigan, of the Greater

Muskegon Women's Club, of the Muskegon Y.W.C.A., and of the Muskegon Branch of A.A.U.W. She has served on the State Board of the Federation of Garden Clubs and the Michigan Audubon Society. She was the organizer of the Muskegon Poetry Appreciation Group and a charter member of Writers, a Creative Writing Group meeting regularly since 1931. These are but a few of the organizations in which she has served in a leadership role.

Teacher: Margaret taught biology at Albion College from 1925 to 1927 and at Albion's summer campus at Bay View, Michigan, from 1927 to 1939. She was camp naturalist for Phil DeGraf's Trout Lake Resort for fourteen years from the 1930's to the Second World War. Although she retired as librarian at Muskegon High School in 1969, her teaching has continued through herb workshops, poetry workshops, writers' groups on various campuses and through numerous local groups. One would expect to find Margaret teaching in the field of natural science, after a Master's degree in Botany and Zoology. But the born teacher, which she is, can teach anything that needs to be taught. I'll never forget my utter surprise to learn, years ago, that she was teaching sewing up in the country somewhere as temporary substitute for the Home Economics teacher. Margaret, teaching sewing? I had never seen her sew anything in my life — oh, there'd been the crocheting of pot holders for the busy hands during a book discussion or poetry reading, but sewing! But it needed to be done, so she did it.

Writer: Margaret published her first poem at the age of 8 for the Sunshine Page of the *Detroit Free Press*. Since then she has authored more than 400 poems and verses in anthologies, newspapers and magazines, 36 juvenile stories, 3 children's plays, 2 pageants, and outdoor articles for 15 Michigan newspapers.

Herbalist: I think the herb interests began in the World War II years when I, who knew nothing about greenhouses, persuaded the Muskegon school board to repair the old greenhouse on the roof of Muskegon High School, so my biology classes could contribute to the war effort by starting home garden produce. Imagine, it meant replacing all of the broken glass and hauling soil by bucket and pulley up over the roof's edge. Laura Carpenter furnished the "know-how" and the pay-off came when a veteran of the Pacific theatre reminisced later how the thought of his greenhouse-started-tomatoes buoyed his spirits in a Pacific foxhole. Well, after school and on Saturdays Margaret and I grew herbs — her idea. Today I still use some herbs learned about in those early greenhouse days, but Margaret went on to become the herbalist — in poetry, (see her "A B C of Indian

Herbs," 1974) prose, lectures, workshops, college classes.

It's been a bit difficult running down the record of the many honors that have come in recognition of Margaret's talents and services to her community. I've had no help at all from her. Since I left Muskegon in the late 1940's my clipping service rendered by mutual friends has helped a little. I turned to the recent volumes of Michigan Poets and of Michigan Writers, but some of their notations call for interpretation which no one gives me. So I know I have omitted a number of honors which should have been included.

Perhaps her most cherished recognition came from the Ottawa and Chippewa tribes when in 1962 she was adopted and named Ag-Kaa-Noo-Ma-Gaa-Qua — Friendly Teacher Lady. Did she wear for the ceremony her white leather embroidered Indian dress with two braids over her shoulders, the costume for her lectures on Indian legends and Indian herbs?

In 1963 she was honored in Muskegon County as Career Woman of the Year. She is a member of the National League of American Pen Women. In 1979 the Michigan Audubon Society awarded her a plaque in recognition of her services to the Society and as a nature columnist. At some point there was an award from the Children's Reading Roundtable. In August of 1983 she was made an honorary member of Michigan Outdoor Writers. I know there have been other awards, but, I repeat, Margaret is reticent and my clipping service faulty.

But this is sufficient to show you Margaret Drake Elliott, the author of this book, as a versatile woman of many parts, whether she is identifying fungi for a group at an Audubon Campout, lecturing in Indian costume on American Indian herbs, answering a phone call on "what is the bird in my apple tree" from a faithful reader of her *Muskegon Chronicle* column, tapping out haiku at her desk, or teaching a Community Education class the origins of words.

In her 1974 book of poetry, "Phoenix Feathers" there is a favorite poem of mine, "Remember." It's been fun remembering back through the long years of our friendship. In those college days of the early 1920's when I didn't know a bluejay from a bluebird, she opened my eyes to the birds while giving credit to her high school biology teacher, Ella Clark, of Alma High School.

I remember she told me once her role models from those early days were three: John Burroughs, Gene Stratton Porter, and Luther Burbank. I recently found a 1940 postcard of Woodchuck Lodge, home of John Burroughs, tucked in a Burroughs book. Paul and Margaret were on a pilgrimage to the country of one of her mentors. A pilgrimage to find frui-tion, no doubt, in a Burroughs lecture. I remember hearing of trips to the Gene Stratton Porter Limberlost State Memorial at Geneva, Indiana. In Margaret's poem, "Lotus" ("Phoenix Feathers," 1974) you will find her tribute to that second mentor. I'm still looking for some written tribute to Luther Burbank. I remember, before the fire which destroyed her home, the shelf in her library which held a complete set of his writings. Treasured from high school days, were they the trigger of all of her nature-questioning in-terests? She doesn't say.

Anne Verne Fuller
Associate Professor Emerita of Biology
Western Michigan University
Kalamazoo, Michigan

# Winter

Winter, the great white bird
Swoops down from the frozen north
On hurried, rushing pinions;
Then soars as silently as death itself,
Showering frost flakes from feathery wings.
Glaring with sharp, cold eye
Searches choice prey.
Its call is crisp and brittle clear.
The song, a lovely, eerie thing.
Winter, the great white bird,
A migrant creature,
Is loathe to leave in spring.

1

# JANUARY

## PICTURESQUE MICHIGAN TREES

Whether one treks on skis or snowshoes, rides a snowmobile or just stays home and enjoys the winter wonderland through his picture window, trees are one of the picturesque aspects of a Michigan winter. Now that the Christmas trees have had their day, the bare, leafless "broad leaves" come into their own. These are days when trees stand out in all their starkness and shapely beauty.

Winter is the time to make friends with the trees and learn their names. Each kind has its own particular shape, branch and twig arrangement, winter buds, color and texture of bark and habitat.

Michigan was one of the early states to establish Arbor Day (later renamed Arbor and Bird Day). One of the Bicentennial projects of the Michigan Botanical Club, in conjunction with the American Forestry Association, was to search out and reevaluate the big trees in the state.

The results were most gratifying, in fact Michigan might very well be known as "The Big Tree State." State champions have been established for 174 different kinds and of these 90 are national champions. This gives Michigan the claim of the greatest number of winners, even surpassing Florida. During the project, 44 new or different national champions were defined.

The results show 11 species of oak, 11 willow, and seven maples in the top ranking. The formula for establishing a national champion is to take the girth at four and one half feet, the height, and one fourth the average crown spread. Only the girth is considered for a state champion.

The tallest tree measured is the champion tulip tree, almost 200 feet, in the Russ Forest of Cass County. The tree with the greatest girth is a white willow, west of Jackson, nine feet in diameter.

Muskegon has its own national champion tree, a witch hazel located in the Muskegon State Park. It was nominated by Paul W. Thompson, of the Cranbrook Institute of Science, chairman of the project. The tree measured out at 17 inches in girth, 43 feet in height, and had a 41 foot spread.

Many small tree species had been previously overlooked as potential "big trees," so the project is being continued. Any data on a potential "big tree" may be sent to the State Botanical Society.

## WHEN SNOW FLIES, BIRDS COME BEGGING

After an honest-to-goodness Michigan winter snowstorm, few persons wonder where their birds are since they show up at their favorite feeding stations for hand-outs.

All during December I had callers asking about the absence of birds at local feeding stations. Humans thought their bird friends had deserted them, but they had not. They are not the lazy little beggars some would say. So when natural foods are abundant and accessible, as they were all through the mild weeks of late November and December, the birds were foraging and finding plenty to eat.

The first storm sent them to their human friends with well-stocked tables and feeders. A glance at my own table Monday morning revealed more jays, juncos, sparrows, cardinals, doves and starlings than I had seen all month. The chicadees, titmice and goldfinches were also on hand for a quick lunch.

Even the downy woodpecker I had not seen for weeks remembered the suet bag and was at it. The little flock of eight evening grosbeaks that has been around apparently was gypsying elsewhere, for I did not see it.

This is the time of year when all serious birders start their "annual lists." Lists are a part of the fun of birding. January 1 sees the birder peering out his window trying his best to avoid seeing a house sparrow, a starling or a rock dove and hoping for something a bit different. Two members of the Muskegon County Nature Club came up with goldfinches at their thistle-feeders.

Very seldom does one in this area come up with an eagle on the first day of the year, but an immature bald eagle was sighted and reported in a tall tree on New Year's Day. There seemed to be some hindrance attached to its foot, possibly a chain, strap or cord. The obstruction did not prevent its flight, for after an audience gathered too sizable for its pleasure, it flew to Port Sherman and took a position at dusk in a tall tree overlooking the channel. It was seen in Pere Marquette Park and the dunes area for the better

4

part of the week and was also observed in Beachwood by several residents.

The sighting of this eagle at the year's beginning was important not only to bird-listers, but also was a good beginning for the Midwinter Eagle Survey which is sponsored by the Department of Natural Resources in cooperation with the National Wildlife Federation. Locally it is being assisted by the Muskegon County Nature Club, which headed it for the area last year. Last year's state survey recorded thirty bald eagles and two golden.

Two other projects local birders may cooperate with are the Great Lakes Beached Bird Survey and the Third Annual Michigan Bird Feeder Survey. The first is sponsored by Long Point Bird Observatory, Port Rowan, Ontario, with Anne Lambert in charge. The second is the effort of the Michigan Audubon Society and entry blanks may be obtained through the Muskegon County Nature Club at the County Museum.

One year the Beached Bird Survey, working with 58 volunteers, counted 85 species and 1,209 birds covering 1.3 percent of the Great Lakes shoreline. Two birds — a coot and herring gull — were noted by the birders on the Muskegon Christmas bird count last week.

## UPSIDE DOWN BIRDS

A low, emphatic nasal "nyank, nyank, nyank," is sure to announce the arrival of interesting bird guests at feeding stations. If one has been offering suet, meat scraps or nuts, sooner or later the reward will come in the form of a stocky, square-tailed little gray and white bird trimmed in black. If lucky, its cousin, the red-breast, will also visit.

These are the nuthatches, acrobats among the winter birds. Closely related to the titmice and chickadees, like them, they eat in any position and cling to the slightest pretense of a branch or perch.

They are bark-tenders, and their natural feeding ground is the trunk and larger branches of trees — "the bigger the better" seems to be their motto, for I recall a western cousin of these Michigan species scurrying about the huge bole of a giant sequoia.

In the cracks and crevices of these bark tables they find their favorite foods, spiders, eggs and larvae of moths, beetles, and other harmful insects. Some of the food of these birds is vegetable, and their fondness for nuts gives them their name. Perhaps the reason they are called "nuthatch" is the manner in which they insert nuts in cracks and hatchet away at them

5

to get their tasty contents. As for all insect-eating birds, the best food substitute is suet, so generous supplies of this animal fat are sure to attract nuthatches if there are any in the vicinity.

Commonly known as the "upside down bird" because they are usually seen on the tree trunk with the head downward these birds are abundant throughout Muskegon and western Michigan in winter. They sometimes become very tame at feeding stations allowing their pictures to be snapped even on the hand of a human friend.

The most common of the species here is the white-breasted nuthatch, some of which remain the year around building their nests of leaves, with linings of feathers or hair, in cavities of hollow limbs and trunks at varying distances from the ground. The eggs, in clutches, are from five to eight, although the more usual number here is six. They are attractive with a white-pink ground color with reddish brown and lavender.

Gay, sociable and comic, the nuthatches are frequently seen in company with bands of chickadees and with woodpeckers at times. They seem to enjoy the companionship of these other birds.

Few bird guests are more welcomed at winter feeding stations than the jolly nuthatch. These birds pay well in entertainment and amusement for the food they receive. More practically they also bring returns to the garden by devouring large numbers of insect larvae and eggs which they find hidden away in the cracks and crevices of the tree bark.

With increasing snow and ice and with insect food becoming difficult to find, nuthatches will be more and more attracted to feeding stations and will be continually dependent upon human friends for aid.

## STARLINGS AT STATIONS

In company with the house sparrow, another European alien is patronizing the feeding stations of bird lovers in and about Muskegon. These are the starlings. It is only within the last three decades that these birds have become conspicuous here, and a real part of the county's avifauna.

Christmas bird counts show a steady increase in this bird's number until during the last few seasons it is second to the house sparrows in abundance among land birds recorded. Time was when the starling was unknown in the middle-west and one who was curious to see it had to go to a zoo to become acquainted.

The introduction of the starling into the United States dates to attempts before 1890, but in that year 80 of these birds were liberated in Central Park, New York City. This attempt proved partially successful and so, on the following March, 1891, 80 more were brought. By the beginning of the present century these birds were well established in the region of New York and during the ensuing decades they have spread rapidly until now they are generally distributed as far westward as the Mississippi and are being reported in the western states.

Like the other foreigner, the house sparrow, the starling is a species successful in adapting itself to changing conditions, and eating a variety of foods, thus being able to subsist where many native species would die out. Also, like the sparrow, starlings prefer villages and cities, the urban life, instead of that of the country.

The starling is sometimes mistaken for the grackle or the blackbird, but can be distinguished from these by its light colored beak, its stocky shape and its short tail. The plumage of the starling differs throughout the year, and for this reason some people do not recognize them in the late fall and early winter. During most of the year they are dark with a distinctly iridescent sheen of purple, green and blue. Then in the late fall and early winter they appear highly spotted with light colors, cream, buff and almost white. Careful attention will show that these border the feathers, and that as the season progresses these spots disappear as the result of feather wear, and that then they again appear in the all-over dark suit.

Just now birds in both these plumages may be seen feeding at the same stations.

Now, in winter, starlings rove about in bands from place to place in search of food. They are gregarious and lead a gypsy sort of life during the winter months. They follow this vagrant life for several months, visiting station after station, sometimes making the complete round only a few times during the season.

In their native home in continental Europe this species is migratory, wintering in the southern regions or crossing the Mediterranean Sea to northern Africa.

Judging by the depredations committed by the English sparrows, it is not surprising that with the increase in starling numbers, some people have become alarmed, fearing these birds, too, would become pests. Their chief misdemeanor is the taking over of nesting places previously used by native songsters. They appropriate holes used by bluebirds, and make it necessary for these birds and others such as tree swallows to look elsewhere for nesting sites. They also compete, of course, with the native birds for food. But this is not as serious a charge, for much of their diet is insectivorous and there are plenty of insects to go around.

Since a bird's status is determined chiefly by its feeding habits, a careful study has been made of the starling and we are told that 57 percent of its food is of animal origin, chiefly insects, millipedes, crustacea, mollusks, suet and carrion. According to a report of the Department of Agriculture, "no bird in this country eats more millipedes."

In Europe it is considered a useful bird and starling houses to attract it to yards and gardens are seen everywhere. It was its record as an insect eater that prompted its introduction into this country. Like the sparrow, it has succeeded too well at the expense of some of the more beloved native species. Control measures for it are difficult to recommend. What is successful in one vicinity does not work in another. Fortunately, when spring comes, the large gypsying flocks pair off and separate for the nesting season. Martin houses are then often overrun with them.

SNOW CRYSTALS

Snow is one of the great marvels of the natural world.

Millions of persons now living on the earth have never seen it. (You wish you were one of them?) Many others, who see it as banks of "cold, white stuff" to be shoveled many days during the winter months have never really "seen" it. Until one looks carefully and appreciatively at the individual crystals which compose the mass of snow, one has looked, but never seen.

Even the formation of snow crystals is one of the "minor miracles" achieved by nature. Seldom is there a change in substances from the gaseous to the solid form, but that is exactly how the snow crystal is born. It skips the usual intermediate stage of a liquid. Probably electricity also has a part in the production of snow, for there are charges on the "crystals," and also there are electrical changes from minute to minute in the air during a snowstorm.

Individual crystals are of multitudinous sizes and shapes. It has been said that no two of the billions that fall are identical. There are certain types which can be classified, and identifying these during a storm helps to make the study of snow in winter one of the fascinating outdoor activities of naturalists and hikers.

Snow crystals are built on the hexagonal, six-sided plan, although in some it may be slightly obscure. The plates are hexagonal and thin, solid or partly snow crystals. Their sizes range from 8/1000 to 3/16 of an inch.

The stellar crystals or "stars" represent only a small proportion of all the snow that falls, although they have become the symbol of the snow and winter. Among the snow crystals these show the widest range of form, from simple knife blade rays through feathery forms to branching ferns. In size these range from 1/32 to 1/2 inch in diameter.

The very smallest of these produce a fall which is called "diamond dust" by meteorologists.

When snow crystals clump together as they often do in feathery or cottony-appearing bundles, they are properly known as "snow-flakes" in contrast to the individual crystals which compose them. Although seldom more than 2 inches across, these snowflakes occasionally reach a 4 inch size.

Frequently the two types — plates and stars — unite to give the most beautiful of all snow crystals: a hexagonal plate from which develop decorative plumes or dendrites, giving the familiar delicate aspect.

The true dendritic (branching) type is close to the stellar form and has numerous small crystals along the six rays. A variation of this, which causes some confusion in identifying snow crystals, is the spatial dendrite. These, too, are of several forms with portions extending out in a three dimensional manner from the center, as rays. These are not common here but one of the great students of snow, Ukichiro Nakaya of Japan found that the storms on Mt. Tokachi and Mt. Asari, were made up largely of spatial dendrites.

The columnar crystals are six-sided prisms that are usually transparent. Commonly flat on the ends, one end may be pointed. They are most often small, 1/64 to 1/8 of an inch, and sometimes include air pockets. High, translucent clouds of these columnar crystals produce the beautiful rainbow halos often seen about the sun and moon.

Among the common crystals are the ice needles. Snowfalls which cover the ground with several inches of whiteness usually consist largely of this type. The individual crystals are slender six-sided rods, pointed at both ends with sharp, jagged tips.

Capped columns or "collar-button" is another type of ice crystal. These are a combination of columnar platal, and stellar or dendritic, appearing as a rod terminating in plates, stars or dendritic forms. Sometimes midway between the ends around the rod will be another plate, star, etc. These are rare and are given many descriptive names, one of the best being that of

Dr. Nakaya who calls them "tsuzumi" referring to the Japanese tom-tom of the same shape.

In addition to these symmetrical crystals which have been outlined: the plates, stars, branching, columns, needles and collar-buttons, there are asymmetrical ones. They look like a formless bit of snow powder. Sometimes these clump together as snowflakes, and as such they often form rime, a pearly coating on trees, buildings, and other objects.

Snow pellets, formed by crystals falling from a high cold cloud through a warmer cloud beneath on their way to earth take on an overcoat of frozen cloud droplets and appear like miniature snow-balls. This is graupel and is often mistaken for sleet, which is not a form of snow.

These various crystals of snow have offered a challenge to photographers for many years. Since William Scoresby pictured some in 1820, many scientists and cameramen have seen the beauty and intricacy of snow crystals, and reproduced them for others to enjoy. Wilson Bentley of Jericho, Vermont, was one of the pioneers in this field. He has been said to have photographed more than 6,000 different kinds of crystals from nature. Very specialized methods are used, including a "cold box."

Other students of snow have been challenged by the problem of producing snow crystals artificially in the laboratory. This was achieved by Vincent Schaefer in 1946. (Perhaps, some of you are wondering why anyone would want to "make snow.")

More recently it has been discovered that snow storms can be produced by seeding the sky and clouds with dry ice.

It is amazing how these minute delicate crystals can build up the tremendous banks and drifts which clog roads and highways, so that traffic is impeded and transportation is tied up. Communities are isolated and suffering and inconvenience are caused.

The blessings of snow are hard to remember when one is stuck in a drift or shoveling one's way out of the parking lot. Yet, we know that they are many, and that much of the rebirth of spring depends on the snow's soft blanket. Cold as it is, it forms a soft, comfortable shelter for many little creatures, both plants and animals, snuggling and crouching under it. It is to the earth what our wool blankets are to our beds in winter; it insulates the earth. The moisture it provides also is a part of the general fertility of the soil in the temperate zone.

Whether we like it or not — it's here — so why not enjoy it? There is much beauty in it.

# GULLS

Sea gull is the name usually applied to the familiar habitué of Michigan's harbors. Few realize there are several different kinds of gulls, and at present Muskegon lakes are hosts to at least three species, herring, ring-billed and Bonaparte's.

Largest and most common in Michigan waters is the herring gull, a well known year-round resident of Muskegon. These are the gulls about the docks and piers, and known to follow boats for great distances to feast upon garbage. These are the ones, well known to Muskegon bird lovers, which become so tame in winter that they visit regularly the feeding stations of friends, and even catch food tossed to them. These birds are present in Muskegon all year, but the individuals of the gull population vary with the season.

At present, the herring gull population is made up largely of young birds, this season's hatch, and birds which were hatched last year and have not yet reached breeding maturity. Later in the season, great flocks of old birds will arrive, bringing the winter gull population of Muskegon to well over 2,000 individual birds.

The juvenile birds, unlike their parents, are decidedly brownish and are frequently mistaken for birds of another species. Herring gulls are the largest of the common Michigan gulls and are approximately two feet in length. The bill of the mature gull aids in distinguishing it from other species because it is yellow with a red spot at the angle.

Next, in both size and numbers in the present gull population of Muskegon is the less known ring-billed gull. The mature birds of this kind often are confused with the larger herring gulls, but the conspicuous broad band of black encircling the bill will aid in distinguishing them. The immature of this species are noticed because of the dark wing tips and the striking black band on the tail just above the light white tip.

A common sight these days about the fishing holes is a flock of gulls fluttering and squawking excitedly as the fishermen make their hauls through the ice. One man had his catch neatly piled a short distance from the hole when he heard a rush of wings and looking around saw the tail of one of his fish disappearing down a gull's throat. This wasn't the first one; the gull had lunched on six already and the fisherman had to start his count all over. Gulls are frequenters of many of the shanties and there's keen competition in this ice fishing business.

The third, the Bonaparte's gull, is easily distinguishable from the other two more common species by its small size and tern-like actions. In flight there is a noticeable white triangle at the wing tip.

In summer, the conspicuous black head, red legs and black beak separate it from the others. In winter, a black spot behind the eye and the black bill are good marks. Immatures are less easy to recognize.

These small dainty gulls are most often seen here during their spring and fall migrations between breeding grounds in the Arctic and Canada and wintering places on the eastern Great Lakes, the Atlantic and Gulf Coasts.

Years ago it was an exciting time when "Bonaparte's Birds" arrived here in April. Their favorite spot was Muskegon Lake at Edgewater, and they came in flocks of 1500 to 2000, spending a fortnight or so here. Mealtime was noisy and the competition among so many birds kept the water stirred up like a whirlpool and was most riotous.

The gulls arrived again as winter neared, but they came in smaller flocks with little of the spring excitement. In recent years they are not seen in such numbers at Edgewater, but are reported semiannually at the Wastewater System.

There are five other gulls which are less frequently seen here but are listed by the Michigan Audubon Society. One should be on the lookout for them — the glaucous, Iceland, great black-backed, Franklin's and the little gull. Strays or accidentals of other species occasionally may be seen here. Never assume all gulls in a flock are one species. Many rare ones have been overlooked.

CEDAR WAXWING GUESTS

The bird population of Muskegon has been augmented this month by large numbers of cedar waxwings, appearing in various sized flocks of from four to four dozen individuals.

These birds are abundant in summer and are among the familiar sights of July when they are nesting. Although considered a permanent resident in much of Michigan, they are less frequent during the winter months. In the fall, southward movement takes many individuals out of the state, but some either remain in their summer haunts or their places are taken by the arrival of other birds of the same species from a more northern region. As banding is continued and more results are obtained, greater information on the exact movement and whereabouts of these birds will be available.

Summer or winter, the cedar waxwing is among Michigan's beloved birds.

Much persecuted in past years and sought for the ornamentation of women's millinery decades ago, these beautiful birds were known as the common "hat bird" of the period. According to the late Dr. W. B. Barrows in "Michigan Birds," "their convenient size, beautiful plumage and gregarious habits, permitting many to be killed at a single shot, all favor their use in this way." Protective laws have checked this practice.

The cedar waxwing, easily identified by the soft grayish brown coloring, the yellow tinted underparts, the golden banded tail and the expressive crest, has been reported from North Muskegon, Muskegon Heights and Lakeside.

Although commonly known in summer as the cherry bird because of the habit of devouring this fruit, in winter the species is better known by the name cedar waxwing, for now they feed largely upon the fruits of the junipers or cedars. Another favorite winter food is the fruit of the mountain ash.

The name "waxwing" comes from tips of the wing feathers which appear ornamented with drops of sealing wax.

Occasionally, western Michigan is invaded in winter by a larger related species of this bird, the Bohemian waxwing. As with the evening grosbeaks with whom they sometimes associate, these birds are known as "erratic winter visitors" and are only seen in this part of the state during severe winter weather or when storms have endangered their food supply farther north. They are easily distinguished from the cedar species by the larger size, decided white and yellow patch on the wings, chestnut under the tail coverts and all-over grayish appearance, as contrasted to brownish in the others.

The cedar waxwings are quiet, refined birds making their presence known by a sibilant lisp or whisper. Because of the quiet, friendly manner of this bird and its modest coloring, it is known locally by the name of Quaker-bird.

The cedar bird is of great value to the farmer and horticulturists, for it destroys great numbers of insects in various forms at all seasons, and devours many kinds of injurious caterpillars in the spring and summer.

Devoted to its favorite, the cedar tree, the waxwing builds its nest in this frequently, but also in orchard trees and in other evergreens.

Winter foods which attract the cedar waxwing to feeding stations are corn, sunflower seeds, sumac berries, suet, bread crumbs, hemp and chicken scratch feed.

## APPRECIATION TIME

Following the spring weather and January thaw last weekend, the winter that since has settled in means hard going for the birds, especially the little fellows that scour their living from the ground.

Game birds, grouse, quail and pheasant, were at a grave disadvantage when drifting snow and ice covered their food supply.

Friends of the birds should be loyal these days and not begrudge them a few table scraps and crumbs. Many people are now providing special diets for the birds, catering to the individual tastes of the common winter species.

Scratch feed, such as is fed to chickens, will attract a variety of the seed eating birds, including juncos, several species of sparrows, goldfinches, redpolls, buntings, jays and any stray robins that may be wintering nearby.

For the insect eaters, meat scraps, suet and nuts are delectable. Chickadees, titmice, downy and hairy woodpeckers, the red and white nuthatches, and occasionally brown creepers are on the lookout for stations offering these.

Some specialized feeders such as the grosbeaks, pine and evening, seek out box elder trees where they feast for hours at a time on the seeds inside the small winged fruits. Year after year these birds will return to the same tree. Purple finches and cedar waxwings are lovers of the wild fruits and berries and congregate where the dried, persistent fruit of shrubs, hedges and trees offer them a winter menu.

More than thirty species of birds have been attracted to winter feeding stations in the Muskegon area.

All manner of food is provided for them, from stale doughnuts tied to discarded Christmas trees for the chickadees, who perform on them like acrobats, to cracked corn for cardinals, sunflower seeds for goldfinches, and nut shells for the nuthatches to chisel out pieces of kernel which were too difficult for ordinary man-made nut picks.

Spring and summer the birds are busy caring for yards and gardens and ridding them of harmful insect and weed pests. During the winter months humans have a chance in a small way to show their appreciation to these feathered benefactors for the incessant watchfulness they offer green growing things the other nine months of the year.

Besides, they reward with gay wings at windows during shut-in days.

Bird guests at Muskegon area feeding stations seen during January included:

House (or English) sparrow, tree sparrow, goldfinch, junco, red-breasted nuthatch, downy woodpecker, cardinal, herring gull, red-bellied woodpecker, cedar waxwing, snow bunting, grouse, crow, red-headed woodpecker, song sparrow, starling, blue jay, purple finch, brown creeper, white-breasted nuthatch, hairy woodpecker, robin, tufted titmouse, chickadee, redpoll, pheasant, quail, flicker, grackle, and screech owl.

## THINK SPRING

With seed and nursery catalogs coming in like a mid-winter blizzard, now is the time to enjoy the rainbow of colors and think "spring."

Spring means birds and the return of the summer residents for many of us. Numbers of these returning birds can be enticed to remain close to human habitations and be a real help in freeing the yard and garden of injurious insects and weed seeds.

The secret to keeping them nearby is to offer plants that they like. In choosing from the newly arrived catalogs plan to add some trees or shrubs to the garden design that includes bird preferences.

Fortunately some of the bird-attracting trees and shrubs are among those with outstanding flowers and colorful fruit, so they are eye-catching for the gardener as well as the birds.

Three trees that are good to begin with are mountain ash, flowering dogwood and cedar or a related evergreen. The ash will invite a great variety of birds, but the robin, other thrushes, cedar waxwings and evening grosbeaks are partial to it. Dogwood berries are so attractive to many of the late summer and early autumn birds, that the gardener hardly has a chance to see them himself. The birds snap them up quickly and finish off a good-sized tree in a few hours. The evergreen cedar is especially attractive to waxwings and often the rare Bohemian is seen in this, feeding with its cousin, the better-known cedar waxwing.

Catbirds, brown thrashers, the thrushes, orioles, cardinals, finches, blackbirds, and even woodpeckers eat berries and other small fruits during summer months and early fall. In addition to fresh fruit and seeds it is important to provide shelter and nesting sites for birds in the garden during the summer. A variety of shrubs and evergreens lend themselves well to this. The seeds of evergreens provide food for the seed-eaters, such as crossbills, siskins, purple and other finches.

Among the useful plants for birds are blackberries, raspberries, dewberries, all the wild cherries, wild grapes, mulberries, viburnums, especially high bush cranberry, wild raisin and sandcherry.

A great favorite among a large number of birds is the hawthorn or thornapple and there are many attractive varieties of these that will enhance the decorative scheme of any yard or garden. They have a long season of beauty while in flower and later in fruit. Autumn olive is very popular.

Gardeners who grow raspberries for their own use will find it helpful to plant mulberries and other wild fruits that mature at the same time as the cultivars nearby, perhaps encircling the berry patch. The birds have a preference for the natural foods, and if there are enough, presumably leave the cultivated ones alone.

Oaks and maples, in their many species, are attractive to birds and provide both food and shelter for them. The box elder of the maple clan is inviting to evening grosbeaks, and they frequently gypsy from one to another throughout a suburb cracking the seeds with their large bills.

Bush plants or shrubs are another source of bird food. Blueberries, pokeberry, trumpet and bush honeysuckle, firethorn, inkberry, hollies, and sumacs, all have their special guests. It is well to plant a variety of these that will fruit at different times so there will be a continual food supply from summer through fall.

Nut bearing trees are important as wildlife food. In addition to the oaks, beeches, walnuts and hazels are recommended. Birches, elms, and alders offer their own type of food and the "little birds" are fond of these.

A favorite in this area is the shadbush, juneberry or serviceberry which ripens early and attracts more than a score of species, when they are "fruit-hungry."

Vines also add to the interest of the yard and garden and birds like them. They provide good nesting sites as well as food. Virginia creeper or five-leafed ivy is especially satisfactory.

In recent years nothing has proved more useful in a bird garden than multiflora roses, and few plants add greater beauty to the garden edge than these, both in flower and fruit. It is a "must" for many birds.

Hummingbirds like red tubular flowers, so the trumpet vine invites them. Even the annuals and perennials in the flower garden can be bird oriented. The "little birds," finches and their friends, are partial to the composite

16

or daisy family so they welcome any of these flowers. They especially delight in China asters, bachelor buttons or cornflowers, black-eyed susans, cosmos, chrysanthemums, marigolds, sunflowers, sweet williams and zinnias. Hummingbirds also like petunias, columbines, salvia, snapdragons, and vervain.

Ground covers which birds like are bunchberry, partridgeberry, bearberry and wintergreen.

Some gardeners have successfully grown bayberries in this area, and if one is lucky enough to have done it, look for the birds, they love them.

Now, if you like birds and want them in the yard all year, go back to those colorful and intriguing seed and nursery catalogs and go all through them again — take a bird's eye view.

# FEBRUARY

## GROUND HOG

February second and the weather sages, rustics, even urbane city folk mutter, "ground hog day."

Few animals have become so closely associated with any one calendar day as has the ground hog, or woodchuck. It is true, as a weather prophet he has been over-rated, but seldom does February second pass without at least a mention of the animal and the superstition of his prophetic power to foretell the length of winter. If he sees his shadow, six more weeks of winter are to follow, the superstitions say.

The woodchuck sleeps the winter away. This animal, along with the bear, the bat and several others, has found a satisfactory solution to the problem of a long, cold spell with his food supply cut off. He sleeps. In fact, so well known is this habit that he familiarly is called one of the "seven sleepers."

As far as scientists have been able to check up on the ground hog, his earliest emergence date in the United States is February 5, and that was in the south where winters are not severe and where six weeks is more winter than they usually have. He sleeps right through February in Michigan and other Lake States. If he did come out, he would not know any more about the length of winter than you or I, and shadow or no shadow, in this part of Michigan we would be willing to bet six weeks is a moderate guess.

The ground hog's a wise old fellow in many ways, but his sagacity doesn't extend to weather wisdom. He does know enough to hibernate in winter, always to build two openings, a front and back door, to his dwelling, where the best hay, clover and alfalfa fields grow, and that dogs are "bad medicine" for "chuckies."

Woodchucks are widely distributed throughout the United States, and have been known since the earliest of colonial times. In fact, it was the early European emigrants that gave these animals the name "woodchuck."

"Chuck" was the familiar word for pig in their old homes, so when they found these animals about the forests in their new land it was only natural to call them "woodchucks." They are known locally by a variety of names such as marmot, whistler, or the French Canadian title of "siffleur."

Frequently the farmer harbors much ill will toward this animal because of its fondness for cultivated crops such as beans, clover, alfalfa, cabbages, young corn and pumpkin vines. In waste land and wooded sections they do little harm, living on many kinds of wild and native plants.

Young woodchucks make interesting and excellent pets and are easily tamed.

Ground Hog Day it is to the oldtimers, but we'd better call it "Candlemas Day" to keep our natural history straight.

## HOORAY FOR FEBRUARY

Now that we are sure of six (at least) more weeks of winter regardless of what the ground hog's shadow told us, the shortest month of the year and the last one of winter passes.

Sooner or later this month, we are sure to get some spring-like temperatures that will turn a day into a thaw. A February thaw is a precious thing of promise because with it comes the assurance that no matter how long or cold the winter, it will pass away.

With this warm winter sun, creeks and brooks are turned into happy, bubbly things that hurry along singing as they go. Each day that brings this February thaw shortens our winter by just that much, and who in February is not looking for a respite from winter? Skiers and ice-fishermen perhaps need a little more time to pursue their favorite sports, but most of the rest of us are glad that these sunny hours presage spring.

Winter birds are still coming to feeding stations throughout the area and seem grateful for the handouts that make winter living happier and easier for them. As many as twenty different kinds have visited one station.

Before the end of the month, the early spring arrivals will be coming. Song sparrows will be here in numbers, robins, bluebirds, grackles, mourning doves, horned larks, redwings and ducks will be winging in. Geese announce the prelude to spring before the month ends.

The woodchuck as well as most of the other "seven sleepers" is still hibernating. Among the early risers are chipmunks. They will be cleaning house and "sweeping" out their burrows long before the month's end. On a woodland trek do not be surprised to find a litter of cone scales at the entrance of a small hole, for chipmunks are very good housekeepers and get this spring duty over early.

The bear, bat and jumping mouse are all sound sleepers and are still napping at month's end. The others sleep more lightly and are often aroused during warm days or moonlit winter nights.

The cold-blooded creatures, amphibia and reptiles, are slow and sluggish in responding to weather changes and not until after February are they apt to be about.

Butterflies may be expected on that day of thaw, and the first of them to appear is usually the mourning cloak. This insect is a hibernator, and on the first really warm sunny day it may be seen fluttering adventuresomely about the woodlot where it has probably spent the winter in an old fallen log or decaying stump. The admirals also hibernate and come venturing out in the late winter sunshine. They respond to the same warmth and sunshine that brings the snow insects out in such numbers. These are one of February's nature treasures and we almost count the month lost if we miss at least one view of a concentration of these strange minute insects that cover the thawing snow like a layer of soot.

The plant world is showing signs of awakening and already pussy willows are blooming in the county and by the end of the month the brown points of skunk cabbage cowls will be thrusting their way through the woodland muck and swamp undercover. This is commonly thought of as the "first flower of the year." If one is lucky, on some slanting hillside with a southern exposure where the sun is at its best even in February, he may catch a glimpse of that early floral treasure, the hepatica or liverwort. Protected by heavy wool on the buds and stem, this flower is well adapted to winter and cold days.

While all this is going on outside, there are small duties that can well be put off no longer. One of these is renovating and refurbishing bird houses and nesting boxes. If one would have bird tenants, he must prepare for them. Spring comes so rapidly after February that there is little time for these tasks in March and April.

Once the migration opens up in spring, there is wave after wave as the birds come rushing in, all looking for nesting boxes and house sites. The bluebirds, which are among the very desirable bird neighbors, want their houses out early, and mid-March is none too soon to encourage these pleasant birds about one's premises.

If you are lucky, you should be able to find a snowdrop in your garden before the end of the month. We keep a sharp eye out, but do not always have a chance to welcome these little "Maids of February," as they are called in Europe, until the short month has slipped away and spring's March is here.

## OWLS SWITCH FEEDING TIME

This severe winter weather has been altering the behavior of some of the birds, as well as humans.

Owls, which usually hunt and feed at night when mice, moles, and rabbits are active, have had problems. With the deep snow, the rodents are not coming to the surface at night, so owls have had to adjust to this scarcity or go hungry.

As a rule, they sleep during the daylight hours, but this month numbers of them have been appearing at feeding stations where there are concentrations of small birds. Birds or rodents? It does not matter much when one is hungry. Since small birds sleep at night and are active by day, owls are shortening their daytime naps and changing their lunch-times.

The snowy owl, visitor from the north, is an exception. It is a diurnal feeder, and the short-eared owl often hunts on dark days or just before dark. Another northern owl, the hawk owl, rarely seen in the Lower Peninsula, also is a daytime hunter.

In addition to the snowy owl, there are six owls which are county residents. The largest and best known is the great horned owl, which is sometimes called "the tiger of the wood."

It is also known as the "five hooter" because of its characteristic call. It is large and strong and able to prey on possums, coons, skunks, rabbits and woodchucks. A pair raised a family in McGraft Park this past season.

These owls have been most frequently reported visiting feeding stations where pigeons and starlings entice them. They are early nesters, and often take over a discarded crow or hawk nest, refurbish it, and are incubating by late February.

The small, dainty counterpart of this large owl is the little screech owl, which also has "horns." This little fellow is more common in the area than most persons realize. Often they warm themselves by sitting near chimneys as starlings do. Like Santa Claus, they sometimes come down the chimney to the dismay of householders. These owls have two color phases, brown and gray. They nest in tree cavities and can be induced to take over a bird house if suitably placed for them. They have been seen at area feeding stations during the past two weeks.

Two other medium-sized owls are the long and short-eared. The long-eared prefers woods near open country, while the short-eared likes open country, near marshes and wetlands. All owls like evergreens — they make good places to sleep unnoticed during the daytime.

Another larger owl without ears and seldom seen in suburban or urban situations is the barred owl — known as the "eight hooter," as contrasted with the great horned. For the most part these are "country cousins" that favor wooded area, swamps and river bottoms. These would probably visit only rural bird feeding stations. None has been reported locally.

The smallest owl here is a little tuftless fellow called the saw-whet (from its call) and is probably more common than most realize. Since they are so small, smaller than a robin, nocturnal and hide during the day, few people have seen this delightful "brownie."

The barn owl, previously seen here years ago, is the "valentine-faced owl," and, as its name suggests, is a rural resident.

Many of the owls nest in holes and tree cavities and accept woodpeckers' old homes. The smaller owls can also be attracted to bird houses if one wants a good mouser nearby.

Less common owls on the Michigan Audubon list are the boreal and great gray. All owls are protected by state law just as such predators as the hawks, eagles and ospreys.

WOODPECKERS AT WORK

People disagree about woodpeckers. Nevertheless, they are one family of birds which does not desert us when winter comes. Several species remain in Michigan during the cold months and take their chances of survival with other year 'round residents.

Woodpeckers do their greatest good in winter. Now it is that they are searching in and out of the cracks and crevices of bark looking for sleeping larvae of insects and devouring enormous numbers of insect eggs. Drilling into infested trees, they bring out large numbers of quiescent insects which are highly detrimental to the wood.

It has been said that woodpeckers will seldom attack a sound and healthy tree. This is not an infallible rule, but it does merit attention. If woodpeckers (other than sapsuckers) persist in drilling in a given tree, it better be examined for infected areas. Woodpeckers know where "bugs" are and they go after them.

Sapsuckers are something else again. They do not hesitate to attack healthy and sound trees and some people are of the opinion that in their case "the healthier the better" — maybe more sap flows. Muskegon country residents do not need to worry about sapsuckers until about the last of March and through to April 20. Then if one has special ornamental birches and fancy cherries, it's well to wrap them with strong fiber or other material to discourage the sapsuckers. It does not take long for one or two of these birds working to make an unsightly and unpleasant scar on young trees.

The woodpeckers here now, patrolling shade and fruit trees, are the downy and his larger cousin, the hairy, the red-bellied and a few flickers which have decided to try a Michigan winter for a change. Most of them winter in the southern states and return in March. In the northern part of the state the pileated or log cock is found in wilderness areas and remains for the winter. Infrequently enough to make it a real thrill for lower Michigan bird-watchers, the two members of the three-toed tribe come south. The arctic and American three-toed are both occasionally reported as far south as Muskegon County and are recognized by the yellow accent with black and white instead of the more common red which is characteristic of most of the other species.

If one wishes to attract the woodpecker family, suet is the best diet to offer. Meat scraps are second-best and members will accept a variety of other things. But, by and large, "suet's the thing" for the woodpeckers. Call them to a station and they soon will be cleaning your trees of injurious insects and reduce your garden pests for spring and summer.

Several species of woodpeckers can be attracted to nesting boxes in spite of the fact that they are the carpenters of the bird world.

TUFTED TITMOUSE — BIRD ELF

Tufted titmice, delightful little bird elves, have been bringing pleasure to numerous feeding stations throughout the county during these winter days.

Slightly larger than the well-known chickadee, the titmouse is a member of the same bird family and resembles the black-cap in many of its antics as well as in its feeding habits.

The titmouse gives a general impression of gray, being grayish above, with a black forehead, lighter underparts, buffish sides, and an unmistakable crest. This latter is an aid in identifying it in the field, as no other common tiny bird has the conspicuous crest.

Titmice often announce their presence by their loud, clear whistle. This they repeat over and over, sometimes to the distress of their human friends who are inclined to find the call monotonous.

The small birds are agile, active and acrobatic and perform on twigs and feeding stations almost as clownishly as the chickadees themselves.

They sometimes visit feeding stations in company with their cousins, the chickadees, and they like a similar diet. Suet and grains likewise attract them. In nature, the titmice feed largely upon insect eggs and larvae which they find about the twigs and bark crevices of trees. They are invaluable to the farmer and gardener and much of their best work is done in winter when the insects are in their dormant stages.

About April, they start nesting and usually choose a woodpecker's old hole in which to place their nest of leaves, moss, bark and feathers. Fencepost holes and old hollow stumps also appeal to them as attractive home sites. The eggs are whitish cream, rather evenly marked with brown.

Few winter birds are more vocal than the titmice as they make their presence known to station operators and advertise the feeding board to other featured patrons.

BIRDS TURN LOVERS

It is possible the ancients were right and Valentine's Day is the day that birds mate.

I was awakened on the morning of Valentine's Day with the soft cooing of a pair of mourning doves. Peeking out the window I saw a couple in the maple, billing and cooing as they have appeared for centuries on Valentines in lacy frames. They were not mourning.

It was a beautiful sunny morning, warm and thawing. At the feeding table was a male cardinal, and I knew his attitude had changed on this special day. For beside him was his mate, and instead of chasing her away, as he had all winter, he picked up a sunflower seed and offered it to her. She accepted it with a graceful nod. Later he sang a love song to her from the pine tree and coaxed her to come near.

At the mailbox I was attracted by the spring love call of a blue jay in a cottonwood tree on the hill. Later he arrived for lunch with a lady friend.

Instead of the usual group of seven or nine quarreling jays, four couples came at different times to eat and display.

I heard cawing overhead and looking up, saw the crow roosts were breaking up and birds were flying over in groups of twos and threes. These triangles are typical of the early mating behavior of crows, but here it usually does not take place until early March.

A flock of starlings came in and were bathing in a puddle of melting snow in the driveway. As they finished and alighted on the fence to preen, the males went into their courting display of crowing, wing-waving and fluffing. About noon, as I participated in the annual Valentine's watch, at the feed table natty little male sparrows were doing their hop-and-bow, tail flick and wing quiver to attract their ladies.

With all this love-making going on in the bird world, I am ready to apologize to the ancients for my skepticism and concede that perhaps they are right.

Birds were active at stations throughout western Michigan as reports came in from Pentwater to Grand Haven. The results indicated that many of the finches that appeared on the Christmas count were still around. Goldfinches accounted for the largest number of a single species. There were 390 of them, seen at all but one station. Redpolls, including some of the rare hoary redpolls, totaled 365. There were 221 juncos and 211 evening grosbeaks.

Other large numbers included 152 starlings, 136 house sparrows, 150 blue jays and 127 chickadees. The chickadees were the only birds this year that were seen at all reporting stations. This is unusual because usually house sparrows and starlings are found on all reports.

Five other species were recorded at all but one station. They were goldfinches, downy woodpeckers, blue jays, cardinals and juncos. Birds considered migrants but remaining and patronizing area lunch counters this month include grackles, redwings, cowbirds, towhees, field sparrows, white-crowned and white-throated sparrows, song sparrows and mourning doves as well as a robin. Two hawks — a red-shouldered and red-tailed — were observed near feeding areas.

The Valentine watch, contrasted with the Christmas count, showed 37 species feeding and 2,245 individuals at stations in February against a December count of 44 species and 2,432 individuals of which 1,555 were waterfowl.

One does not need skis or snowshoes to enjoy cross country treks in winter. A strong, warm pair of boots will take the rambler over hill and dale and through duneland where there are many things to see and secrets to discover.

With so many sunny days this winter, such trips have been especially enjoyed by old and young alike, and revelations have been fun.

There is a whole world that few, except fishermen hunting bait, know anything about. This is the world of galls, those strange, abnormal growths commonly seen on various plants. This is a mini-world of insects, and the galls are generally the nursery for the young.

The first stop on our snow-trek was a patch of brown goldenrod stalks with the frayed, feathery seed plumes. Right away we saw the ball galls on the stem. Many of the stems in this patch had the spherical hard growth on them, and a closer look showed another kind, a spindle-shaped one, smaller in diameter but of greater length. It is the ball gall that is very familiar to fishermen. They know the secret of it. Cut it open carefully and inside, curled up comfortably, is a pale little "grub" — do fish like that tasty morsel!

This creature is the larva of a fly, which laid its egg on the goldenrod stem in summer. As soon as it hatched, it ate its way through the stem to the center, and the plant responded by the swollen growth which provided the cozy little "room" for the larva. Here it has eaten and rested and in late winter will pupate and emerge in a few weeks as an adult fly about the size of a house fly with attractive red, brown and white wings. Ordinarily galls do not harm plants on which they occur, unless in great numbers, but many persons think them unsightly.

Sometimes a ball gall larva is parasitized by another insect, and a tiny beetle will emerge instead of the fly. In the spindle gall there may be the larva of a small moth or it may be empty, the adult having "left home." Toward the top of the stalk there may be another type of gall, more slender than the spindle. This is the taper stem gall and it is less common here than the others. Another common one on the goldenrod is the leafy bunch gall. This is a cluster of distorted, misshapen leaves usually at the tip of a branch. The crumpled leaves can even be found in winter. This is the result of another fly's work. Along with the egg the fly deposited a chemical which caused the leaves to form the untidy cluster for its nursery. These are empty now unless some other tiny creatures — thrips or mites — have taken them over for the winter.

Like the goldenrod, oaks are favorite hosts for gall insects and have at least four common ones that attack them. Since many oaks retain their leaves in winter, we found them on our snow-trek. The four we saw on the oaks were the bullet, made up of several round, hard nodules in a neat cluster; the oak apple, a large, round thinner-skinned growth on the leaf; the hedgehog, a spherical smaller one covered with spiny bristles and the gouty, an irregular swollen growth on the stem. Each of these has its own individual insect that produces it and lives within. The amazing thing to me about the world of galls is that they are very specific, an oak apple insect from the tree could not possibly produce a ball gall on the goldenrod. In few places is the saying "To each his own" more applicable than in the world of galls.

Look for the oak apples in the spring also when they are newly formed and brightly colored, reds and greens, like Christmas ornaments in the oaks. Then you will know the reason they are called "oak apples," for they look like fruit.

Our snow trek had shown us so many galls, we remembered a wild berry patch and went there. Sure enough, we found several of the hard, knobby growths, the berry knot gall, on the stems. These are communal dwellings, each made up of many cells, and each cell contains the wintering over larva of a small white wasp which will emerge in spring.

Following a hunch we hunted out some wild rose bushes and again were rewarded with the mossy rose gall which looks like a tangled mass of threads on the bush. This, too, is communal and houses wasp larvae.

There are many aphid galls, and one that causes trouble in spruce plantations in this area is the spruce-gall, which attacks the tips of the twigs and branches. Most aphid galls are on leaves, and many of them can be seen in the spring shortly after the new leaves appear.

Another winter, one we found near a duneland pool was the pine cone willow gall. They look like small gray pine cones growing on the willow. In the spring, the gall fly lays an egg and a growth inhibitor on a bud that is ready to open and develop the new branch. Instead of growing into a normal branch with leaves properly spaced, the bud grows about an inch, with the leaves overlapping like shingles. They go through a seasonal color change — first green, yellow, brown and for winter, gray. In the center is the bright orange larva which rests well protected.

With the exception of the aphid gall on evergreens, the gall insects do little damage in making their winter nurseries, and in the early days galls were even utilized, such as the oak galls in tanning and also in making a very fine grade of ink which was used to write many of the old historical government documents. Today they have little commercial use and to many are still a "secret world."

This dozen seen during a two hour snow-trek give some idea of the number of them that can be discovered if one is alert to this mini-world so close to us.

## SUGAR BUSH

With the early spring sun shining invitingly, there is nothing that gives one the thrill of this season more than a visit to a sugar-bush.

Western Michigan has its share of these delightful woodlands, and one of our favorites is near Montague where we were told the trees had been tapped regularly for more than a century. They had been used by the Indians during the days of the first white settlers. Another favorite "maple orchard" or "sugar orchard" as they are called in some states, was that on the Old Mills Homestead near Hesperia.

Our best remembered excursion was several years ago when Muskegon was playing host to an Irish exchange teacher, and one of the things she had heard most about in the "Old Country" was maple sugar and the sugar bush.

So it was our great pleasure to take her on the annual visit and give her a treat of American traditional culture. She has never forgotten the experience and the taste of the sap as it was boiling down in the steam-filled shanty.

Michigan's history and economy have been closely associated with her trees. Three kinds stand out especially. The pine, which was the king of the lumber era; the apple, whose blossom is the state flower, whose fruit fills storehouses and marts in the golden days of autumn, and the maple, the tree which meant so much to the everyday living of the pioneers and early settlers.

It is this tree that comes into its own, spring and fall. In the spring the harvest of sap, which makes the syrup, is its chief attraction, and in the fall the beauty of its brilliant autumnal foliage. Twice a year the maples call outdoor-lovers to the groves and woodlots.

For some time now, maples along many of the state's highways have worn their buckets suspended from the old-fashioned "spiles" or the newfangled "faucets."

These are the invitation to take that excursion to the favorite "sugar bush."

Toward the end of the season, Vermontville in southern Michigan celebrates with its annual "Maple Syrup Festival." It is well worth a trip to this attractive little Michigan village to see sugar-making at its best. A number of Michigan farmers still supplement their income by harvest of the sugar bush. In fact, in a good year there are about 100,000 gallons of syrup produced. Michigan is a top ranking state in maple sugar production, and annually ranks fourth or fifth behind Vermont, New York, Ohio and Pennsylvania.

Similar to the festival at Vermontville, Chardon, Ohio, has one, and many southern winter tourists stop there on their return trip to find it's a wonderful introduction to the northern spring.

How long will the maple syrup season last? No one can tell. But, the old-timers will tell you that as soon as the buds break, the season is over "because the sap becomes buddy." "Buddy?" They know what buddy sap tastes like, and they don't like it. Others say when the frogs croak all night, the season is over.

Maple sugar farmers are even glad to see the season come to an end. Oh, they like it, and they like those first few days, but, when the season's on, the syrup has to be cared for 24 hours a day, and that means "long hours" in anybody's language. So, not until the sugar season is over will the sugar farmer know a full night's sleep again.

But, any of them will tell you, it's worth it.


SEVEN SLEEPERS STIR


The bright sunshine of the last few days has made us wonder if some of the winter sleepers would be awakening. Low temperatures will keep them sleeping.

Before the month is past, some of the seven sleepers will be rousing themselves. The lighter sleepers will stir and their tracks in the snow will tell of their wanderings. Raccoons, skunks and chipmunks are among the early risers.

Almost any thawing sunny February day one may see signs of chipmunk activity in the woodlots and thickets. Very shortly they will be chipping and scolding at woods-wanderers on the winter trails.

Bear, jumping mice and bats sleep later and seldom do they waken before March.

This is the month when the first of pussy willows bloom, and with the usual seasonable sunshine and warmth, there should be alder catkins shaking golden curls along the brookside by the end of the month.

Spiders are astir already and water insects are becoming more active in lake, stream and pond.

The bird population is at its winter best right now, for in addition to the permanent residents and the winter visitors, there are sure to be some stragglers, and before mid-month some of the summer residents returning.

The first of the birds to return from the south usually is the song sparrow. Often before the middle of the month the cheery song of these attractive little sparrows is heard in the yard or along one's favorite willow-bordered stream.

They are easily distinguished from the common winter sparrows by their streaked and striped breasts with a large median spot which looks like a brooch. The tail has a longer look than that of the tree sparrow, a common winter sparrow. The bird appears slightly larger as it sings from its favorite perch, often along a waterway.

They are lovers of thicket and shrub-bordered stream, although they are equally at home in evergreen plantings in city yards and gardens.

The song sparrow is a true harbinger of spring, just as the pussy willow and hepatica are in the flower world.

Other birds which should be watched for this month are bluebirds, redwings, meadowlarks and grackles. These return in February in normal seasons.

Birds are still interested in patronizing feeding stations, so do not forget the daily handouts.

CHECK EXPECTATIONS

While feeding winter bird visitors, renovating bird houses for spring, and before there is new foliage on the trees, check the yard and garden and discover the homes of last year's neighbors and learn whom to expect this year. In other words, make an inventory of the nesting sites birds used in and about your premises last year.

It is a great surprise to most residents to learn how many different kinds of birds lived near them during the spring and summer. Tree and shrub foliage obscure most of the nests so they are inconspicuous during the nesting season. That is as it should be, for their greatest protection is this obscurity and concealment.

Nests can be divided into ground nests, platforms, holes and open cups. There are some specialties like the orioles' long woven pendant pockets, the chimney swifts' brackets and the ovenbirds' covered nests.

Trees and shrubbery offer the most common situations for the yard and garden birds. The materials from which nests are made differ considerably, but in the passerines (song birds) twigs, grasses and other vegetable matter are basic. Robins and some of the other thrushes as well as swallows use mud in their nests, while chipping sparrows and several others include an inner cup of hair. Some prefer feather lining. Crested flycatchers are partial to a snakeskin in their nest.

To attract birds to nest about the yard, proper planting is important with natural food and water in close proximity.

Several years ago I inventoried my neighbors by nest-hunting after the leaves had fallen and came up with a surprising group on or adjacent to our one lot at Pere Marquette Park. Wrens, a pair of tree swallows, and bluebirds accepted the boxes we had put up for them. House sparrows and starlings built in the eaves and a pair of robins on the bedroom window sill. A chipping sparrow nest in a small spruce tree near the porch had its typical inner cup of hair (human combings had replaced the conventional horse hair.) In the next bush, a spirea, a yellow warbler family had been raised and the architects had woven toilet tissue into the nest. Later investigation showed the unusual material had been obtained through a broken window in the park's restroom.

The lilac bushes protected the catbird's nest, while a tangle of bittersweet was the location of the brown thrashers. Cardinals nested near the house in a trumpet vine. The barberries were not yet large enough to offer the height most of our bird neighbors needed; but since then chipping sparrows have chosen them often.

A utility pole at the corner of the lot houses a red-headed woodpecker and the neighbor's garage on the other corner (northwest) had several barn swallows nesting. They had entered through a missing window pane. The old martin house we had left on Beach Street continued to have its colony of martins, I discovered. As I visited lots adjacent to ours, I found a hummingbird nest on the branch of a cottonwood. It was lichen-covered and

31

looked very much from the ground like a natural knot on the branch. I knew killdeer had nested in the sand over the hill, but by now there was no sign of this simple ground nest. There was still evidence of the nest of a pair of mallards I had seen earlier in the season at a small duneland pool.

A plantation of pines, between our lot and the Naval Reserve proved to be a good hunting place. Here were the nests of jays, crows, mourning doves and goldfinches. I had to go a bit farther, toward Port Sherman to find the tall oak which has harbored an oriole nest for years. Then, on the way back I found a flicker's hole in a dead tree.

Since that year I have moved from the top of the hill to the base and instead of the abundance of shrubbery and vines have only three trees, a white pine, maple, and box elder and one shrub, a burning bush. Wrens nest in the bird house hung in the pine, robins build in the maple, and chipping sparrows in the burning bush. A pair of barn swallows tried very hard to move in. The backdoor was blown off in a severe May windstorm. The repairman was not able to come for two days and during that time the swallows located the situation and thought it was an "open invitation." They carried nesting material, including mud pellets in and out continuously, which I industriously removed. It was touch and go for the two days, but swallows in one's utility room are just a little too close, even for good neighbors.

# Spring

Spring is the time I love the best
For, then in verdant lacery drest
The trees are joyous brides.
The rains are happy, tinkling things
That waken dreaming wildings.
Then flowers peep from leafy mould
And mystically their hoods unfold
As if they fear the season's stealth
Will rob them of their colored wealth.
But, best of all I love
The silvery notes that from above
Tell me my birds are here again
For, not until I hear them sing
Am I quite sure it is really spring.

# MARCH

## GARDENS DRAW BIRDS

"How many kinds of birds may we expect in our garden?"

This question is frequently asked as someone describes an unfamiliar bird visitor to his yard or garden.

In a modest town, city, or suburban garden and surrounding yard, records show it is not unusual to have half a hundred different bird visitors in a nine months period — spring, summer and autumn. Winter may bring a few more.

This number is predicated on the fact that most of the gardens checked had bird baths or pools and most of the residents had been accustomed to feeding birds in winter and had one or more bird houses offered for occupancy during the spring and summer.

Needless to say, not all the birds paid daily visits. Some were seen only during the spring and fall migration but nevertheless they were conspicuous enough or useful enough in their feeding habits to be recorded.

Among the year-round inhabitants, welcome or not, are the house sparrows, starlings, blue jays, chickadees, nuthatches and woodpeckers. Cardinals also are year-round providing they can find suitable nesting sites in shrubbery or vines about the house or grounds.

Bluebirds, tree swallows, wrens and martins are sure to come if nesting boxes are available.

Then there are the foliage tenders which are so useful in destroying harmful insects that infest the leaves — these include a variety of vireos and warblers. Goldfinches are common and eat dandelion, thistle and salsify seeds. Cedar waxwings are attracted by berry bearing shrubs and trees.

The whole flycatcher family is sure to come if there are some dead twigs, branches or a pool near which they can perch and snap unwary insects. Redwings, cowbirds, grackles and blackbirds are quite sure to patrol the lawn, at least in spring and fall, for insects.

The thrushes are more secretive and like lots of shelter. Catbirds and brown thrashers not only visit many gardens in this region but prefer to nest in them if there is a tangle of shrubbery or a massed planting of bushes.

Hummingbirds are sure to patronize gardens that offer tubular flowers as lunch counters. They are partial to trumpet vine, honeysuckle, petunias, foxglove, delphinium, lilies, bergamot and columbine.

During spring and fall the native migrating sparrows come in flocks and it is possible to see as many as eight species in a small garden at once.

These are only a few of the many kinds of birds that may be expected in Muskegon gardens. In the rural sections there are many more species which can be enticed from the fields and meadows.

Of course, no Michigan garden would be complete without its robin family.

## HORNED LARKS NEST EARLY

While most birds are still hovering about and visiting winter feeding stations, some already are at their domestic duties and nesting. There are two in Muskegon County busy with home tasks right now. The great horned owl is the first of the Michigan birds to nest and usually is incubating by the last of February. Their nests, in the cavities of trees and similarly protected places, are more comfortable than those of the little horned larks placed in open fields and waste places with sometimes only a clump of grass to shelter them.

The larks are now very active and may be seen about the highways and fields throughout western Michigan. They often fly up almost from under the wheels of the traveling motorist. They are sparrow-like birds, easily identified by the black outer tail feathers displayed in flight and the black eye mark. They are the American representative of the Old World lark family, and, as their European relatives, they sing on the wing having a low, sweet, clear song. The alarm note and call is different from the ordinary song and is a sharp, high pitched whistle, repeated a number of times. These larks are also characterized by their walking or running as distinguished from the typical hop of most of our native birds.

Because of the habit of early nesting, it is not unusual for these birds to have their first nests destroyed by snow, ice and sleet. Sometimes several are built in a season before a successful family of young ones is raised.

Living in fields, pastures and waste places, the food of these birds is largely injurious weed seeds such as pigweed, ragweed, sorrel, amaranth, and bitterweed. Also, they destroy many harmful insects and in this way prove beneficial to the farmer and gardener.

In the past they were killed in large numbers as food in the northern part of the state where they were known as "yellow-breasts."

The name "horned lark" suggests the two tufts of dark feathers sometimes observed on the head resembling horns.

## SKUNK CABBAGE BLOOMING

Bringing spring to the swamp and marshy lowlands of the county as surely as the pussy willow brings it to the streams, the skunk cabbage is now unrolling its dark striped hood. It is a bold adventurer among the flower clan and appears while arbutus is still budded and before the hepatica has broken the ground.

Because this first floral bloom is somewhat inconspicuous in the moist woodland or inundated marsh, the seeker must look sharply for the treasure. The flowers appear before the cabbage-like leaves, which give it a part of its name, and the club-like spadix is protected by the large curled spathe which is variable in color through purples, tans, browns, and yellows. The plant is a relative of the jack-in-the-pulpit and the calla lily and betrays its relationship by the type of bloom. After the blossom disappears or withers, the leaves put forth a prodigious growth and soon are conspicuous in the damp lowlands. Then it is that the wood-wanderer wonders how he could possibly have missed the numerous plants which are now revealed.

The name "skunk" comes from a somewhat disagreeable and penetrating odor. It is also called swamp cabbage and is found in eastern states, as far west as Minnesota, and south to Florida.

In the early days the roots and seeds of this plant were used medicinally for whooping cough, asthma, nasal catarrh and bronchial irritations according to "The Herbalist." The Indians used it for "consumption" and all diseases of the lungs as well as for snake bites.

Flies, beetles, early bees and occasional butterflies visit this first flower and pay their respects while nectar hunting is a dubious task. Later there will be an abundance of blossoms, offering multitudes of sweets to the insects, but now pussy willow, alders and skunk cabbages are gracious plant hosts.

# GINSENG, A VALUABLE HERB

It doesn't matter whether March comes in like a lion or a lamb; it is the month of awakening.

With the retreating of snowdrifts, the first spears of greening grass appear. The rosettes of dandelions, mulleins, cress and other plants begin to show. In Michigan woodlots, and wild places, one of the plants which many look for is ginseng.

Ginseng is a fascinating herb. Its history goes back for many centuries, both in the Occident and in the Orient. It is a plant of mystery and superstition. The Chinese value it above all other herbs as a cure-all, a choice panacea.

The ideal root is "man-shaped," with four parts representing the extended arms and legs. The word "ginseng" comes from the Chinese word, schinseng, meaning "like a man."

Whatever the true medicinal value of ginseng, the monetary value is high. Ginseng is grown in the United States, but the cultivated product does not seem to have the effectiveness of the wild form, so mountain-men, hill people and herb gatherers throughout eastern and southern states search for it.

Michigan has its ginseng-hunters and this fall they will be in the woodlands looking for a good harvest.

The search for this plant goes back to Indian days. Even George Washington and Daniel Boone engaged in the trading of this herb. From an average price of 42 cents a pound in 1822, when it was carried round the Horn in clipper ships, it has risen to almost $100 in 1977. In 1975 a record 248,854 pounds of the magic herb was exported.

It's gathered in the fall, when the plant is golden and the berries red. Careful diggers always replanted the seeds. Now some people dig all year, taking the plant even before the leaves appear. This is of great concern to botanists and veteran diggers, for the plant is decreasing in many sections of the country.

As a result, the Endangered Species Authority, following a state-by-state assessment, said it was unable to find data to justify the continued exportation of the herb. Therefore, the ESA, which is responsible for permits to export or import wild flora and fauna, has banned the export of ginseng from all states except Michigan.

Michigan is exempt because it has very strict rules on the gathering and handling of the plant. The rules are so stringent that few diggers find it worthwhile here. The ban, however, may bring additional numbers of harvesters into Michigan.

New York, likewise, has rules to protect ginseng. Wisconsin has gone so far as to establish a collection season.

Some drug companies and individuals do not agree with the ban, and prefer state control, but do not favor such strict control as Michigan exercises. For more information, read "Ginseng" by A. R. Harding.

So March is the time to get out in the woodlands and wetlands and see what is there. If you find a patch of ginseng, guard it carefully for as some other native plants, it is "endangered."

## SHAMROCKS

Irish or not — on St. Patrick's day many people will be a-wearing of the green.

It's shamrock day and in honor of the spring, as well as of Ireland's patron saint, there'll be bits of green on coat and blouse.

To many of true Irish extraction, the green will be a three-parted leaf from a treasured house plant which several generations ago came right from the Emerald Isle itself. In the past it was a happy custom to bring cuttings of the shamrock from Erin.

There are two plants in the United States which are commonly called and sold as shamrocks: one is sorrel, or oxalis, and the other is a white clover. The origin of the true Irish shamrock is lost in antiquity, and the Erse word "seamrog" from which it comes means simply a three-parted leaf and therefore describes both the oxalis and the clover.

In early Irish history, it referred to an edible plant associated with cresses. This reference points to the oxalis or sorrel which is frequently used in salads for its tart taste. It is an attractive plant with bright green leaves.

The shamrock is worn on St. Patrick's day because legend has it that it was this plant's leaf which the Saint used to teach the lesson of the Trinity to Irish Christian converts. Later it became to the Irishman his national floral emblem, typifying the three virtues of love, heroism and wit.

In many modern homes there are cherished house plants of shamrock kept alive and tended for their ancient symbolism and bright green freshness. In the old days they were kept for a much more practical reason, to ward off evil spirits and witches and kindred malcontents.

Today, in fields, roadsides, and pastures of Michigan, both clover and sorrel are common. And, if one really wants to be lucky, the Upper Peninsula, so-called "cloverland," offers innumerable "shamrocks" for the picking.

## WINTER IS OVER

"Lo, the winter is past, the flowers appear on the earth and the time of the singing of the birds is here;" thus the wise man of old described this time of year.

Even though the calendar does not say it is spring, nature announces it. Snowdrops are blooming in the herb patch and skunk cabbage in the swamps; pussy willows doff their dark brown caps, and birds are singing everywhere.

Friday was Buzzard Day at Hinckley, Ohio, where thousands celebrated the arrival of the great black birds. Last year we were there to greet them. Tuesday, St. Joseph's Day, the swallows are expected to return to Capistrano, but many of our birds are already here from the south.

Since mid-February, the robins have been slipping in each warming day and joining those that wintered over here. The returning ones seem to like to proclaim their arrival from the top of the tallest neighborhood tree. There is nothing shy about them. They want the world to know they are here.

Meadowlarks are noisy, too, but they prefer fence posts and telephone wires for their choirlofts. All through the rural sections of the county they are heard. Like noisy children, song sparrows are often heard before they are seen, and many have joined their winter cousins, the tree sparrows, at local feeding stations.

The early bluebirds are here, and if you plan on having them for tenants, you'd better have that bird house in readiness so you can put it up at a moment's notice.

Several big flocks of redwings came in during the first week of the month and hundreds are now in the cattail marshes of western Michigan. Almost daily more are arriving. Flocks of mourning doves are on the move. Since late February crow roosts have been breaking up and pairs setting up housekeeping. Grackles have moved in and are among the early nesters here.

Horned larks, horned owls and possibly eagles are already nesting in some sections of the county, and, of course, house sparrows and starlings are always "acting domestic" on the first sunny days, no matter what the month. They, like rock doves, have been reported nesting the calendar around — every month of the year.

## ROBINS ADOPTED MAN

Unless winter stages a sharp comeback there'll be eggs in the robins' nests in another week or two.

The flocks of friendly redbreasts are back from the south. Those hardy ones which stayed for the winter have abandoned the thickets and are questing for sites and materials with nary a building restriction to worry about.

Occasionally robins in numbers are viewed as pests by orchardists, but by and large the robin is beloved over its entire range, which includes most of the United States and Canada, much of Alaska, parts of Mexico and, now and then, Cuba and Bermuda.

The robin was a favorite of the early colonists. It was known to the southerners as fieldfare. Later, because of its resemblance to the English robin redbreast, eastern settlers gave it the name robin, but the American bird is markedly different from the European. In fact, it is of another bird family, being closely related to the thrushes and bluebird.

Part of the charm of the robin, in the northern states, is its migratory habit. It comes happily back in March and early April from the gulf states and south Atlantic. Each year a few birds remain in the north to brave the rigors of winter. If these are fortunate in finding natural foods or in patronizing a feeding board, they are here to greet their wandering cousins in the spring. Two things have contributed chiefly to the increase in reports of robins in Michigan during winter. One is the increase in the number of interested bird-watchers who maintain feeding stations and the other is the greater watchfulness exercised by bird students, demonstrated by the spread and popularity of the Christmas bird count. At best, robins have a difficult time enduring a Michigan winter.

Next to winter, the robin is least seen in August. This is molting time. After the busy days of nesting, incubation, and care for their several broods they are tired and need a rest before starting their southern flight. Retiring to the deep woods or swamps, they remain silent while they change to fall feathers. Then in September they become plentiful again and are seen in small flocks. They frequent lawns, parks, and grassy plots everywhere, eating their fill of insects and grubs. The flocks gradually enlarge and finally, usually in October, most of them head for points south of the Mason-Dixon line. Virginia, Georgia, the Carolinas, Florida and Louisiana are favorite winter resorts.

There was a time when these birds met a barrage of guns in the south. They were considered a choice table delicacy in potpie. However, robins are now protected everywhere in the United States by federal law. Dr. F. C. Lincoln of the Division of Wildlife Research reports that "such cases have been most uncommon in recent years."

Robins naturally are birds of the wood and forest, like their thrush cousins. With the coming of white settlers and the clearing of forests, they became dooryard birds and have retained this affection for human company. The robins even followed the pioneer into Death Valley, California, the low, dry desert stretch between the Paramints and Funeral Mountains. A date ranch and a green golf course were all the invitation they needed. The story is always the same. Wherever man goes, the robin follows. It is our closest bird friend.

Although not accepting nesting boxes, as do wrens and bluebirds, the robin does like a covered shelter, with a floor, top and back. The sides should be left open. Ledges, gables, fence posts and shade trees are among the favorite nesting sites for their neat, compact, mud-lined cups which hold their blue-green eggs. Robins often rear more than one brood of nestlings a season in the north. They seldom nest during their southern stay.

SKYWAYS ARE HIGHWAYS

Skyways are highways above Michigan these early spring days as bird arrivals pour in from Florida, the gulf states, Mexico, the West Indies and Central and South America.

The spring flight is on. It will continue for three months, and not until every tree, bush and shrub has had its visitors will the great mass trek come to an end.

Winter visitors are leaving or have left. Daily the population of spring migrants and summer residents is being augmented.

Most popular among these early arrivals are the beloved bluebird and robin, but even before these are seen, the song sparrow is sure to be here. Grackles often beat the robins and bluebirds, and meadow larks are often heard before snow is off the ground. Redwings and cowbirds also help to make up the vanguard of feathered fliers. Frequently the males of these species arrive first and may be seen in large flocks in marshes, pastures or fields.

These first arrivals are among the omnivorous feeders. They are not particular about their diets and therefore can eke out a living, even though winter has scarcely left and the food supply is scanty. They have wintered in the southern states, some no farther than southern Indiana and Kentucky.

Late March and April bring the seed-eaters. The finch family makes up the bulk of this group, with many species of sparrows. Some do not remain to nest here in Michigan. The white-crowned and white-throated sparrows stop only long enough to pay a call, rest a bit, and have a meal or two.

The tree swallow and hermit thrush are the first of their families to arrive. The tree swallow has a great winter range from the southern states through Mexico, Guatemala and Cuba. The hermit thrush spends the winter in the southern states, especially those bordering the gulf.

Along with the seed-eaters the phoebe, a flycatcher, is sure to come. Probably the secret of its early appearance is that its winter home is within the United States, south of latitude 37 degrees, and that it can subsist on other fare if insects are not abundant. Most of its family go much farther south, returning later in the season.

It is not until May that all the insect-eating birds arrive. Among the last are the warblers, nighthawk and whip-poor-will. Almost the last of the common birds to arrive is the little ruby-throated hummingbird. Tanagers also are late-comers, as they make a long journey from Colombia and Peru.

In Michigan the scarlet tanager is known as one of the very brilliantly colored and showy of the state's birds. We can hardly realize that in its winter range it is an olive-colored inconspicuous bird, yet that is the case. In the south the male tanager assumes the plumage of the female and is rarely seen in its bright red plumage.

The hummingbird likewise has a long spring trip. Its winter range is in southern Florida and Louisiana, through southern Mexico and Panama.

The two most conspicuous phases of the spring migratory parade pageant are the flight of thousands of ducks in late March and April and the warbler flight. The ducks cover ponds, small lakes, bays of the Great Lakes, rivers and marshes with gigantic rafts which sometimes number many thousands. These, along with the early flights of wild geese, announce that the spring migration is in full swing.

In May the onrush of wave upon wave of warblers fills every tree and shrub with bird-fairies. Many of them pass through Michigan to nest in the north. Small, vivacious and brilliantly colored, they are among America's choice birds for they are found on no other continent. May is the time to see them at their best, and then every day counts for they are constantly on the move and may be in one place only a day or two. Many species of this family travel together. The first to arrive is the myrtle warbler, coming sometimes as early as March.

Chimney swifts are laggards in the spring procession, but it is not because they do not get an early start. Like some of the others they have vast distances to travel, and because of their insect fare they must wait for warm weather. They go south of the United States into Vera Cruz and even farther than that to winter.

Water birds often pass more or less unnoticed in spring, but in the fall their flight is one of the most conspicuous parts of the autumn migration.

Although there are many well defined flyways or migratory routes which are used by all species of birds, there are a few so popular that they can be generally outlined. One route is that typified by the mourning warbler, following the land from Mexico around the east end of the gulf to the Mississippi Valley and then northward, avoiding the Atlantic coast. The second popular one is that of the bobolink, northward in Florida from Cuba and South America or to Louisiana from Yucatan and overland from South America. This route is followed by many species. The redstart makes a mass flight north both by land and water from Central and South America.

The hummingbird's route takes it directly across the gulf from the southern Americas to the gulf states, and then there is a general scattering to its summer home.

Some species have highly developed flyways which are used by them alone and which are phenomenal in length. Such flights are those of the golden plover and arctic tern. This latter has been called the champion migrant of the world, for it travels more than 20,000 miles annually.

An eerie twittering at night, a familiar bird song in the morning unheard for months, silhouettes passing over a bright moon, fresh-plumaged visitors at feeding stations, prospective tenants at bird houses left up all winter — these are the things that announce the great annual pageant which brings back the cheery songs, the color, the grace and gaiety of bird friends for another year.

# REDWINGS BRING SPRING

Although the spring peepers may be singing their frog chorus, spring, for many bird lovers, does not come to the swamp until it is heralded by the pleasing, liquid "ok-a-lee" of the red-winged blackbird.

These brilliantly colored blackbirds, among the more beautiful of their family, are widely distributed throughout this state and are familiar to all accustomed to roam the countryside. They may be found throughout Michigan, wherever marshes and cattail swamps provide their favorite nesting materials. They are a cousin of the grackle, the cowbird, the crow, blackbird, and oriole.

The spring march of these brilliant "soldier-birds" is now on, and almost daily individuals are added to the ranks. The dapper males come first in a group. It is from this sex that many of the most common names are given to this blackbird, for the female is inconspicuous, one of nature's fine examples of protective coloration, fitting in so well with the surroundings of her nest that even a careful observer frequently misses her. The male is a glossy jet black with the "shoulders" adorned with flaming epaulets of scarlet bordered with buff or gold. It is from these that the names redwing, red-shouldered blackbird, red-winged starling and red-winged oriole are given. Its habitat provides another common and local name, "the swamp blackbird."

The shy and modest brownish gray females follow the early migration of the others and by the end of March or first of April the entire population of redwings has arrived. Next follows a long period of courtship and building nests. This period is particularly interesting among these blackbirds, because unlike many of our native birds, the redwings are polygamous — one male taking for himself several females and accepting the protection and lordship of their scattered nests.

Almost any cattail marsh during the spring months reveals these birds singing their songs as they sway on the narrow rushes and cattails. Their song has been variously interpreted by a group of nature lovers, but to all of us it is a pleasing, liquid one. It seems to be a part of the marsh itself these early spring days. During these courting days the brilliantly colored male is an ardent suitor and bows and antics before the ladies in the most devoted fashion. He spreads his plumage, struts, bows, and sways, showing in innumerable ways what an attractive swain he is.

Actual nesting does not take place until May and after that it is not difficult to find the nest of redwings. The nests are most often composed of the most available material, which in their favorite habitat is cattail leaf. These they fashion and weave into bulky somewhat suspended nests. The rim is well constructed and the whole structure withstands considerable weathering.

The nest contains some of the more beautiful eggs of our native species, although they are variable in coloring and markings. They range from white to bluish or greenish white and are marked by dots, spots and penmarks ranging from lavender through purple and brown to black. The scrawls on them are interesting hieroglyphics and within one nest a variety of eggs may be discovered.

The food of these blackbirds is also variable. Investigation has shown that the greatest percentage of it consists of grass and weed seeds, many of which are obnoxious. Likewise, they eat a great many harmful insects including cutworms, grasshoppers, click beetles, span worms, weevils and other plant-eating beetles. In some sections, especially during the fall migration, when congregated in huge flocks, these birds sometimes visit grain fields and do considerable damage. On the whole, however, it is felt that beneficial feeding habits far outweigh any harm they may do.

## MIGRATING CRANES

After mid-March many eyes turn upward to the blue of the spring sky, for there is always the hope of the glimpse of a flight of cranes.

Last year I was lucky, for three of the huge birds flew high, right over my house at Pere Marquette Park, headed northward over the State Park. These were the common sandhill cranes for whom sanctuaries have been established in both of Michigan's peninsulas. Michigan Audubon maintains nesting areas at both its Baker and Haehnle Sanctuaries. In the north, Trout Lake and Seney areas are crane haunts.

Cranes offer one of the success stories of modern concern and activity. While havens were being established for the sandhills, it was discovered their large cousins, the whooping cranes, were decreasing alarmingly. In 1941 the entire national census showed them at an all-time low of only 15 birds.

Many innovative procedures have been used by the scientists in charge of the crane project, and this spring is showing good results.

This year showed a record number on the wintering ground (Aransas National Wildlife Refuge) in Texas. Now the main flock of 78 birds, two more than last year, is preparing to leave the Texas Gulf Coast for its long migratory flight to Canada.

Meanwhile, a transplanted flock of 17 whooping cranes is already migrating with their "foster" sandhill crane parents from the Rio Grande Valley of New Mexico to the Rockies. This total of 95 birds is the largest number of whoopers to migrate for years. In addition to these, there is a group of 24 birds which have been raised in captivity in the Patuxent Crane Propagation program in the charge of Dr. Scott Derrickson.

Six young birds hatched last spring are among the 78 whoopers at the Refuge preparing to leave for the 2,600 mile flight, which they successfully accomplished last fall, to Canada's Wood Buffalo National Park. Only through the concerned cooperation of the two countries, Canada and the United States, could the crane project have succeeded, for birds know no national boundaries and are not citizens of one country.

The Aransas birds are conducting their spectacular courtship rituals — dancing and leaping into the air with huge outspread wings. They form pair bonds at the age of two or three, but it is not known what the exact breeding age is. They begin mating before reaching Canada, some at Aransas and some en route to Canada.

During April they make their long flight northward.

The "foster" flock has a less arduous flight of only 750 miles from Bosque del Apache Refuge, New Mexico to Grays Lake in Idaho. Fifteen of these have already arrived at a favorite midway stopover in Colorado's San Luis Valley.

When these birds are moving we may expect the Michigan cranes to be on the way, and April is usually their arrival month. To see them on a trip to either of the two state Audubon sanctuaries can be most rewarding. It is important to go early after their arrival before nesting is under way because at that time they should not be disturbed or annoyed.

For several years Muskegon birders were especially fortunate to have Dr. and Mrs. L. H. Walkinshaw living on Scenic Drive, for he is a world authority on cranes and has authored two books on them, "Sandhill Crane," (©1949 Cranbrook) and "Cranes of the World," (©1973, Winchester). Dr. Walkinshaw was instrumental in helping with the establishment of the two Michigan Audubon areas where cranes are nesting.

A sight of these majestic birds flying leisurely over the city is a never-to-be-forgotten experience. One of my choice moments was seeing a trio fly over Hackley Park in downtown Muskegon a few years ago.

# MEADOWLARKS ANNOUNCE SPRING

Seeing robins and bluebirds tells us spring is here, but not until one hears the clear, sweet, musical whistle of the meadowlark is spring announced with certainty. On bright, sunny days during the past week, the musical somersault has been turned over and over again in cities as well as in rural areas. Migrating from their winter homes in the southern and gulf states, the meadowlarks may be heard and seen in vacant lots and even close to populous business centers.

Not closely related to the skylarks of the Old World, these birds are members of the well-known blackbird family and are cousins of the grackles, redwings, orioles and bobolinks. They are omnivorous feeders and, as many of their relatives, are among the earliest of the spring birds to arrive. They are often heard before they are seen.

Typically birds of the meadow, pasture and open field, they are ground nesters, building their usually arched nests of grasses and lining them with finer and softer plant material. The eggs, four to six, are of a white ground color with spots and specks of cinnamon and reddish brown.

The bird itself is more or less protectively colored and the brown and white upper plumage makes it almost indistinguishable from the field grasses where it hunts its food and spends most of its time. White outer tail feathers are sure field marks, and these birds may be recognized as far as they can be seen in flight. The flight is direct, straight and frequently low. They are often seen from the highways throughout the state.

Meadowlarks select a singing post or station from which they will pour out the musical strains of their song, time after time. This is frequently the very top of the highest tree in the locality, or a favorite fence post within its territory. Day after day, the bird mounts these sites and sings lustily, calling attention to its joyous life.

From these vantage points it is easy to see the expanse of yellow breast with its conspicuous black half moon, characteristic of this species. With the sun shining against it, it has even been considered as additional protective coloring.

Within recent years occasional reports from Michigan tell us that the western meadowlark, a closely allied species to our common meadowlark, is finding its way into the state, and there may be increasing numbers of these birds as time goes on. It is chiefly distinguishable by its song, by its lighter upper plumage, and by the yellow on the sides of its throat.

Daily meadowlark numbers will increase until this becomes one of the abundant of our summer species.

## PALMS AND WILLOWS

Today is Palm Sunday throughout the Christian world, and it is a happy time as spring awakens all nature in much of the earth. So today, the question arises, "When is a palm not a palm?" English children have a little chant that answers this nicely for us:

"The people call it Palm, they do
They call it pussy-willow, too
And when it's in full bloom the bees
Come humming around the yellow trees."

Most of the countries of Continental Europe, as well as England, do not have native palms, and so it was not possible for them to celebrate in the early days with palm; they substituted branches of various kinds to decorate their homes and churches. In Germany it was common to bring branches of fruit trees in the house early in the year and force them into bloom for this particular day. More Europeans took what was at hand at the time and used the early blossoming willows for the celebration. In some rural churches in Britain I found the day is still known as "The Sunday of Willow Boughs," as in Germany it is "Blossom Sunday."

The blooming of the pussy willows here is one of our early spring signs, so I like to have a bouquet of willows gracing my table today.

## EGGS FEW AT PRESENT

Eggs, a major symbol of Easter, are uncommon in the bird world this month.

Crows have been pairing for some time as the roosts break up, and, although some are already about the task of building nests, eggs are in the future. The horned larks, known for their early nesting, are delayed this year, and so far I've seen no indications of nesting.

Killdeer are selecting nesting sites since their recent arrival from Latin America. They are among the early nesters.

If you desire an egg hunt this Easter, you had better take advantage of one sponsored by a park or similar place where candy and eggs predominate. Don't count on Mother Nature to entertain you. In case you were wondering, taking any egg from a wild bird's nest is illegal.

While eggs are few at present, birds have come from the south in flocks. I was greeted the first day of spring by a flock of hungry grackles at my feeder. Their grating conversation was really "music to my ears" after the long winter.

A flock of redwings also arrived in my yard and greeted me with their ok-a-lee, ok-a-lee, which is one of my favorite spring songs. The song sparrows have been singing for two weeks. More than three weeks ago, the cardinal tuned up his spring song to attract his mate.

One sunny morning, a fortnight ago, I was awakened by the soft, persistent cooing of a pair of mourning doves that have been my guests all winter. I knew spring was not far off, though my back door was still piled high with snow.

Chickadees and titmice have been singing spring songs for some time. There has been a happy, joyous rhythm in the pounding of my downy and red-headed woodpeckers. Even the house sparrows have been more vocal as they hurry about courting their favorites. They are among the early nesters, as are the starlings.

Both of these birds, imported from Europe and now an established part of our wildlife scene, have been known to nest at every month of the year. Don't be surprised if you see them carrying nesting material on a mild sunny day next winter.

The flocks of grosbeaks, siskins, tree sparrows, redpolls and juncos are lessening at feeding stations as they heed the call of the north and slip away in small groups, almost unnoticed.

Birds with spring songs are celebrating spring and Easter. We cannot neglect the Easter Rabbit — that is any cottontail that happens to be about this week. Because of the deep snow and mountainous drifts this past winter, rabbits have found their way to bird feeding stations and are enjoying leftovers that have fallen on the ground.

So it is that on this last day of Wildlife Week, these creatures, birds and rabbits, bring us a "Happy Easter."

# APRIL

## EARTH REJOICES

April is the month of the year when the earth is in its youth and full of rejoicing.

Bird songs, unheard for many months, again resound through swamps, pastures and fields. Redwings and meadowlarks are just two of the many birds tuning up for their annual vernal concert.

Stream borders are vibrant with the music of the song sparrow, the honking of wild geese and the trumpeting of cranes. Their music floats to earthbound ears as the birds beat their trackless way north.

Skunk cabbages push upward and unfold their protective hoods as the flowers appear, welcomed by the first flies and other insects. British soldiers and fairy caps are among the brilliant little plants that catch one's eye.

Hepaticas carpet the woodlot and flower the sunny slopes of hillsides. Willow and alders bloom about duneland pools while killdeer and sandpiper wade at the edges. The first shadbush may burst into bloom to surprise woods-wanderers in early April. By the end of the month the diaphanous shadbush veil will spread through much of western Michigan's wooded acres, changing them to a fairyland.

Water is again teeming with many creatures. Scuds, fairy shrimp, daphne, striders, skaters, water scorpions and whirligig beetles are a few of the conspicuous inhabitants of pools and ponds.

The bird population is rapidly changing — both by day and by night — as winter visitors leave for their northern nesting grounds, and the summer residents return to us. Transients are streaming through, and one has to be very alert to catch a glimpse of the more wary of these travelers.

Spiders, snakes, and turtles venture out on the first sunny days of April as the air warms. They soak up the heat to give activity to their cold-blooded bodies.

Baby squirrels, chipmunks, woodchucks, rabbits, and skunks are being born this month. Many homes are already overcrowded with the younger generation.

In April, the maple sap run slows down, and toward the end of the month the sugar bushes close down for another year. So, if you would see this fascinating activity of rural Michigan, do not delay. The sap draws birds such as woodpeckers, robins, phoebes and titmice, as well as a large variety of insects.

Butterflies are increasing as the days warm, and where a few weeks ago there was only an occasional mourning cloak, there are now groups of red admirals, whites, and commas to join them.

Snowdrops and crocuses welcome April and soon jonquils, daffodils, and other narcissus varieties will add to the parade of spring garden flowers.

By the end of the month gourmets of native foods will be seeking fresh dandelion greens and new milkweed shoots. Both are very good eating.

April to the Michigan Indians was the Green Grass Moon. The grass is greening and by month's end, the summer carpet will be laid.

## HEPATICA AND ARBUTUS RACE

After the skunk cabbage, it is difficult to say which blossom wins the race. In some sections of the country and of Michigan, it is the hepatica or liverleaf, and in others it may be the arbutus. Both of these have been honored in poetry as the "first blossom of the year."

In Muskegon country and western Michigan it's especially hard to say which gets second place, for here both the arbutus and the hepatica are common. During the past two weeks both of these have been blooming and have delighted the hearts of many a woods-wanderer. The wooded dunes along the shores of Lake Michigan are choice places for these early flowers, and many a sunny, south-exposed dune is dotted with their delicate shades.

The blossoming of one plant is often overlooked because it is so small and because it has the unfortunate word "weed" attached to its name. That is the chickweed with its minute star-like blossom. Scarcely has the snow disappeared from the ground before this mite of a plant puts out its wee stars. This neglected plant is close on the heels of the skunk cabbage, and in this section really comes before either the hepatica or arbutus.

Dandelions are springing up everywhere and if early numbers count, this season presages well for the "tribe of lions."

Spring beauties, or claytonias, are plentiful about the area, and the grassy knolls about the bases of many large tree trunks along the highways are beautified by these dainty little plants. Do not try to take them home for they soon wilt and are unsatisfactory as cut flowers. Enjoy them in the grass where they are.

To the fishermen, no plant is more familiar than the adder's tongue or trout lily. True to their name, they are out now to welcome the annual trout season. Their mottled leaves are almost as attractive as their yellow, lily-like blossoms.

A few marsh marigolds are already blossoming, but they will be at their height a little later. The hepatica and arbutus have the stage at present.

## PROTECTED FLOWERS

"April showers bring May flowers" may be the general rule, but this year wildflowers didn't wait for the proverbial April showers. They're here.

Another rule that woods-wanderers and flower-lovers would do well to brush up on these days is one enacted by the state legislature, Michigan's protective flower law. This state was slow among the 50 to recognize the need of protection for its floral wildings, but with this law it took 11 kinds under its legal wing. They are trailing arbutus, trillium, climbing bitter-sweet, North American lotus, bird foot violet, flowering dogwood, club mosses, Michigan holly, all native orchids, gentians and pipsissewa. Evergreen trees and boughs also come under this ruling.

The rule states that these plants are not to be picked or transported without a written permit from the owner of the property on which they grow. This is important to Muskegon country outdoor enthusiasts because a number of these species are not only found here but are "common." The bird foot violet is one of the county's abundant spring blooms and great stretches of the sandy wastes are favorites of this interesting violet. In other parts of the state it is becoming scarce. Orchids mentioned in the rule include the lady's slipper, or moccasin flower, found in Muskegon's wooded duneland, the ladies' tresses, yellow lady's slipper and all related forms.

Bittersweet is the berry which is frequently sold on the farmers' market in the autumn. Venders should realize that this plant is protected.

Arbutus is a plant which has been abused most shamefully in western Michigan. Likewise, flowering dogwood has been gathered promiscuously about the county in the past.

Lotus is a rarer species and is usually protected by those adjacent to the streams and bayous where it grows. The nearest bed to Muskegon is in the Grand River south of Grand Haven. This is under private supervision.

Club mosses, including ground hemlock, pine and deer-horn, were badly exploited in the past, making it necessary to place them under protection. They have been used extensively for holiday greens in garlands and wreaths.

Muskegon country has a fine share of Michigan's wild flowers, and through the aid of this state ruling and the interest of outdoor folk and conservation-minded sportsmen, her forests, fields, dunelands and waterways may be kept beautiful for years to come.

## THE EGG — SYMBOL OF LIFE

The egg as a symbol of new life, even life itself, is older than Easter.

Mythology from many parts of the world and from many times tells that the universe came from a great egg. Many people used eggs as a fertility symbol and as the sign of new life awakening in spring.

Christians saw in eggs the symbol of the resurrection, and as such eggs became an important part of the Easter festival and its celebration. Many legends, charms and myths grew up around eggs and have come down to us today.

However, in the natural world there are few eggs to be found as early as this year's celebration. Many of the birds are back from their winter sojourn in the south, but few of them have prepared their nests and laid eggs yet.

If the courting and mating activities now noticeable are any indication, it will not be long before clutches of eggs are hidden in many nests. Grackles, cowbirds, redwings, jays and starlings are courting. The males are displaying all sorts of visual and auditory behavior in front of the hens. Bowing, fluffing, wing-spreading, flapping, crest-raising and bill-tilting are just a few of the activities in which these males are now engaged.

Roosting birds, such as crows, are now leaving their large assemblies and pairing for their nesting. Common as crows are, their nests are not easy to find because they build numbers of preliminary nests. Having once finished a nest, they breed from late April through June.

Birds that may have some "Easter" eggs in their nests are the house sparrows, starlings, pigeons and hairy woodpeckers. The first three of these have been known to have eggs during every month of the year in favorable weather and are considered early nesters.

Mallards are already about their nesting. This is not surprising as they began courting in September and will continue through April. Some of the robins that came in mid-March may already have their nests made and egg-laying started.

It is a sure thing that the great horned owls have either eggs or nestlings by now for they are the earliest of our birds to start their domestic duties. The song sparrow, the first migrant to return, breeds in April and just might have some eggs by Easter.

These eggs are not the brightly colored ones that we call "Easter eggs," but are white, spotted, streaked and speckled, pale buff, light blue, shades of brown or robin's egg blue.

## EASTER SYMBOLS

Rabbits, chickens and eggs are Easter's symbols from the animal world and one may take a choice.

In the world of flowers there is one that stands out preeminently from all the rest. That is the lily. Traditionally, no other plant holds the position of honor at the spring festival that this one does. The cultivated lily is widely used as the symbolic flower in churches and in the religious celebration.

The common garden lily of this area does not bloom until summer, too late for Easter, and is the Madonna lily. In the 1880's Mrs. Thomas Sargent of Philadelphia became acquainted with the lovely white Bermuda lily, which naturally blossoms in the springtime. She introduced it to a nursery-man, William Harris, who popularized it among other growers. Soon it was America's Easter flower.

When Easter arrives late, it is possible on one's Easter walk to see our own wild lilies. They will be more abundant after Easter and into May, but still two of them stand out in the woodland and streamside scene as "Easter Lilies." One is the trout lily, with its golden chalice and spotted leaves that likes to grow in moist, open woods and thickets and on brooksides.

The more familiar and conspicuous of the wild Easter lilies is the trillium, whose very name suggests the Trinity. This rule of three dominates the plant as it has three leaves, three sepals, which are white like the three petals, three styles, three-celled ovary and twice three stamens. It is also called the white woodlily. John Burroughs, the early American naturalist-writer, called it wakerobin. He said when it bloomed that was the sign that all the birds had returned from their winter vacations, and that robins were nesting.

In the 1930's the wakerobin had almost disappeared from Michigan's outdoor scene due to of a variety of causes, mostly overpicking. When this flower was gathered, the large green food-producing leaves were taken with it, so that the plant could not make and store food in its bulb. Because of this, all trilliums are now protected by state law, as is the dogwood, another symbol of the Easter season. Since protection was afforded it, the plant has made a tremendous comeback and every spring many acres of Michigan woodland are carpeted with the pristine beauty of this small white lily.

## MOURNING DOVES RETURN

During the early days of April, the mourning doves arrive in flocks. They soon separate into pairs and for the rest of the season are generally seen as devoted couples.

Since the disappearance of the passenger pigeon from the woodlands of Michigan, the mourning dove is the only native representative of the family. Investigation of scattered reports of the occurrence of passenger pigeons usually reveals that the common mourning dove is mistaken for its larger and extinct relative.

The mourning dove receives its common name from the sad, monotonous cooing which it makes continuously. Locally it is also known as the Carolina dove and the turtle dove.

Mourning doves are easily identified by the well-developed body, small head and pointed tail displaying white edged feathers. The general color is olive brown with shades of pink, rose and blue and buffy-gray beneath. Above the iridescent neck patch is a conspicuous black mark.

The food of these birds is varied, consisting of seeds, berries, grain and insects.

They frequent orchards, wood-bordered fields, and open woodlands. Here the rather slovenly-built nest is placed precariously in trees or bushes. Thorn trees are preferred by the doves. The nest is a frail platform of twigs and roots with no comfortable lining of down. The most remarkable aspect of the nest is that the eggs and young succeed in staying in the flimsy structure.

Two eggs commonly are laid and these develop into grotesque looking young which are fed by the parent by regurgitation. The young mature slowly and are the constant care of the adults for some time.

Mourning doves are common throughout the state and are frequently seen dusting themselves in gravel roads. Caution of motorists is needed at these times because the birds are relatively slow of flight and easily may be killed by the careless driver. Again the doves are often seen toward evening sitting in pairs on wires bordering the highways.

Economically, because of their feeding habits, the mourning doves are beneficial to agriculturists. Because of their beauty of plumage, gentleness of manner, and admirable habits of life, the mourning doves are made welcome as they return from their winter vacation.

## SPRING PEEPER HEARD

Heard but not seen.

That is the usual story of the spring peeper, that tiny frog, about an inch long, which is the smallest member of the springtime amphibian chorus.

There is scarcely a person in Michigan who has not heard the shrill, piping voice of this little frog as it echoes over marshes and newly-plowed fields in April. Yet there are only a few who have actually seen these minute musicians at their performance.

Peepers congregate in ponds and pools shortly after the ice is out, leaving their upland haunts to mate and lay eggs. The piping is a courting song.

Usually the frog sits in the water or is supported on a grass with only the head protruding. With each note he inflates the skin of the throat into a singing pouch, simply huge for his size. He stretches the skin tight as a drum, and it appears as a yellow bubble under the chin.

The pouch acts as a sounding board and helps to carry the sound more than a mile across watery fields and meadows. Peepers are very sensitive to vibrations, and as an observer approaches the pond or pool the footfalls quickly warn them, and there is ominous silence. "Stop and go" is the procedure if one would see these mini-minstrels playing.

The females are attracted to the pond by the chorus and there the eggs are laid and fertilized. Shortly they become tiny wiggly pollywogs swarming about the grasses and other water weeds near the bottom. Later the adults retire to their terrestrial haunts where they remain until fall hibernation or spring courtship calls them to the water again.

Before the peeper chorus ends, other breeding amphibians will seek the ponds and add their voices to the spring chorus. There will be the green frog, wood frog, the leopard, the dainty little tree frogs, and the bullfrog with its deep bass voice. Intermingled with them will be the bird-like trill of the common garden toad, which is a joy to hear on a moonlit, balmy night in late April.

Already woodland pools are full of activity as the salamanders have invaded them to breed and lay their eggs. Red-backed, three-toed and the spotted are among the ones which mingle with the frogs and toads during these mid-April days.

Water insects are awakening and are conspicuous in these same pools. Whirligig beetles, great diving beetles, skaters, backswimmers, water scorpions and giant water bugs are among those to be seen this week. Tadpoles that have over-wintered and flatworms are other inhabitants of ditches and spring pools now. Leeches or blood-suckers have awakened and are active also.

There is great activity when the ice goes out of these woodland pools, and the announcement is always given by the spring peepers.

BEAUTY ALONG THE STREAM

The creel take may be dubious this week, but there is no question but that every fisherman that wades a stream or even fishes from the bank can catch two beauties — the trout lily and the shadbush. Both of these plants, one an herb, the other a shrub named for popular fish, are blossoming now and by May first will be at the height of their season.

The shadbush blooms earlier than the dogwood and is just as conspicuous in the open woodlands now as that shrub will be later. It is one of the earliest to flower and presents a diaphanous element of green lacery in grove and forest. The name shadbush was given this small tree or shrub because its blossoms appear at the time of the shad run on the eastern seaboard. Early settlers watching the tree knew when to make their shad catches. In this part of the country it is better known as juneberry because in that month it is conspicuous with bright red berries which are beloved by birds as well as humans. The berries are sometimes used for jell and other delicacies. In the south it is the familiar service or sarvis-berry of the uplands.

The white flowers, slightly tinted with pink, are in drooping racemes and appear before the leaves, which makes the shrub stand out now in its bridal array. Bees are partial to it and assist in its pollination. It will be a poor fisherman in western Michigan who doesn't get a shadbush on the opening weekend.

The trout lily must be sought on the ground close to the forest carpet. Although trout lily is one of the earliest and most appropriate names for this small plant, it is known by a variety of others. It is the dog-tooth violet and the adder's tongue of childhood. Although not as plentiful as once, it is still a common spring wild flower.

The mottled leaves grow in great patches, and in among these are the delightful golden bells which hang down so modestly in the woodland sunshine. Occasionally if one is lucky, he may find a white one — an albino, perhaps.

Trout lilies got their name from their habit of early spring blooming when the trout were running. They are an indicator for trout as the shadbush is for shad — or so the old-timers say.

If these blossoms are gathered, care should be taken not to disturb the leaves which are responsible for the food-making of the plant, and the food storage in the bulb. Like many of the early spring blossoms, the adder's tongue is dependent upon a bulb for its growth.

Shadbush and trout lilies will add interest and beauty to any fishing trip, whatever the creel may hold. There'll be a floral rainbow on every stream bank — may it bring good luck.

## MARIGOLDS IN MARSHES

The forest's full of flowers;
The meadow's growing green;
But, the cowslips in the marshes
Are the gayest sight I've seen.

This year nature has strewn her floral gold early in the marshes and swamps of western Michigan, for even now Muskegon country lowlands are shining with these gay blossoms.

In fact, housewives who were planning on "cowslip greens" this spring had to be about early, or they missed out entirely. For to be at their best, marigold greens should be eaten just as the flower buds appear and not after yellow tints them. Lucky, indeed, were those who were in the swamps early and got their selection of these delectable wildings. They are milder than dandelion or dock greens, have a delightfully appealing taste and will enliven almost any monotonous menu.

One never regrets too much when the blossoms get ahead of him because few wild flowers, this time of year, give the massed glory of spring that these moisture-loving plants do. Their gold, shiny character brightens up many acres of Michigan swampland before the trees are leaved out and before many other splotches of color appear. Most of the early spring flowers are delicate, dainty hideaways that one must search for, but the marsh marigolds seem to want to be seen and flaunt their golden floral treasures at every passer-by. Their blossoming season is short, and they surely make the most of it.

Bees and butterflies are welcome visitors at their yellow chalices, and four-footed wildfolk frequently get their first taste of spring greens from the succulent leaves. Toads and salamanders often lay their eggs at the base of the marsh marigold seeking anchorage and protection under its glossy leaves.

Woods-wanderers and rural folk, one and all, greet the coming of the cowslips with a light heart, and cares seem less heavy because of this precious gay blossom which throws its gold away.

## SPRING FISHING TRIP

Yes, we, too, opened the trout season. And the luck certainly was good on Sand Creek.

We started at midnight, just like the rest, so we were almost too late to get Regulus, star of first magnitude and one of the more brilliant in the heavens. Next there was Vega in Lyra, harbinger of spring and beautiful for her blue white intensity. Antares in Scorpio, marking his blood-red heart, completed our first "big three."

Of course, we got Pisces, the fish, thrown in.

Thanks to the pewee, we didn't need Big or Little Ben — At 4:10 a.m. we started our long "catch" of birds for the day. There were 52 in all, including Michigan's smallest, the ruby-throated hummingbird, and the largest — the great blue heron and the bald eagle — take your choice. We caught both.

Despite the lack of April showers, the May flowers were within an easy cast. Skunk cabbage, arbutus, two anemones, cowslips, violets, spring beauties and the dandelions were on the line.

Among the insects not caught by the fish, but counted by us were the mourning cloak, red admiral, tortoise shell and a cabbage butterfly.

True, it's out of season, but a deer made our list.

Suckers, crayfish and lamprey eels were landed successfully, but the turtle escaped with our bait.

What more could one expect of a single fishing trip?

Oh, by the way, we did catch enough brookies for a hearty breakfast. Good takes of brook trout were reported by a few fishermen, mainly from the smaller streams.

As is usually the case in late April, dry fly fishing was almost totally unproductive. The warm weather Saturday brought out a good hatch of insects along the streams, and a lighter hatch appeared Sunday afternoon, despite the cold wind. For all the hatches, however, the trout displayed little interest in dry flies. Live bait easily held first place as a fish getter. Spinners and minnows accounted for the bulk of the really large trout, and worms took credit for most of the full creels. Muddlers and shiners lured many big rainbows and browns to the net.

Nymphs were used by some anglers, but with only fair success. A few good catches were taken on wet flies. On the Au Sable, wet fly fishing after dark produced two or three of the best creels of brown trout taken over the weekend.

EAT YOUR WEEDS

Don't complain about the dandelions in your lawn, just eat them.

To most home owners the dandelion is an enemy; but it can be a friend. It had many friends back in the 17th century when it first came to America; in fact, it was brought here because of its usefulness. It was valued as an important ingredient of salves, ointments and tonics recommended as cures for everything from gallstones to dropsy. In early America, the settlers and Indians depended on "greens and grasses" to keep them alive when other foods were scarce.

Almost every part of the dandelion plant can be used: the leaves as greens in salad or boiled as a vegetable; the flowers for fritters and wine; the roots, dried, roasted and ground, provide a substitute for coffee; dried leaves make a satisfactory tea. As for the seeds, you do not need them so save them for the birds!

Dandelions start the parade of native plants (weeds) that can be used for the spring menu. Pigweed, lamb's quarters, purslane (pussley), curly dock and burdock, watercress, cowslips, wild salsify, skunk cabbage and milkweed are a few of the wild plants available in nature's spring garden.

Some of these plants were here before the white men came. The Indians used over one thousand native plants in their culture. Since the coming of the Europeans, new plants have been added to the flora. Michigan's first list of weeds in 1839 included 47. By 1912 there were 150, and since that time an average of one a year has been added.

Among the late comers, since 1900, are Queen Anne's lace (wild carrot), tumbleweeds, flax and hoary alyssum, and four recent arrivals are knapweed, orange hawkweed, viper's bugloss and purple loosestrife. Many of these were originally brought here because of their usefulness in the Old World, but in recent years they have come in as stowaways.

To bring down those mounting food bills, while your garden is maturing, try some of these native plants, rich in minerals and vitamins, and add variety to the salads and vegetables on your menus.

CLEAN WATER

All living things, both plants and animals, need water. Of course, they need it in varying degrees from the desert kangaroo rat, which never sips water but makes its own from starch and seeds it eats, to the fish and other truly aquatic creatures that never leave the water. Likewise there are the desert plants that go years without a drop of rainfall to the great kelps and submergents that wither and dry on the air-cooled beaches. Somewhere in between these extremes most of our wildlife species live. A former Conservation Stamp sheet depicts colorfully and dramatically three dozen of these plants and animals, including 18 seen in Michigan.

Michigan, the Water Wonderland State, surely has its own concerns about water and wildlife and is ever on the alert to keep the waters clean. One does not have to be a crusading environmentalist to display concern. We all need clean water, and ten million students, teachers, and members of state, national and local outdoor groups emphasized this fact during Conservation Week.

Here in western Michigan we have been cognizant of the importance of clean water and have a history of active concern to keep lakes and streams unpolluted and improve those that have been. We can point to the Wastewater System with pride as we talk of clean water, for we have become a showcase for the nation with this installation. It has drawn tens of thousands of water birds into the area, both spring and fall, and has become the mecca of thousands of bird-watchers throughout the midwest — a true tourist attraction in more ways than one.

Other water areas here, lakes and streams, have their attendant wildlife, and birds are a large part of it. Of Michigan's 350 estimated species, fully half are closely dependent upon the water and wetlands for their livelihood. From the tiny marsh wren to the great sandhill crane and eagle, birds depend on wet habitats to survive. Among the waterbirds commonly seen here either throughout the year, or on spring and fall migration, are loons, grebes, heron, egrets, cranes, rails, gallinules, coots, plovers, sandpipers, dowitchers, godwits, phalaropes, gulls, terns, ospreys, eagles, cormorants and a very occasional pelican. Redwings, marsh wrens and yellow-throats are among the common dwellers in the marshy wetlands.

Let no one tell bird-watchers that swamps, marshes and river bottoms are "unsightly wasteland." They are some of the most prolific hunting grounds for birders and outdoors persons. Clean water? Sure, we all need it, so let's keep it!

## CHICKADEES LIKE HOUSES

Winter, summer, spring or fall, there are few birds that are better beloved than the chickadees.

In winter they are among the most regular patrons of feeding stations, and many people complain that they "disappear" in the spring and are not seen around the premises until snow flies again. These human friends regret the absence of these cheery little birds and wish that they were as neighborly in summer as in winter.

Chickadees are easily attracted to nesting boxes, and that is the easiest way to assure their companionship during summer months. Their food habits are as commendable in summer as in winter, and any garden that shelters a family of these birds is a happy one, for they reduce the insect population considerably. Young chickadees have voracious appetites, and it takes a large number of insects of many kinds to satisfy their hunger.

Chickadee families are interesting and entertaining to watch and bring many hours of enjoyment to their landlords besides paying well in eating insects.

Chickadees are two brooded and consequently are kept unusually busy about their domestic affairs, so perhaps they do not have as much time for human companionship in summer as in winter; but be assured, if houses are provided for and used by them in nesting time, they will delight you with their acrobatic antics in winter and even learn to eat out of your hand, if there is the patience to teach them.

Their houses are easily constructed and one need keep in mind only a few dimensions. Their favorite nesting place is a posthole or a knot hole in branches and tree trunk. Simulating these places gives the best results, and a section of a small log makes an ideal home for chickadees.

The depth of cavity should approximate that of the bluebird's house, about eight inches; and the entrance, one and an eighth inch in diameter, should be eight inches from the floor. The floor space itself may vary but four by four inches is a standard measurement for it. Then, since chickadees naturally nest some six to fifteen feet from the ground, that is the approved height for location. Taking into consideration the exposure, direction of sunlight, prevailing winds, protection and position for observation there is just one more thing to concern the landlord. Take the advice of Herbert Job, authority on bird study, and "Think bird."

## LURING MARTINS

Many persons who have fed a variety of winter birds are now concentrating on the spring arrivals and how they can entice them to become "near neighbors" during their summer residency.

Foremost among these desired tenants are the purple martins, and rightly so, for few birds are as effective "mosquito traps."

Since the earliest days in North America, people have attracted these birds to catch insects. The Indians placed a series of gourds on cross bars to encourage them. Audubon noted this. He commented, "The martins are so audacious they chased away the vultures attracted to the Indians' hanging venison."

The artist also saw many bird boxes for martins at the inns he visited across the country. He noted, "The handsomer the box, the better does the inn prove to be." The houses were attached to the upper part of the inn's sign-board.

A list of points to check for a suitable house according to the *Purple Martin News*, are:

(1) Lightweight for easy raising and lowering. Aluminum is ideal because it is durable and cool.

(2) Coolness, material, color and ventilation are all important factors. White is the coolest, and regardless of material the exterior should be light rather than dark. Holes in each compartment, providing cross currents, are useful.

(3) Size. The house should be three and a half inches wide and the entrance two to two and a half inches in diameter, with its bottom one inch above the floor.

(4) Bright inside. A much overlooked aspect of the interior is that it should be light color to help discourage starlings, who prefer a dark, dingy hole.

(5) Guard barriers. All porches require guard rails or barriers high enough to prevent young birds from falling to the ground. Metal poles prevent many climbing predators.

(6) Easy cleaning. Compartments should have an easy way of cleaning.

(7) Telescoping poles are especially helpful. A crank-up winch or rope flagpole-type lanyard is recommended. It is important to raise and lower it vertically so as not to disturb the nests.

(8) Place in an open area at least fifteen feet from overhanging branches or buildings, 14 to 25 feet high and near a body of water if possible.

If a new house remains unoccupied for a couple of seasons, try relocating its place and height.

Houses here should be in place April 10 as scouts arrive then. Following that time, the rest come, and nesting takes place during late April, May, and, for younger birds, as late as June.

## THAT'S JUST A SPARROW

"Oh, that's just a sparrow!" is a common retort as one glances out the window and sees a brownish medium-sized bird. By such a statement, one usually means the English sparrow or house sparrow, which really is not a sparrow at all, but a member of the weaverbird family. However, right now when one says "sparrow" you had better ask what he means, for it can be any one of the fourteen native sparrows that are here during April and May.

It is not easy for the amateur bird-watcher to distinguish all of them, but it can be done, and it's a lot of fun. It takes a little organized thought and attention to detail to come up with the correct answers fairly quickly, so we will make a few suggestions that may help to interest you in this fascinating group of birds which is here now.

To begin with, take a quick look at the breast — if it is streaked and striped, place it in one group; if on the other hand it is generally plain with only one spot, segregate it into the other group. Now you have already cut down the fourteen to eight and six. The plain breasted ones are white-throated, white-crowned, tree, swamp, field, chipping, clay-colored and grasshopper. (We are speaking now of mature birds, not juveniles which are another problem.) The streaked breasted ones include the fox, song, vesper, Savannah, Lincoln and Henslow.

Now each of these birds has its own distinguishing characteristics. We look for one that can be seen easily in the field, and this "field mark" is the detail to watch for as you check on "that little brown bird" in your yard or garden.

There are two common sparrows and one rare one that have pink bills. These are the white-crowned, the field and the rare Harris. Now let's check through the plain-breasted ones for field marks. If, in addition, the bird has a white-striped crown and white throat, count it the white-throated; if on the other hand it is white-striped with a pink bill and grayish throat, it is a white-crowned. Both are transients here and nest to the north of us as a rule.

Look for a reddish cap and central black spot on the breast and it's the tree sparrow. They are winter visitors and have been lunching at feeding stations for the past months. Soon they will leave us for the northern tundra. Another reddish crown with a plain breast and white throat is the swamp sparrow. Then there's the rusty cap and the pink bill and that's the field. Another very small sparrow with a reddish cap and plain breast is the chipping. Easy, isn't it? Watch for a striped crown and a brown cheek patch and you've seen the clay-colored, and then the grasshopper has a striped crown with a dingy, buffy breast. Now you know the plain-breasted ones.

Let's take a look at the sparrows with streaked or striped breasts. First, there is a big one with much streaking and a reddish tail; that's the fox sparrow, and it is a beautiful bird. It is not unusual for amateurs to confuse it with the thrushes, but once you identify it you never make that mistake again because the birds are of very different builds. The sparrow is chunky, while the thrush is slender.

The song sparrow is one of the very common native sparrows, and sometimes stays here through the winter. It is marked by the darker splotch in the middle of the striped and streaked breast, a breast-pin as it were. The longish appearing tail is significant also in helping to identify it.

The Savannah has a shorter tail, yellow eye stripe and notched tail. The Lincoln is best known for the finely streaked breast and all over streaked aspect. The Henslow has been described as having a greenish crown and nape along with fine streaking in black and pointed tail feathers. Watch for the sparrow with the white outer tail feathers, reminiscent of the junco, and you have spotted the vesper sparrow.

These few suggestions should give you a beginner's guide to the native sparrows you may see during the next few weeks, but there are many other ways to learn the sparrows. One can learn to distinguish them by their songs and calls, and that is very helpful because these birds are highly protectively colored and often blend so well with their surroundings that only their voices make their whereabouts known to the observer.

The habits of these birds help a great deal in distinguishing them. Little behavior tricks are distinctive for the different species, but these are best learned in the field, so we will not try to confuse the issue by putting it on paper.

Remember, first check for a plain or streaked breast and then for the specific field marks memorized for each. Before this season is past, we can almost guarantee you will be a sparrow expert, and you will never again say, "Oh, that's just a sparrow."

## HERB GARDENS

Long before there were flower or vegetable gardens, there were herb gardens, and in recent years they have again gained popularity.

The plants grown in the herb garden can be used for a variety of purposes. They are useful as seasoning, as potherbs, teas and in green salads, some have medicinal value and cosmetic qualities, and some are used to rid the house of insects and to freshen air and clothing.

Many of these herbs originated in the coastal region of the Mediterranean Sea and are found to do equally well here because of the climatic effects of Lake Michigan. Herbs, for the most part, like good drainage, full sunlight, little fertilizer and only a moderately rich soil for best results.

Of the many herbs that can be grown in the western Michigan garden, twelve are especially recommended to answer the common needs of the gardener. Although culinary, several are also used medicinally. These favorites include nine perennials — mints, chives, tarragon, sage, oregano, sorrel, comfrey, thyme, parsley — and three annuals, marjoram, savory and the basils.

Others that are desirable are rosemary and scented geraniums, but because of Michigan winters these have to be brought inside during the cold months. Lavender, very popular for sachets and sweet bags, should be in each garden.

Herbs can be placed in a variety of settings in the garden and one does not have to have a special herb plot for them. Introduce them in borders, place them in the vegetable garden and use them for backgrounds and edgings as well as in containers and planters and as contrasts in the flower garden.

The grayish green foliage of many of them is very attractive and lends itself effectively in bedding and with many flowering plants. The wormwoods, of which there are many, including the so-called "dusty-miller," give a dramatic touch to a planting.

## SANDHILL CRANES IN CORNFIELDS

Several sightings of sandhill cranes have been made during the past two weeks by bird-watchers in Muskegon and Oceana Counties. Along with the eagle, this large bird always gives birders a thrill.

Billed as Michigan's largest bird, it has a wing-spread of six to seven feet and stands four feet high. The mature bird is grayish, often stained a rust color, with a red bare spot on the head. The young are brownish and do not have the red crown.

At present, these large birds are migrating through western Michigan counties and in several cases have been seen feeding with Canada geese in old cornfields, near wetlands. In flight they are easily identified because, unlike the herons which fly with an 'S'-curved neck, these extend both the neck and legs straight from the body. In flight the cranes alternate between gliding and flapping and the upstroke of the wing is very rapid.

My first glimpse of sandhill cranes in Muskegon County was one April day as I crossed Hackley Park, and hearing a strange call note, I looked up to see three of these huge birds flying northward at a surprisingly low altitude over the area.

The Michigan Audubon Society's first sanctuary was established to give refuge to these birds. It was donated to the society by the late Bernard W. Baker, of Marne and Spring Lake, in 1941 in the area of Calhoun County, then known as the Big Marsh.

Later, in 1955, Caspar Haehnle of Jackson donated 497 acres to MAS, known as the Mud Lake Marsh in Jackson County, now the Phyllis Haehnle Memorial Sanctuary. Both of these have continued to attract and provide protection for these magnificent birds.

Their numbers have noticeably increased since those years and nesting in Michigan is more common. Upper Peninsula counties offer similar refuges and acceptable sites for these spectacular birds.

# ARBOR DAY

What did you do for Arbor Day? Did the day pass unnoticed as far as you were concerned?

There was a time when every school child in Michigan took part in some sort of tree-planting ceremony. Then there came a period when this phase of environmental improvement was almost forgotten, with only a few oldtimers remembering. Happy we can be that again citizens are realizing the importance of trees and again Arbor Day is observed.

When J. Sterling Morton migrated from Detroit to Nebraska Territory in 1854 he missed the trees of Michigan which at that time were the very economic lifeblood of the state. He saw the open prairies where the wind swept unhindered with devastating results. He saw that trees were needed for windbreaks, fuel, lumber and shade. As editor of Nebraska's first newspaper he spread the doctrine of conservation and reforestation. In 1872 Morton presented his plan for an Arbor Day before the State Board of Agriculture and it generated so much enthusiasm that on the first Arbor Day, April 10, 1872, over a million trees were planted.

Later the legislature legalized the holiday, naming April 22, Morton's birthday, as the official day. The nickname of Nebraska became "The Tree-planter's State." It is significant that this year Michigan's Arbor Day falls on the 22nd, Morton's birthday. Michigan is one of the few states that frequently has two days set apart for the celebration — differing in the Upper and Lower Peninsulas, due to weather conditions.

This year a theme, "Plant for Wildlife," was chosen for the state's endeavor. In addition to the many school children who are participating here this year, the Muskegon County Conservation Club, The Garden Club, and Nature Club all held special observances. In keeping with the theme, packets of trees and shrubs suitable for wildlife were available from the Michigan United Conservation Clubs, Lansing.

Planting for food and shelter is very important. Mammals and birds alike can profit by this project and many fruits and nuts are eaten by both groups. Non-game, as well as game mammals, game birds and song birds are all considered in this year's program. More than 22 species of plants from ground covers of wintergreen, bearberry, through the shrubs to trees such as apple, sassafras, sumac, juneberry and wild cherry are suitable. Ruffed grouse will eat many of these. Mountain ash (rowan) and mulberry are popular, but the latter are messy near dwellings and buildings. As for

69

birds, there are some plants that stand out preeminently for them. One hundred and twenty species have been attracted to the elderberry, the most desirable for numbers, along with blackberries which have hosted 149. Dogwood and sumac both attract 98 and wild black cherry and blueberry 93 species. Among the conifers, pines and cedars are tops, attracting 63 and 54 and both offer good nesting sites, another consideration when planting for wildlife.

Grapes, hawthorns, chokecherry, wild cherry, and bayberry all have entertained over 80 different kinds of birds. In recent years the olives — Russian and autumn — have proved to be exceptionally fine for wildlife. It is well to plant some trees and shrubs that retain their fruits the year around. Box elder is a favorite of evening grosbeaks.

Study the feeding habits of the creatures you would entertain and plant accordingly for your favorite guest. There are many good helps for this, one of my favorites being "Songbirds in your Garden," by John Terres, Thomas Y. Crowell Co., N.Y.

If you did not get your planting done on Arbor Day, do not let that deter you. While planning your flower garden include some "bird and butterfly" plants. Butterflies and their cousins the hummingbird moths should not be overlooked. They are "wildlife" too.

From deer to ladybugs, there is something tasty for all.

MAY

MERRY MONTH OF MAY

The Merry Month of May — Wabigon gisiss, the Flower Moon of the Indians.

This month has long been associated with flowers. A custom of by-gone days was the hanging of May Baskets on the first. This paid tribute to the coming of the spring flowers, which were once so plentiful. Now some of these are on the state's protected list; nonetheless, more than one hundred native plants (wild flowers) are blossoming this month.

Shadbush is late this year, and at present, is decorating the woodlots of Muskegon country with blossoms of beauty. Next will come the white and pink blooms of the dogwood in many of the same areas. Toward the end of the month look for the rosy blossoms of the hawthorn. This is a May special, and in England these thornapples are called "May" because of their blossoming season.

These are busy days for birds and bird-watchers. The spring migration reaches its height with wave after wave of warblers and its culmination with the arrival of the chimney swift, nighthawk, cuckoo and hummingbird. It is not unusual to run up a list of a hundred during one May day. As December brings the Christmas Count and Valentine Day the February Bird Watch, so May brings "the Century Run," when birders try for "more than a hundred."

Frogs, toads, salamanders and snakes enjoy the warming sunshine in the wetlands as the sun mounts higher each day.

Insects are plentiful in May with hatches of caddis, may, dragon, damsel and stone flies along the streams and lakes. The fishermen watch for these and adjust their trips to hatches.

Some fish are "nesting" now and before long the little stickle-backs will build their bird-like nest.

Woodland trails are beautiful with the varied greens of mosses, ferns, liverworts and lichens. Of course, this is the time of that most famous of all Michigan mushrooms — the May morel. April brings maple syrup festivals to many small communities, but May brings the mushrooms and the morel festivals to the northern part of the state.

Day and night, May is a wonder month with surprises hidden for anyone with an adventuresome spirit, seeing eyes and hearing ears — May is the time for an understanding heart.

## MORELS, CHOICE MORSEL

May is the month of spring wild flowers, but it is also the month of morels. Morels are the first edible mushrooms to appear in plentiful numbers in Michigan.

The damp weather of April and early May has been conducive to a good crop, and all that is needed is warm days to bring in a bumper one. Mushroom enthusiasts throughout Muskegon country have been in the field during the past week finding their share of these delicious fungi. They are easily identified and offer a good species for the beginner to learn. Commonly spoken of as the "sponge mushroom," they are somewhat egg-shaped, brownish-grey and the pitted cap is set on a lighter almost white stem, which is hollow.

They are found in a variety of places. Overgrown, bushy lowlands carpeted with leaves offer a favorite spot, whereas some may be found on grassy plots and about burned-over areas where wood ashes have been abundant.

There are numerous ways of preparing these mushrooms for the table. To some they are a favorite adjunct to chops and steak when fried, to others they form the base for soup and still others prefer them baked with crumbs, fried, broiled or even stewed. However the morel is served, it is one of nature's choice offerings from the wild garden of the out-of-doors.

Before the morel season is past, other culinary favorites will be appearing. Inky caps, puffballs and the meadow parasol are three that will add interest and variety to May's menus.

## BATS IN THE BELFRY

Bats in the belfry? Very few, if any. One reason is that there are not as many belfries as there were a few years ago, for in modern church architecture, they seem almost passé. So, bats have had to accommodate themselves to other places for their long winter sleep.

Their favorite old orchard trees with comfortable holes and cavities have been bulldozed down, and fallen forest trees which might have attracted them have been cut and taken for firewood.

These hibernating bats have solved the problem fairly well, to their own satisfaction and comfort, but not to that of all their hosts. Bats are encroaching on their human neighbors and are taking up residence in garrets, attics, behind shutters, in unused chimneys, in the shelter of awnings and crawl spaces. It takes very little room for a bat to find a winter sleeping place.

Here, for the most part, the hibernating ones are unnoticed and create no problem until early spring. Then, during the first warm days, and even before, if the sun is streaming through an attic or garret window, they begin to stir and awaken to the warmth and fly about. They find themselves in a sterile environment as far as insects, their food, are concerned, and so they seek the first exit they can find. In doing this, they frequently arrive at the main living floor and during the daylight hours hide in dark closets, under beds, behind furniture, and in similar quiet places.

Then when dusk comes and a light is turned on, they come from their hideouts to search for food. This is all most ordinary and normal for the bats, but highly abnormal for their hosts who have not seen a bat since summer. Sometimes, they winter in the basement and then come upstairs "where the folks are."

For the most part, all the creatures want is their freedom and a supply of food. The problem is that often they emerge, because of the warmth in the house, before their natural insect food supply is here. However, in spite of this, it is best to free them, and in no case, should they be destroyed, for they are among humans' good friends and are highly beneficial in yards and gardens and about the city as well as rural areas. They take over the hunt of annoying and injurious insects at dusk and continue all night, while the birds are sleeping. They work the night shift.

There are many misconceptions about bats, and they are not the most beloved of our wild creatures. However, once one takes time to learn a little about their way of life, and the many hardships they have to put up with, we can only admire them.

They do not wish to alight in one's hair — so if standing when one approaches, sit down. It is only because one's head is sticking up like a tree that they might seem to be "attacking." As to parasites, normally they carry fewer than the common house cat and are not the bearers of "bedbugs."

There is a larger bat population, in any given area, than most persons realize, and this is, of course, because they are nocturnal. Usually, they start their flight at dusk and continue about street lamps and other likely places until dawn. Their metabolism is very high and it takes many insects to satisfy them. If one has a yard lamp, sometimes they will play around it all night and rid the area of mosquitoes, flies, gnats, midges, and other nocturnal pests.

In Michigan, there are eight species of bats, not all of equal distribution and abundance. The most common one here is the little brown bat, which is only about three and a half inches long with a wingspread of nine inches. It is this most popular bat, characterized by highly swift and erratic zigzag flight, which is seen in rural, urban and suburban areas. Its chief article of diet is mosquitoes.

Two others, the keen bat and the Indiana, are so similar to the little brown, that they are not easily distinguished in flight. In hand, though, the little brown has much shorter ears than the keen.

Two larger bats are the big brown and the hoary. The hoary is the biggest and the least common of the bats here. It is migratory and in summer appears after dark, when it is most difficult to see it. It has a wingspread of fifteen inches and sharp, narrow wings. Its name comes from the frosted appearance of its brownish fur. The big brown appears later in the evening than the small ones and usually flies closer to the ground snapping up insects.

The evening bat is much like the big brown, but it is smaller and hunts earlier in the night. All Michigan bats are harmless, not a vampire among them.

The red bat is my favorite. Its fur is ruddier than the others and, although not as common as the brown, the red is still found in the area. My introduction to it was when an Ivy Street householder called and asked about an injured bat. Upon arrival, we found the little mother red bat with her three young clinging to her breast. Her flight was somewhat impeded by them, but nevertheless, she was hawking about the yard and garden with her burden. Red bats come out the earliest in the evening and may even be seen flying and feeding on a dark, cloudy, overcast day. During the bright daylight hours, they hang in a tree or shrub alone, unless they have young.

Another choice encounter with these reds was in October after the leaves had dropped from the Michigan holly. I came upon one of these brilliant red-berried shrubs with three red bats hanging from a stalwart branch. Their dark fur along with the twigs of the black alder, contrasted with the ruddy fruit, made a never-to-be-forgotten sight.

Bats are specially endowed with an echo-location system which has been likened to man's invention of radar and sonar. It directs them in their night-flying and helps them to avoid obstacles and locate their food.

Bats are usually thought of as black, so remember, "Black is beautiful." Why not befriend our helpers, the bats?

## BROWN THRASHER CLEVER SINGER

Few musicians in the April and May chorus of nature are more melodious and versatile than the brown thrasher, the "mocking bird of the north." This bird, cousin of the southern mocking bird, vies with the hermit thrush in claiming the laurels among northern singers.

Widely distributed throughout our state and this region because of his preference for dry land, sandy and gravelly stretches and the margins of woodlands, he is found on almost every farm and is well known by rural folk. No farm lane or woods seems complete without at least one pair of nesting thrashers.

The thrasher's song is his greatest claim to fame. It is a difficult song to describe and interpret, most varied and seeming to include many moods expressed in a truly lyrical manner. It has been described simply as a "bright and cheerful carol," but this does not do justice to the soft, whispering and somewhat plaintive strain that is always heard if one will listen long enough. Then there are the loud, full, rollicking measures which seem almost to burst the throat of the singer. Besides the song, the thrasher expresses himself in sharp clicks, hisses, and smacks.

The thrasher, along with the catbird and southern mocking bird, belongs in the family of mimics and seems to take great pleasure and delight in exhibiting his ability. Like many birds, thrashers often choose singing stands, and from a familiar perch day after day they pour out their medley of songs. Here they mimic the calls of other birds, frequently with such success that the victims of the prank are deceived and not only answer, but are attracted to the same tree.

In the dunes along Lake Michigan one day I heard a goldfinch, a robin and a cardinal calling in quick succession. It was a bit mechanical and unnatural because the intervals were so perfectly spaced. As the calling continued, others of these species answered. The calls and answers went on for several minutes until the cardinal, goldfinch and robin all came to a huge oak tree, and then the secret of the spaced intervals and quick changes was revealed. There in the very top of the oak, on a branch barely large enough to hold his weight, was a beautiful brown thrasher, trickster of the bird world, playing his roguish pranks on the innocent. The goldfinch, robin and cardinal soon saw through the trick and were not long in flying quietly away to find members of their own clans with whom to exchange confidences.

Not only is the thrasher a mimic but he, also, is somewhat of a ventriloquist. This ability causes many interesting confusions in his world, and we can almost read some glee into the thrasher's performance and a certain amount of appreciation of his own jokes.

Few of our birds are more entertaining than this beautiful cinnamon brown creature. In common with his catbird cousin he has the expressive habit of jerking his tail as he sings, a trait that has given him his name.

Sometimes the thrasher is confused by amateurs with the thrushes, but this is unnecessary for the thrasher is a large, bright brown bird, having a conspicuously long tail and a decidedly yellow beak and eye. The favorite habitats of the thrasher also differ from those of the thrushes. Roadways, lanes, brush-bordered pastures and briar patches are the common haunts of this bird.

As a rule the thrasher is a ground feeder and divides his menu between plant and animal matter. He takes large numbers of insects, especially ground beetles. Caterpillars, grasshoppers and crickets all come under his sharp beak. His vegetable foods consist of berries, wild fruits, grains and weed seeds.

The thrasher's nest usually is well hidden in tangles of bushes and briars, and because the materials used are similar to those around the nesting site, it is easy for the bird to conceal its nest. In approaching her nest the female is secretive and stealthy and so avoids advertising its whereabouts to curious observers.

The brown thrasher is known locally by a variety of names. Among the more common are ground thrush, brown mockingbird, French mockingbird and mavis.

# WRENS AND ORIOLES VISIT GARDENS

Wrens and orioles are not much alike, but they are two of the favorite birds in the Greater Muskegon area during May.

Gardeners, birders — and just plain people — like to see them about their yards and gardens, and they go to some length to attract them. It is houses for the wrens and oranges for the orioles. These should be out the first week in May. My wren house is already swinging from the pine tree, and the orange half is out for the orioles to find.

Already the martins have taken to their houses, as have the bluebirds, tree swallows and chickadees. House sparrows and starlings have appropriated some, much to the landlords' disgust. But they, too, pay rent in the numbers of insects and weed seeds they eat. I was interested in England to see fewer of these two species than in our state. Natural competition is probably one factor. In addition, they are highly adaptable and "quick learners," so their success here has been outstanding.

Grackles, doves and robins are also nesting.

Wrens get busy with house-hunting as soon as they arrive. They are highly territorial and will seldom allow another pair to nest near them, even in the same yard. They are inclined to fill every available house with nesting material and choose one in which to nest. Both sexes carry nesting material, and the male especially is indefatigable in this. Wrens are experts in keeping insects down and are good protection for shade trees and other ornamentals.

Orioles, on the other hand, seldom nest near humans unless there are tall mature trees for their pouch-like nests. They eat our oranges and seek one of the taller trees in the neighborhood to locate their woven nursery.

One way to help these beautiful birds in their domestic life is to provide nesting material. Lengths of yarn, string or cord will be snatched up and woven into the nest. Care must be taken, however, to offer pieces no longer than eight or nine inches. This is very important because longer strings tend to tangle, and the bird could be caught and hung by them. Occasionally, an oriole will attempt to weave an entire kite string into the nest, and the whole thing becomes a tangled mass hopeless to handle.

Elms for years were the favorite tree of orioles, but now with the scarcity of these, they have adapted to maples, oaks, and willows. Occasionally, a large cottonwood with drooping branches will be utilized.

In addition to wrens and orioles, May brings literally hundreds of wood warblers to this area as wave after wave arrive from the south, spend a few days, and then pass on to their breeding grounds. From May 12 to 20, Michigan's own warbler, the Kirtland's arrives at its breeding grounds near Grayling, Mio and Roscommon.

## WREN FRIENDS HAVE FAULTS

Wrens are among the admired and very familiar of our bird friends. Because it is easy to attract them to nesting boxes, and because they love human companionship, almost everyone has a wren friend. A friend is one whose failings and mistakes we know but whom we love just the same, and even the jolly little wren has some failings.

Devoted and courageous parents, they will tolerate no other wren family in their territory, and sometimes take drastic steps to remove the rivals. Two cottonwood trees on the same city lot housed nests of wrens and one of these hatched before the other. A young bird was found on the ground under one nest. It was replaced in the nest and again the following day it was found. This seemed too regular for an accident.

The third day a young wren nestling was on the ground so we determined to discover the cause. It did not take long. After careful observation, it was discovered the male wren from the other tree was forcefully removing the young, doubtless in an attempt to rid his territory of the other family.

None too nice neighbors!

Likewise eggs of other species have been pierced and even thrown from the nest by these energetic little busy-bodies. They brook no interference in their own domestic affairs and will roundly pursue and even battle intruders who may inadvertently alight in their tree. They are pugnacious and frequently attack birds much larger than themselves, such as blue jays, crows, robins and sparrows.

Oftentimes the wrens meet the problem of keeping their territory to themselves by building "cock" nests. These are usually built by the male while the female is concentrating on the real nest. We have known as many as six nesting boxes — all those available — filled by one pair of wrens during the building season. Occasionally one of these may be used as a "nursery nest," it has been observed. Wrens usually have more than one brood of young a year, and their clutches number from six to twelve eggs. Perhaps that helps to account for our large wren population.

Although the house wren is the most familiar one, other wren cousins summering in Michigan are less known but as interesting. Of the thirty species found in the eastern hemisphere, six may be observed in Michigan. Two of these are considered among the better songsters of the family — the Carolina and the winter wrens. The Carolina wren, of more southern distribution, is found in the southern part of the state and is a trifle larger than the house wren. It has similar habits.

The Bewick wren likewise is found in the southern part of Michigan and is about the same size as the Carolina. It is sometimes known as the "long-tailed wren." The winter wren is the smallest of the Michigan species and is of northern distribution, rarely coming into the lower penininsula to nest during summer. The short-billed marsh wren (sedge wren) is slightly larger than the winter wren and smaller than the house wren. It is usually found in cattail marshes and reedy swamps and swales. It is a noisy bird, often building cock nests and hiding them among the swamp grasses and sedges. The nest is a fine example of bird architecture in which plant material is woven together to form the top and sides of a deep cavity.

The long-billed marsh wren (now marsh wren) builds a similar nest, is slightly larger than the short-billed and is found in similar places along streams and waterways. All of these wrens are much like the house wren in action and in nervous behavior. It is not difficult to distinguish them from other bird families. Their characteristics are well pronounced and all are small brown birds living primarily on a diet of animal life. Insects in various forms are their chief menu, and they do great good in ridding vegetation of many obnoxious and injurious kinds.

It's not hard to build a wren house. These jolly little birds will nest in anything from a tin can or suit of underwear flapping on a clothesline to the most ornamented and elaborate house that can be devised. Materials such as wood, clay, pottery, beaverboard and wallboard — almost anything the ingenuity of the builder can offer — are suitable. Use of metal is to be discouraged because it overheats and kills the young birds.

The more inconspicuous the color, the more attractive is the house to the wren. Green and brown are most desirable. General shape and size of the nesting box are not important, but a floor space of at least four inches square is the minimum. The larger the house, the more twigs the birds will carry in.

The most important single item in wren house construction is the size of entrance. It should be 7/8 inch in diameter, or approximately the size of a quarter. This will prevent the intrusion of sparrows and other competitors.

Depth of the nesting cavity may vary from six to eight inches, and the height of the entrance above the floor may be from one to six inches.

Wrens also enjoy a perch before their door. A small ventilation hole will add to comfort during warm weather.

A site from six to ten feet above ground is satisfactory. Poles, posts, buildings, trees and wires, all offer locations which will attract wrens.

MAY IS MOTHER MONTH

Today is Mother's Day and all over our land we are honoring mothers.

May is mothering month for many of the wild folk. Already baby rabbits and small squirrels are out learning the ways of the world with their mothers. Just this past week two calls told of finding rabbit nests in area yards. In them the young, with open eyes and new fur, were about ready to face life and its hazards.

The most charming of May babies is the fawn, spotted like sunshine dappling through the new leaves. Fawns are often left unattended by their mother while she seeks food. Because of their mottled appearance, they are exceptionally well protected. Nevertheless a sharp lookout may be rewarded. Should this happen, by all means, leave the little one alone. It is not lost or abandoned. Being left alone is a part of its training. The mother knows exactly where it is and will return to care for it. Few wild babies are "lost" or "abandoned" by their parents. Toward the end of the month many other wild babies will be about. There will be baby woodchucks, chipmunks, gophers (some think too many) and muskrats.

Families of raccoons, opossums, skunks, minks and flying squirrels will appear in late May and June. The mink may be seen in daytime, but the others are nocturnal feeders. A ride through rural sections sometimes reveals these little families out for an evening meal. The coons, possums and skunks are seen crossing the highway in a family line-up that warrants slowing down or even stopping the car to view the group.

The flying squirrels sometimes nest in bird houses that have been left up during the winter. They may continue to use it, instead of a hollow tree, during the summer. Should one discover he has such delightful neighbors, a handful of food tossed out each night will bring them closer.

Equally playful are baby foxes as they frolic about the doorway of their den while mother is away. They dash inside at the suggestion of danger, only to cautiously peep out when they think the danger has passed.

Mice, rats and moles do not wait for the mothering month. All are many-brooded and produce a succession of babies through the season. They are among the choice prey of hawks, owls and other predators.

The last of wild babies to appear here are the little bats. Not until mid-June are these infants born. They cling to the breast of their mother for some time. Thus, heavily laden, the mother bat flies in and out in the early evening seeking food for herself and family. When the purple martins and swallows go to bed, she takes over the constant battle against insects.

Animal babies, like human infants, are the most attractive and entertaining of their kinds. Whether it be a baby bunny standing on its hind legs sniffing a daffodil or a firstling squirrel scolding a saucy blue jay, each is a rewarding sight.

Parental devotion may be strong or tenuous depending upon the species. For some, like mice, the maternal attention and concern may last for only a few days. For others it lasts weeks or years. Some mammals do not have young every year, and these give greater assistance to their offspring.

From late May through the summer months, these families will be abroad, especially at night, and a good motto for this Mother's Day and the summer days ahead is, "Let's give them a brake," for highways are often disastrous and fatal to young wildlife.

## BABY SITTERS — BIRDS ARE BETTER

Bird brains are better than ours. That's right, when it comes to taking care of baby birds.

Bird parents are better than humans when it comes to training their youngsters; they are not nearly as indulgent as we with our offspring. A "lonely" little fledgling "crying" (squawking) incessantly on your front lawn or under the shrubbery is probably not "abandoned." Doubtless, its mother (or father) is watching from an inconspicuous vantage point and at the proper moment will swoop down to feed it, comfort it or lure it to a hunting ground where it may learn to get its own food.

Kind-hearted humans all too often interfere when they are attracted by the youngster's wails; they pick it up, take it inside and then comes the question, "What will I do with it?" Or children find these little birds and, thinking them lost or injured, bring them home, and then what? Usually the small one dies, for this time of year, in the changing temperatures, it is very difficult to raise these adopted ones. Some people have successfully done it, but for every one which survives, from my own experience and knowledge, at least twenty die.

It is hard for parents to hear a baby cry. They want to go and comfort it, but for its own good, they learn to let it cry. So it is with bird babies.

Of course, there are exceptions. During a severe storm, with wind and hail, a birdling may be cast from the nest; or the nest may be violated by a predator and one or the other of the parents killed. Such cases may need the intervention of "kind" humans, but be assured if you take on such a task, it is a tedious one. All you have to do is watch the trips Jennie Wren makes back and forth to her young to know the devotion and attention you will have to give. So think at least twice before you adopt one of these little ones. Robins, blue jays, catbirds, waxwings, grackles and thrashers are the birds most often involved in human foster homes, because they nest in residential areas, city parks and yards as well as in gardens. If you are in doubt about a "lost bird," watch for several hours and see if an adult comes or notices it. These "hours" are nothing compared to the time you will spend if you take the little stranger in with the view of raising it.

Sometimes birds themselves will adopt a "stranger," but this is unusual, and most interesting to observe. Have you seen a pair of small birds feeding a large dark-colored youngster which follows them about chirping and fluttering its impatient wings? This is a common sight now as young cowbirds are being fed and reared by their foster parents. A variety of small birds, including the Kirtland's warbler, is parasitized by the cowbird, and so different kinds of birds are now feeding them.

You hate to admit it, but there are cases where bird brains are better than ours — much better!

MAY IS WARBLER TIME

May is the month of warblers in Michigan. Forests and open fields, thickets along the streams, trees on city streets all teem with them, for the wood warblers are winging northward. Up from the steaming jungles of Peru and Ecuador, up from the tropical forests of Guatemala and the moss-hung swamps of Louisiana, the myriad horde streams toward breeding grounds which extend as far north as the timberline. It is a bridal procession so vast that its ranks take weeks to pass a given point. Unless you keep your eyes turned upward you may not know of its passing.

The east shore of Lake Michigan is one of the two main migration routes of this purely American family. The other is the Atlantic seaboard. So western Michigan bird-lovers have one of the very favorable positions in the world for enjoyment of the flight. In this month they are everywhere just above our heads with their exquisite coloring, their charming ways and infinite variety. Here is a whole month of foreign, ever-changing beauty which one can enjoy without leaving home.

The birds fly by night and stop to feed by day, each species with its own migration schedule. The transients in your dooryard or the park in the heart of downtown may vary daily. There may be black and white warblers to-day, yellow palm warblers tomorrow, black-throated blue warblers the next day. Anything which stays more than two days seems like an old friend. As many as 14 different species may be observed in one area on a given day.

Warblers are a strictly New World family and are found only in the western hemisphere. They are a very beneficial family of birds living to a large extent upon insects that prey upon foliage. They are sometimes appreciatively spoken of as "foliage tenders." With a few brilliant exceptions they are insignificant songsters. They stay in the treetops and put on no concerts. Their family name "warbler" is somewhat misleading as the majority of species do not have strong voices and scarcely can they be said to "warble." That name might better be applied to the vireo family.

The warblers are small birds, measuring from four and a half to six inches in length. They are also among the very exotic of the spring visitors and lend a tropical air to the landscape during the time they are here.

Warblers are at once the delight and the despair of the amateur field student because of their bewildering variety. There are about 116 species (Reilly) in the family. In most species the sexes differ in coloring or marking and the young differ from their parents. Multiply these by the seasonal variations, and the number of classifications is staggering. Small wonder the beginner often throws up his hands and says, "When it comes to warblers, I give up."

In the first place, about thirty species breed in or pass through Michigan, and amateur field identification must almost of necessity confine itself to the male in spring. To the dismay of the beginner, the bird guide descriptions of about half these thirty begin alike: "Upper parts olive-green, under parts yellow," and then run off into a feather-by-feather account of primaries, secondaries, inner webs of tail feathers, under-wing coverts, eyelids, etc., which would be impossible of identification on anything except a dead bird in the hand. And bird lovers consider a bird in the bush worth a score in the hand. An on-the-wing identification is in the same sporting class as the hunter's wing-shot.

As a matter of fact, however, a systematic breakdown of the problem brings out some amazingly simple rules for identifying many species. The simple and easy way to spot a species is to give it a tag. Learn one unmistakable characteristic and forget the feather-by-feather description.

The black and white warbler, for instance, is probably the easiest of all to identify. His description in the bird books is painstaking and complicated, but never mind. If you see a bird striped lengthwise in sharp black and white — a regular feathered zebra — you are safe in writing it down as a black and white warbler.

The American redstart is another easy one. One glimpse of that gay, half-opened orange and black tail is enough to identify him. He couldn't be anybody else. If the bird you are watching has a back of soft blue and a black bib on a white breast, he is a black-throated blue warbler, and you need not worry about the color of the eye-area.

Even some members of the "upper parts olive-green, lower parts yellowish" fraternity have one feature so unmistakable that a glimpse will serve to name them. The Maryland yellow-throat, now called the northern yellow-throat, wears a black mask across his eyes exactly like a lady at a masquerade. His general coloring is the same as that of half a dozen other warblers, but the black mask is his exclusively. In the same way the hooded warbler wears a black hood tied under his chin like an old-fashioned sunbonnet with his yellow face peering out from it. Wilson's warbler wears a little black skullcap with his olive-green and yellowish garb. His design is exclusive, too.

A few warblers have striking songs which will give you a clue if you cannot get a good look at the bird. The northern yellow-throat's bubbling "witchery, witchery, witchery, witchery," and the black-throated blue warbler's endless reiteration of "zur, zur, zur, zr-e-e-e" can set you scribbling their names confidently in your notebook.

When you have memorized the one-of-a-kind individuals and progressed to the almost identical varieties, there are still short cuts. The bay-breasted warbler and the chestnut-sided warbler both have streaks of reddish chestnut down their sides. But on the bay-breasted the streaks are connected by the chestnut of the throat. That one distinction is enough. The mourning warbler and the Connecticut warbler are almost identical except for a slight difference in the depth of color on the chest, but the Connecticut warbler has a conspicuous white eye ring. So waste no time on the chest. The eye ring will tell you.

It's as simple as that. Look for the tag!

## MICHIGAN WEEK

"Michigan, My Michigan" will be heard throughout the length and breadth of both peninsulas, for this is "Michigan Week." There are many festivals and special weeks throughout the year, but this week is set aside that all may take stock of our state in all its aspects, its commerce, industry, and agriculture, as well as its natural heritage.

In spite of pollution of air, water and soil, the dire threat of overpopulation, the energy crisis and all other unpleasantries of modern life, our state has succeeded in keeping a maximum of its wildlife. Each year hundreds of thousands enjoy Michigan's outdoors, attracted by its natural beauty, its flora and fauna.

Birds are flocking here in such numbers this month that every day adds new ones to the birder's list. Michigan's avian emblem, the robin, has been here since March and is now busy with domestic duties. Likewise Michigan's "own" bird, the Kirtland's warbler, has returned to its northern nesting grounds and is busy nesting.

Michigan's fish, the trout, has almost been displaced in popularity by the newcomers, the king and coho salmons. The fishermen are among those who really appreciate Michigan's treasures as they wade the streams and fish the lakes for a greater variety of fish than even the old days offered. It is good to see the fishermen again lining the arms of the breakwater and rejoicing in the perch's "comeback."

Although this is the Wolverine State, the animal was never "official," and so in 1970, just in time for Michigan Week, the timber wolf was recommended for the honor.

The white pine has long been the State's tree, and rightly so, for of Michigan's more than ninety different kinds, none has contributed so much to the state's economy and history as the pine.

Yes, for the rockhounds there is a state rock and gem. The Petoskey stone, a fossilized coral, was named the state rock, and later the greenstone, a favorite of Isle Royale visitors, became the Michigan gemstone.

This is an ideal time of year to get outside and get acquainted with some of the natural treasures our state offers. Why not save a little gas and oil and try shank's mare for a change. Get on your own feet and tramp the highways, byways, and trails, or canoe the streams, sail the lakes, climb the dunes and trot the bogs. Walking is wonderful exercise, so find the enjoyment of it by visiting a spot nearby with seeing eyes and listening ears.

Do not sell your children and young people short — take them with you that they, too, may know the natural legacy Michigan has in store for them.

Remember our two nearby state parks, Muskegon and Hoffmaster; our ten county parks and city ones are ideal places to begin your "Michigan Appreciation."

## MYRIAD GREENS JUST WEEDS

Nothing could be more appropriate than a dish of native greens to go with that meal of freshly caught trout this month. They are easy to find these days, too, for any of the choicest native greens are free for the taking because they come from the common weeds. Modern science rids us of weeds with chemical sprays and similar devices, but our forefathers had a much simpler way. They ate them.

The state health commissioner advises the use of these wild greens in filling one of the "basic seven" food requirements. Like other green, leafy vegetables these plants belong to the group of "protective foods" which are high in iron and vitamin A content. Because they also contain considerable amounts of calcium and other minerals and vitamins B-1, C and G, they are valuable. They also afford roughage and bulk for the diet. If children are tired of spinach, take them out and let them gather their own dinner greens of pigweed, mustard or parsley.

The average family knows the value of dandelion greens and picks the verdant rosettes to cook, and also many take watercress from country streams to add to salads or replace the customary lettuce.

Less familiar is the use in this country of such commoners as milkweed, pigweed or lamb's quarters, marsh marigold, mustard, sorrel, chicory, wintercress and purslane, the pest of the home gardener.

Milkweed is one of the more useful of these and can be eaten in a variety of ways. A choice dish is to cook the young shoots and serve them as one would asparagus tips.

When selecting greens, choose the young and tender ones. Wash well in several waters. Cook in very little water — little more than what clings to the leaves. Salt them before cooking. Cook only five to ten minutes, preferably with the cover removed after wilting to preserve green color. They may be seasoned in a variety of ways and served attractively with hard boiled eggs, bacon slices, bits of crisp pork, sliced peppers and onions.

The fresh greens are attractive and palatable in spring salads in combinations with other vegetables.

## LOOK AT DANDELIONS

Dandelions, a common harbinger of spring, are late this year. They are beginning to pop up here and there on lawns, in parkways and in wayside fields and pastures. The name, dandelion, is from the French and means "tooth of the lion" referring to the toothed edges of the leaves. Perhaps the golden shaggy flower head reminded an early botanist of the lion's mane.

"Weeds" to most householders and gardeners, there are those of us who consider them the "first spring vegetable," and make good use of them. Few plants offer themselves — root to blossom — so completely for human consumption. By the way, it is thought that seeds of this plant were brought here and grown in the colonial gardens to provide leaves, roots, and flowers for the kitchen.

Everyone is familiar with dandelion greens, the favorite spring tonic of the pioneers and early settlers. The leaves are usually cooked as potherbs, but can be wilted and served as a hot salad or chopped for a tossed one.

The floral heads are most often used for wine, but they are also delicious dipped in batter and fried as "little fritters."

Most recently, however, the roots, for a long time neglected, have again come into use. In winter the roots are at their best for baking and boiling. Two popular ways to prepare the roots any time of year follow: Wash the roots, remove root hairs and place in boiling water for twenty minutes until soft, but not mushy. Drain and add butter and seasoning to taste. These make a very attractive and delicious "second vegetable." To bake, prepare in the same way and then bake in oven for thirty minutes at 375 degrees. The time may vary depending on the age and size of the roots. Butter and season. Roots can also be sliced, boiled and creamed or prepared in a casserole. To add attractiveness to the latter dish, sprinkle some of the yellow floral rays over the top and add some snipped chives or parsley.

Many persons are now interested in dandelion roots as a coffee substitute, and it is easy to prepare. Wash several dozen roots in warm water. Dry in a moderate oven for two hours or until the roots are brittle and dark brown (coffee colored.) Cool, then crush to a powder or grind in a coffee grinder; an old fashioned one is just the thing. Use one teaspoonful of the powdered root for each cup of boiling water. Stir and let steep fifteen minutes. A glass or pottery container is preferred. The dandelion may be added to regular coffee. This same process is used for chicory roots, which are a favorite additive to coffee these days.

Dandelions are not only appetizing, but they are highly nutritive and easy to find. Take a good look at these weeds and consider the other side of the little golden floral coins that are flung broadcast these spring days.

## SWALLOW FAMILY HERE

One swallow may not a summer make, but when the six common species of this family have returned to Michigan, one can be sure that spring's over and summer has begun. During the last few days the most tardy of the swallows have arrived, and now the whole swallow family presents itself to the bird lover as the home makers seek nesting sites.

Two of these species take kindly to nest boxes and houses prepared by humans. In fact, one of the well known of the family, the purple martin, has become almost dependent upon the aid of men. These birds generations ago nested in colonies in hollow trees and natural cavities, but with the disappearance of the forests they have adapted themselves not only to city life but to apartment houses. Some landlords find that these birds are most particular about their houses and that they make numerous demands as renters. They are particular about the size of the house, the location, the height, the surroundings and neighborhood, their neighbors, the ventilation, the size of entrances and at times it is not easy to see the reason for reaction to seemingly attractive homes. Fortunate indeed, therefore, is the person who has successfully established a colony of martins — fortunate, if you don't mind bird noises. For these birds do not hesitate to let their presence be known.

Another swallow cousin which is easier to attract to one's yard is the tree swallow. This dapper fellow is the first of the family to arrive in the spring. Not long after arriving he goes house hunting and is a very curious and thorough "hunter." Nothing seems to escape: bluebird houses, wren homes and almost anything with an aperture into which he can stick his questioning head. Gourds seem to provide very satisfactory houses for tree swallows, and they are not long in taking possession. They are pugnacious and do not hesitate to defend themselves against all comers, even their own species. In fact, is is not unusual for them to "pick a scrap" with other birds. The tree swallows are distinguishable from others of the family by the upper plumage which in the male is steely, bluish green. This contrasts with the shining white of the breast plumage.

One of the loveliest of the family, less often seen in cities, is the barn swallow. This bird takes its name from the habit which it has developed of nesting in barns and similar outbuildings where it attaches its nest to rafters, ledges and other projecting timbers. The bowl shaped nest is made of pellets of mud which the bird cements into place with saliva. Usually a soft lining of feathers is prepared for the nest. The opening is at the top.

The barn swallow is characterized and easily identified by a deeply forked tail, by upper plumage of metallic purple and by the brick colored forehead, throat and underparts. As in all these birds the female is duller plumaged.

The cliff or eaves swallow, like the barn swallow, attaches its home to barns, outbuildings and bridges, usually placing them under the eaves. These nests may be distinguished because they are flask or gourd-shaped rather than like a bowl and the opening is in the side. The name cliff swallow is derived from the habit in less inhabited regions of placing the nests on the sheer faces of cliffs.

Two very closely related species are the bank and rough-winged. These birds are somewhat alike in coloration of plumage and have similar nesting habits. They nest in colonies in holes in banks and frequently honeycomb sand banks. The holes are prepared by the birds themselves and are usually just below the sod line. Both birds are dark grayish to black above and lighter underneath. The rough-winged has a dusty throat while the bank has a dark breast-band.

The swallow family is insectivorous, and therefore all are migratory. As a rule, the insect eaters are the last of the birds to arrive in the spring and the first to leave in the fall. During August, the swallows will be noticed assembling in huge flocks, lining the telephone and telegraph wires preparatory to their fall flight. Theirs is one of the very interesting and conspicuous phases of the autumnal bird migration.

SPRING BIRD MIGRATION ENDS

When the whirr of dainty, almost invisible, bird wings is heard about a blossoming shrub and the darting beak of a bird fairy is seen probing the honeyed depths of flowers, bird lovers know the spring phase of the annual migration is over for another twelve months. The hummingbird is the last to arrive from the south. Since mid-February when the gay notes of the song sparrow were first heard, there has been a continual procession of returning birds to lighten the gardener's battle against insects. With the whirr of the hummingbird's wings, all this ceases, and the birds settle down to the routine of domesticity, nest building, egg-laying, incubation and the care of countless broods of youngsters.

For the next three months birds' lives are a round of toil and trouble. It is during this period they are most valuable to farmers and gardeners, for with the heavy demands of young growing birds, the quantity of food consumed is vast. Many baby birds eat several times their own weight in insects and weed seeds during these growing days.

The hummingbird is the busiest of these bird parents. For although they usually have only two mouths to feed, the appetites are prodigious, and the parents are kept constantly on the wing to provide fare for the birdlets.

In all of Michigan there is just one species of hummingbird; this is the ruby-throated, and the name is given from the bright coloring of the male. The female does not have the glowing throat, and therefore sometimes people mistake her for another species. They are frequently called tobacco-birds by residents from the south where the bird visits acres of this plant. Poets speak of them as "feathered jewels" and "bird gems." Indeed, with the sun shining upon their glinting infinitesimal feathers they are gem-like.

Flowering shrubs are playing host to hummingbirds now throughout Greater Muskegon, the county and western Michigan. Our bird wanderer has returned from wintering in Mexico and Central America, and no bird in the garden brings us more of the exotic and romantic thrill of the tropics than this "smallest of Michigan's birds."

For nesting sites, they prefer large trees — oak, maple and apple are favorites. They saddle their tiny nest of plant fiber, spider silk and lichen on the limb horizontally, and thus it is disguised to appear as a knot. Inside this miniature nest are placed two white eggs about the size of navy beans. From these come the gluttonous youngsters that keep father and mother visiting parks, gardens and porch boxes every hour of the day. Only at night can they rest from the demanding appetites of these elves.

To see a mother hummer feed her young is a disconcerting scene. The babies do not have the long, slender beaks of the adults, but wide mouths and small, slightly horny beaks. The mother places her beak into the open mouth of the little one and "pumps" the food which has been carried in her own crop for it. It seems as though her beak would pierce the infant "from stem to stern" as she forcefully feeds it. The birdlet must not mind, it only asks for more.

See them attack an intruder or would be marauder at their dainty, lichen-covered nest and they become a bundle of fury and madness. They are fearless and furious in defense of nest, eggs and young. Birds many times their size are put to rout by the whirling onslaught of these bird mites.

Hummingbirds are partial to gardens, especially where there are flowering shrubs. Petunias will also lure them to porch boxes and fuchsias to hanging baskets. Later in the season glads entice them, and they are fond of salvia, borage, bergamot, delphinium, impatiens, balsam, and foxglove. If there is a trumpet vine in the vicinity it will be a favorite rendezvous of the hummers. The funnel-shaped flowers and red color of the bloom make it a "natural" for these birds. Contrary to rumor, these birds do have feet and do alight.

## MAY CALLS OUTDOORS

May is the mother month of summer, and perhaps at no time of the year is the call of the outdoors more tantalizing than right now.

Bird calls unheard for months invite one to investigate the songsters; bright glimpses of color from a roadside or field beckon, and subtle fragrances come floating on almost every breeze, trying to lure one from inside work. These are days when it takes a forceful character and perseverance to follow the prescribed indoor tasks and routine. Even a fleeting glance from a partially washed window reveals birds of tropical splendor, the oriole, cardinal, rose-breasted grosbeak, scarlet tanager and the host of intriguing tiny warblers with their dash of brilliance. While scrubbing the porch or taking down storm windows you will be entertained by the goldfinches and indigo buntings with their side show on the lawn. They are helpful in ridding the lawns of dandelions, and right now are busy eating the newly formed seeds.

When shaking rugs or a dust mop from the back porch, many people will hear the catbird and brown thrasher serenade if shrubbery and bushes have any share in back yard plantings. Robins, wrens, tree swallows and martins are just as busy with their domestic tasks of spring as are bustling housewives and householders. Feeding the family takes as much or more of their time as shopping for the humans.

91

Just as spring housecleaning renews the indoor scene, Mother Nature is changing the looks of her house. New spring carpets of blue lupine and sand or bird foot violets are spread throughout the county; shadbushes form curtains of lacy white, cherries are hung with blossoms for all to see, and lilac tapestries accent the varied greens of our walls.

Fresh spring winds and gentle southern breezes air her house, and fragrance like incense drifts here and there; the climax will come when the whole atmosphere is perfumed with locust and clover. But, no sooner does that scent make one heady with spring fever than — spring will be gone — summer arrives.

## RAINBOW OF BIRDS

Everyone likes to see a rainbow. Saturday I saw a rainbow of birds. It was on the field trip sponsored by the Muskegon County Club and led by George Wickstrom.

Of course, these birds were not all lined up in that special order — red to violet, but they were all there. For the most part the birds were recent arrivals and for the rest of the spring and summer it should be possible to see this colorful array.

It was the two red birds that thrilled me most — a cardinal and the scarlet tanager — in the same small tree. When one focused his field glasses there they were both in view and there is a difference in their shades — a real distinction between "cardinal" and "scarlet." Seldom, however, does one see the contrast as clearly as we did this day.

Then there is orange. It was the northern oriole (formerly Baltimore) that added that color to our avian spectrum. In spite of the bad April they were just about on time, May 1, and it did not take them long to find the oranges that admirers had put out for them. I had six brilliant males feasting at one time and with them an extra-special guest, an orchard oriole. They ate and bathed and even argued a bit in both the front and side yards.

Gold is for goldfinch and those little males are really decked out in their new spring feathers. Have you seen them among the dandelions as they take off, seemingly a flying flower? They are spring yellow but a newcomer, the yellow warbler, is summer yellow, in fact, it is sometimes called the "summerbird."

There is a lot of green in birds' plumage, but two we saw have it in their name also. The vireos' name comes from the Latin "to be green" and one of their local names is "greenlet." The green heron is often silhouetted against the sky and its verdant color is not easily seen.

The indigo for the bird rainbow came from a recent arrival and a favorite summer resident of many birders, the indigo bunting. This shade is very special and can not easily be confused with any other. It is the male that is this color. The hen is a demure little brown bird, unnoticed most of the time.

We have blue in the jays the year around and they were beautiful against that backdrop of snow that stayed with us too long this year. The blue most birders prefer is the blue seen when that first little "harbinger of spring," the bluebird, arrives. Then there is the gray-blue of the heron, but some scarcely count that as blue at all.

For violet one has to settle for a darker shade, say "purple" and then there are the purple finches and purple martins to round out the complete arc of this colorful array of birds.

No doubt there are others you will see and wish to add to your own spectrum, but these satisfied me.

# Summer

I hear spring with singing birds;
I feel winter in wind and snow;
I see fall in flaming leaves
But, summer is hard to know.
Then, when I smell the clover,
That for me is the day
That spring is surely over
And summer's here to stay.

JUNE

## APPRECIATE ALL BIRD LIFE

These are gala days for bird-watchers. Now birds move right into one's yard and garden and make themselves known in shrubbery and at the dooryard. The nesting population of the county is greater than it will be at any other time of the year. Robins, bluebirds and wrens are busy with the second broods, and the late nesters — cedar waxwings and goldfinches — have just finished nests and are setting. They are among the latest of the common birds to nest. Many of the others are now accompanied by their young, and watch for the small birds, warblers and sparrows, and their "giant" offspring, a cowbird.

Field, meadow, swamp, marshland, stream border and woodlot are all overflowing with bird music in late June. These are days when one can learn to recognize birds by their songs and calls, for they repeat them over and over again.

There are books available to help bird students to identify birds by their songs. The author of one of these, and a pioneer student of bird songs in America, Dr. Aretas Saunders, has been in Michigan this month studying bird songs. He attended the Wilson Ornithological Club's annual meeting last week at the University of Michigan Biological Camp at Douglas Lake. His book, "A Guide to Bird Songs," is recognized as the best in America on the subject, and he has devised his own special system of noting the calls.

Another good work on the same subject is "Fieldbook of Wild Birds and Their Music," by F. Schuyler Mathews. Beginners like the birds that are accommodating enough to tell their own names. The killdeer, towhee, chickadee, pewee, phoebe, chebec (least flycatcher) and whip-poor-will are some of these.

In coloring, the June birds run the gamut of the spectrum from red to purple, from tanager and cardinal to purple finch, with the orioles for orange, goldfinches and warblers for yellow, vireos and kinglets for green, bluebirds and jays for blue and the bunting for indigo.

Color, grace, beauty and song are but a few of the birds' gifts to us.

Then there are the insects they eat. We may praise the nighthawks, martins and swifts for their eccentric taste in mosquitoes, the rose-breasted grosbeak for its fondness for potato bugs, and the cuckoo for its dietary choice of tent caterpillars.

The weed seed eaters are also appreciated these days when weeds seem to grow faster than the garden plants. The goldfinch feasts on dandelion seeds and later on thistles, the native sparrows on many weeds including ragweed.

If one watches the birds when they are feeding, he soon learns to appreciate them for their economic value as well as for their beauty, grace and song.

A garden or yard without birds would be a sad and desolate place.

## HOME MONTH OF THE BIRDS

There is no question around here but that June is the home month of the birds. If there's any doubt in anyone's mind, just count them — the nesting birds, that is.

I remember one June day a few years ago when I set out to find out who my summer neighbors were, and I discovered I had thirteen different nesting birds on, or very close to our city lot at Pere Marquette Park.

The house sparrows and starlings chose the sheltered vent from the gas water heater close to the roof. Houses we had provided in the cottonwood trees had families of tree swallows and wrens. Robins took a southern window ledge and raised a brood. A pair of yellow warblers built in the drooping spirea bush in front of the house, and catbirds and brown thrashers in the lilacs, on the west and south. A bittersweet tangle on the north held the nurseries of cardinals, bluejays and chipping sparrows. Song sparrows built in our neighbor's evergreen close to our line, since our own spruces were not large enough. A woodpecker drilled its home in a pole on the corner of the lot.

The hummingbird came daily and flew back and forth through the spray when we watered the herb patch, and I was sure it was nesting in one of the cottonwoods, but I did not find the nest; it was too well camouflaged for my eyes. Just across the street in the sand of the oval was a killdeer nest with four eggs.

The barn swallows nested in the garage next door where we kept our car, and the martins in our old bird house four doors away. Then there was the piping plover just over the small dune that backs up the herbs. Yes, it is surprising how many summer neighbors one has, and until you really go calling and list the nests, you do not appreciate them.

For years bird-watchers have observed this month in temperate zones to be the nesting time for many species. In fact, it has been recorded that more than eighty species are nesting during June. This is not hard to believe when fifteen to twenty can be found so easily.

Besides an easy walk or stroll about the yard or park, we have found a canoe an excellent device in which to visit nesting birds. A canoe is quiet and makes many stream and lake borders accessible to the bird watcher without disturbing the area and sites.

Two of our friends, Dr. Lawrence Walkinshaw, on Scenic Drive and his guest, William Dyer, both eminent birdmen, had the pleasure of such an excursion recently when they canoed on Muskegon Lake and River.

Perhaps the most thrilling to Dr. Walkinshaw, because it was his first for this area, was the nest of the orchard oriole. Even the experts still have firsts and that is what makes this bird-watching game so fascinating.

Two wood thrush nests were found, and that reminded us of the June day a year or so ago when we stopped in at the Vasa Lodge Cottage to help celebrate Midsummer's Day, and our hostess showed us a beautifully made nest with the mother thrush setting on her eggs. She had gotten quite used to the members coming and going and placed her nest in a small shrub close to the road entrance.

A least bittern nest was not a surprise to us because again we remembered our own canoe trip in Lakeside when, behind the lumber company and right opposite the business section, we found eleven least bittern nests and one of the American bittern down at the other end near the Causeway.

Walkinshaw and Dyer also found nests of five yellow warblers, Traill's flycatcher, several redwings, red-eyed vireos and back home one of a piping plover, which Dr. Walkinshaw had been watching for some time.

Almost as big a thrill as the orchard oriole was that of a chestnut-sided warbler, for this was the first nesting record for the county. Mr. Dyer, who is a special student and photographer of warblers, was also grateful for others, the black-throated green, Canada, redstart and prothonotary which were seen.

In addition to the usual common birds mentioned above, Dr. Walkinshaw reported the nests of the least flycatcher, the pewee, phoebe, red-eyed vireo and hummingbird about his place.

Most of the swallows are now nesting, and many persons are reporting colonies of martins in their yards. A few have been disappointed since they put up new houses and have no tenants. These should not be discouraged because sometimes it takes two or even three seasons to establish a colony.

## IT'S NICE TO HAVE A MALE AROUND THE NEST

There used to be an old saying, "Everybody works but father, and he sits 'round all day."

That certainly isn't true of most bird fathers.

Most male birds work very hard in domestic life and help during the breeding season with the young. It is surprising how many species of birds mate for life.

For many of the smaller birds, this does not cover a long period of time. The life span of many is short, depending upon predators and the exigencies of migration.

Most birds mate seasonally and change mates. Some even have more than one mate at a time. In many cases, both the parents assist in the domestic duties.

To begin with, the male usually selects the territory for the nest and often the exact nesting site. The hen chooses the placement of the nest. Species vary as to the amount of help given by both birds. In many cases the male helps in the nest building, although it usually is the female that completes the nest and its inner lining.

In many of the common species of songbirds, the two sexes share the responsibility of feeding the young. After fledging, the male usually cares for them. This is especially true in those who raise more than one brood. It is not uncommon in many familiar species for the male to feed the female while she is incubating and to even take his turn on the nest.

Already young birds have hatched in the area. For instance, notice the care and attention of both parents given to the young goslings that have hatched at the Causeway park. Likewise, the swans on White Lake have cygnets and, although usually accompanied by both parents, only one adult was reported with them this week.

There are some species which tend to young considerably more than the norm. Red-winged blackbirds are polygamous. They may have as many as six "wives" in a season. The average is three. He cannot spread his attention so widely over the marshland nests, so his duty is mainly protection. Male redwings are often seen perched on a vantage point in the marsh home where they have clear view of the nesting areas.

The nest is entirely built by the hen. She does most of the incubation and feeding of young. After fledging, the male may assist in the feeding.

Even less responsible for their young are the cowbirds. This species is parasitic. After mating, the female lays her eggs in the nest of another bird, usually smaller than herself. It is doubtful whether the cowbirds ever see their own young until they join the later summer and autumn flocks. The cowbird young are raised entirely by foster parents, usually at the expense of their own offspring, which often die in the nest or are pushed out by the larger intruder.

Not all bird fathers have it so easy. The phalaropes, which are seen spring and fall at the Muskegon County Wastewater System, have wives that are real women's libbers. Contrary to most species, the female wears the bright colors, and the male wears the drab shade, for it is he who protects and incubates the eggs.

The female selects a male with whom to mate. She scrapes a slight hollow in the ground, and after laying the eggs, leaves incubation and care of young to the male. She may even leave the territory before the young are hatched. The young usually take to the water shortly after hatching and are soon able to feed themselves.

The feeding process of a young bird is tedious. Often nestlings eat their body weight and more each day. Some parents have been known to make five hundred feeding trips a day.

FLORAL COLORS FOR FLAG DAY

As today is Flag Day, there's no argument concerning our subject — flags.

Ever since June 14, 1777, this day has been set apart to honor the flag of the United States, the Stars and Stripes or Old Glory, as it is affectionately called.

After the Declaration of Independence on July 4, 1776, the new nation needed a flag to symbolize its unity and this independence, so eleven months later, June 14, 1777, the following resolution was adopted by Congress: "Resolved that the Flag of the United States be thirteen stripes alternate red and white, that the union be thirteen stars, white in a blue field, representing a new constellation.''

From that day to this, the national colors have been flown, now with fifty white stars, on this special day, the birthday of the flag.

Not only are these popular colors in the flags of the world, but they are common in nature, especially at this season of the year. I want to mention three red, white and blue flowers that are spectacular now — the blue vetch, the red hawkweed and the white daisies. These intrigue me on this day because, just as our nation was, and is, made up of immigrants, these three flowering plants have come in from foreign parts, insular and continental Europe. They have become so well established here that they are typically ''American Wildflowers,'' that cannot be denied citizenship here in Michigan or elsewhere throughout the fifty states.

However, today let us visit about some other plants — the flags, no less. Wild flags are the irises, and just as they are beautifying home gardens and parks now, they are added interest and charm to the wild garden.

The iris family is closely associated with orchids and lilies but is different enough to have a group of its own. There are some 1,500 different kinds all over the earth, mostly in temperate climates and they have been well known since earliest times, when some of them were used medicinally and later commercially.

In Michigan, there are two general types: the blue-eyed grass and the true iris of which there are four or five.

The form of the iris flower is well known, with its conspicuous falls and standards. The floral form and beauty of it have given the iris the nickname ''poor man's orchid.'' The name ''iris'' comes from that meaning ''rainbow'' and is appropriate, for the cultivated varieties come in many colors, almost vying with the rainbow.

The wild forms are as attractive and exquisite as their cultivated cousins, and it is always a delight to run upon a bed of these wildings when one is woods-wandering or bog-trotting.

The most common is simply called the wild iris, or blue flag, and the flowers are very showy, being violet-blue and occasionally white. The claw is long and narrow, of greenish yellow or white with purple veins. The leaves are long, narrow, blade-like and a fresh lovely shade of green. The whole plant gives an oriental air to the lowland where it grows. These prefer damp, moist, sunny spots in low pastures, marshes, or along stream and lake borders. We are at the height of the blossoming season now which is from

May to July. Fishermen haunting the streams and inland lakes of Michigan at present get some of the best views of these attractive flags waving in the early summer sun and breeze.

The southern blue flag is very similar to the former species and can seldom be distinguished except by a skilled botanist because there is a tendency for these two to hybridize and there are all manner of intermediates, especially near the Straits of Mackinac as Helen Smith tells us in her "Michigan Wildflowers."

The yellow iris, or water flag, is another which is seen, but less commonly. It is called the European wild flag and fleur-de-lis. This, doubtless, is an escape from cultivation but in many sections has become "wild." It is larger and hardier-appearing than the two blue forms and has larger showy yellow flowers. My own observation is that it is becoming well-established in several sections of the state and is a fine addition to our wild flora.

Probably, this, along with other flags, was brought here in early days by the pioneers and colonists who knew the medicinal value of the plants. The rhizome or rootstock is the part utilized and according to old herbalists, it was used as a cathartic, emetic and a favorite in the treatment of jaundice. Yellow flag was roasted, ground and used as coffee. Orris powder, which is used in rose jars, pomanders and perfumes is a favorite to scent powders, hair preparations, other cosmetics and toiletries. Orris powder is the basis of the familiar violet scent in these products.

The flower of the yellow flag had an unusual use as the basis for dye and ink.

Early settlers have learned the medicinal attributes of wild flags from the Indians because some tribes cultivated them for their rootstocks in ponds.

Michigan's most famous, and least known iris is the dwarf lake which can be seen at its best in Wilderness State Park near Mackinaw City from May to July. The blue showy flowers have the usual iris form, but are on a very short stem so that the large patches of them present the aspect of a beautiful purple-blue and green oriental rug spread out on the woodland floor. Their habitat is given as "on beaches and cliffs, in sandy woods and bogs." So far they are found only in the Upper Great Lakes region, highly localized on the shores of Lakes Huron and Michigan and at the Tip o' the Mit.

This is Michigan's own floral flag and it seems especially appropriate because it has the same blue, white and yellow that is found in the state's official banner.

This is truly Flag Day in more ways than one.

## DELICATE ORCHIDS BLOOMING

June is the month of orchids. Throughout the state this month many of these choicest of wild flowers will be blossoming, and Michigan has its share; for of the 146 species recorded as native to the United States and Canada, this state claims 53, better than a third.

Commonly thought of as tropical, orchid plants are widely distributed throughout the temperate zone as well. They thrive in a variety of places and in Michigan are found in the three areas designated as deciduous forest, pine plains and lake forest. Of these three, Muskegon lies within two, the lake forest and pine plains and therefore has a variety of orchid species. Wild orchids are found in many locations from the high, dry wooded uplands through to the dense coniferous forests to the low sphagnum bog and tamarack swamp. Each of these places has its choice blossoms.

According to a study of distribution of orchid plants made by Sister Mary Marceline, Keweenaw, Michigan's most northern county has the greatest number of recorded orchid species with 40, next comes Emmet county, most northern county of the Lower Peninsula with 36. Muskegon is listed with 13. As study is advanced throughout the state, doubtless there will be additions to these figures.

One of the more plentiful species in Muskegon country is the stemless lady's slipper, commonly known as the mocassin flower. This is found in Muskegon State Park, at Winnetaska and throughout the wooded duneland of the region. It is the showiest of the family and is generally beloved. It is one of the state's widely distributed and according to "Orchids in Michigan" by Marjorie T. Bingham, botanist and former president of the Michigan Wildflower Association, is found in 35 counties.

Other Muskegon species found blooming this month are the smaller yellow lady's slipper, larger yellow, showy lady's slipper, green orchids, purple fringed orchids, rose pogonia, grass pink, ladies' tresses, rattlesnake plantain and coral roots.

Of the state's orchids, perhaps the rarest according to Mrs. Bingham, is the ram's head, a small and very attractive species. She says of it, "The Great Lakes region is the home of the ram's head. It grows from Maine to

104

Minnesota between the 40th and 50th parallels. Fond of a cool climate and a shelter of evergreens, these small moccasin flowers bloom in cedar swamps, cold, damp coniferous forests, on dry sandy hillsides beneath pines and on evergreen heaths. The diminutive flowers grow singly at the summit of slender leafy stems from six to twelve inches tall. A side view of the pouch and curving sepals and petals resemble very much the head and horns of a ram.''

Michigan's orchids are perennial herbs and are dependent upon a stored food supply. Many of them depend both on the multiplication of the bulbs and tubers as well as upon seed to reproduce. Picking flowers prevents the production of seed. Few native plants are more in need of protection and conservation than these choice wildings which have been driven back into isolated swamps, bogs and swales by the continuing onrush of civilization.

Orchids are among the native wild flowers which the Department of Natural Resources and the Michigan Botanical Club say must not be gathered. Removing the blossoms causes the destruction of the plant and, if they are plucked, it will be only a short time until Michigan cannot boast native orchids. These plants do not transplant well for wild flower gardens, so should be left in their natural habitat. The orchid family is now protected by action of the legislature.

CHIMNEY SWIFTS CONSPICUOUS

During June, the "home month" of the birds, perhaps no single species is more conspicuous than the chimney swifts.

Sometimes these birds are referred to as "chimney swallows" but this is really a misnomer inasmuch as the swifts are not closely related to the swallows, even belonging in a different order of birds. They are the cousins of the hummingbirds and the goatsuckers, being akin to the nighthawk and the whip-poor-will. Like these relatives, the swifts have wide mouths and graceful sickle-like wings, especially adopted for aerial life.

The tail is highly modified for the life which the bird leads. Each tail quill terminates in a sharp bristle which assists the swift in climbing and clinging to the interior of chimneys.

Time was, when the chimney swift was not known by this name and took up its residence in hollow trees and stubs. With the encroachment of civilization and man's influence and the disappearance of many forests, these birds have adjusted themselves to urban life and are now found in the most thickly populated parts of our larger cities. Nothing is more acceptable to them than a large, unused chimney, and if such is not available, they do not hesitate to build in one which is still being used. They seem to be unmindful of the smoke and soot and only in occasional cases are they tumbled down from their homes and, escaping into rooms through open fireplaces, they are received as unwelcome visitors.

The color of the bird, deep sooty gray to black, lends a suitable attire for this chimney "sweep."

The name "swift" is altogether as appropriate for this bird as the modifying "chimney," for among our native birds few are more agile and tireless on the wing than this one. Many speed records in flight have also been attributed to it. This species on migration has been reported by aviators winging its way northward at terrific speeds. Relatives of these birds are found in the Old World as well, where they are also known for their unusual flight.

So aerial and untiring in flight are these birds that even the nesting material is collected on the wing. The nests, pockets of twig lattice-work, are glued to the sides of the chimneys with the bird's own saliva. The twigs, which are loosely woven together, are snipped from trees as the birds pass in flight. The eggs, usually numbering three to five, are whitish and somewhat long and narrow.

These birds are highly social, and so it is not unusual to find scores of them nesting together in one large chimney. Chimneys of cottages and summer hotels seem especially to attract them, and many resorters have found it desirable to investigate the chimney each season before starting their fires or the room is likely to become an aviary of wildly excited swifts seeking exit.

The number of swifts sometimes living in one chimney seems almost unbelievable when the observer sees a dense cloud of these birds come noisily winging their way from the brickwork. Circling round and round their home, they fly out later in all directions, scouring the air. For many city blocks they assume their herculean task of ridding it of insects. They are assisted in the undertaking by their friends, the swallows and their cousins, the nighthawks.

As twilight and dusk approach, they gather in from their excursions and seek the comforts of their dark, chimney home for the night and there, safely clinging with the aid of their bristled quills and claw-like feet, they may be heard several hours after dark jostling each other and twittering until they finally quiet down after a day of ceaseless activity on the wing.

These birds are easily identified on the wing by their swift, somewhat mechanical flight, and by the silhouette which they present against the blue sky which suggests a drawn "bow and arrow," so perfect is the arc of their wings and so straight and slender is the position of the body and tail.

## TOADS HARMLESS AND BENEFICIAL

Everyone likes birds in their yards and gardens since most of them have bright plumage and are conspicuously active and are pleasant songsters. But most of them aren't too dependable and come and go as they so please.

There is a more constant garden friend that is often overlooked, and these past rainy days have brought them especially to my attention.

They are my garden toads! I say mine because generally toads don't wander far once they become established in either a yard or a garden. Some have been known to live several years in the same yard. It's true that constant friends are few, but the toad is one of them.

Perhaps no creature is more harmless than the toad. It's chief protection, in addition to coloration and sluggishness, is an acrid substance secreted from glandular warts when attacked by a dog, bird or any other assailant.

By the way, toads don't cause warts . . . they have them.

It's the common garden toad we are considering, and for the gardener they are all good. They live almost exclusively on small insects that are harmful to both crops and garden plants. They are so well thought of in France that they are often bought and released in gardens to do their work.

Someone once figured that one average toad in a vegetable garden is worth $20 a season. The service of this hard worker is not generally appreciated and although most people overcome earlier aversions to them, toads still are not given the protection and encouragement they so deserve.

I've always regretted the fairy stories that picture toads as evil and ugly creatures, since it's better to see them as "handsome is as handsome does."

I have mentioned my little friend that sits on the step by my back door and accompanies me around the yard whenever I go nest-viewing.

Perhaps you, too, have had a toad follow you around your yard or garden. A biology teacher friend of mine insists they make very good pets and, because of their lethargic, easy going manner of life, are not constantly trying to escape.

Toads don't drink as most creatures, but absorb water through their skin, therefore it's important to have a shallow pool or container of water available for them. Toads in my yard enjoy cement basins in front of St. Francis and Mary statues. Nearly every summer morning I find one or more soaking in them.

Being amphibians, toads are cousins of frogs and salamanders, and as such, spend part of their life on land and part in the water.

In spring, long strings of eggs embedded in a clear jelly-like substance are wound about water plants in pools and ponds or in roadside ditches. The adult toad migrates to water during the spring mating season.

It's then the wonderful music of the toad is heard and, of all our amphibians, it's the most musical and birdlike, often putting many birds to shame. I shall never forget the exciting and melodious concert I heard for three nights last spring in Pere Marquette Park. Some who heard it said, "It can't be toads!" But, it was!

One toad may lay 20,000 eggs which hatch into tadpoles or pollywogs in from three to twelve days. As such, they are vegetarians, spending all the late spring and most of summer eating algae in their home pool.

BEAUTIFUL MOTHS

June is the month of the large, night-flying moths. Warm early summer nights are enlivened with the flutter of noiseless wings as the great moths emerge from their cocoons and their half year long sleep.

Already, in spite of cool May days and evenings, some of these giant insects are about. Among the most beautiful and delicately colored of the group is the luna, or moth of the moon. This beauty is pale green, with a touch of lavender and yellow on the wings. The hind wings have long trailers which make the luna exquisite in flight and among the most graceful of the insects hosts. The luna is the result of long months spent in a cocoon hidden among the brown fallen leaves and a larval period spent as a voracious fat green caterpillar with tubercles of red, green, blue and yellow. Not a pleasing sight to many who disdain "worms," the luna is a lover of woodland and is found about Muskegon country throughout the wooded dunes.

Largest of the common moths is the cecropia or robin moth, so named because of the "robin-red" with which its wings are ornamented. The cecropia is sometimes called the American silk moth because its cocoon is made of a silk-like substance spun by the caterpillar. The cecropia cocoon is hung on the small outer twigs of maples, elms, and oak trees. These moths are just beginning to emerge.

The polyphemus is another large moth which is sure to be attracted by porch and street lights before the end of the month. These moths are numerous even in metropolitan areas.

The promethea is partial to lilac bushes, and the paired cocoons are most frequently found about these shrubs. The sexes in this moth species differ in color and are predominately of wine or brownish hues.

The yellow emperor is a beautiful, large moth less frequently seen but occasionally found on corners about street lamps at night. Last year two were found on Western Avenue during the summer. This is the moth made famous by Gene Stratton Porter in her fiction story, "A Girl of the Limberlost."

The io, a smaller cousin of these giants, is an attractive moth but its caterpillar sometimes plays havoc in the corn fields where it feeds upon the young plants. Another moth, whose caterpillar is unwelcome in the garden, is the tomato sphinx. The caterpillar is the well known and ill thought of tomato hornworm.

The poplar sphinx is a moth of modest and delicate coloring occurring more frequently than many people suspect about Muskegon in the vicinity of cottonwood trees.

The underwings make up a large clan of protectively colored insects, whose upper wings blend harmoniously with the bark of the trees upon which they rest, but whose underwings are brilliantly colored ranging from pinks, rose, through reds, yellows and orange, even to white.

Many nature-lovers miss the joy of seeing the beauty of these giant insects because they confine their outdoor wanderings to the daylight hours. Really to know these charming winged ones it is necessary to wander at night and canvass street lights and bright windows. Sometimes one will be fortunate and the moths will pay a visit to the porch or dance flutteringly about one's own lighted window. These are choice moments that every June can bring to the lover of the out-of-doors if he but has the patience and will to see.

## POISON IVY TAKES TOLL

"Leaflets three, quickly flee," is advice which many people have not been properly heeding this spring, for with the coming of warm outdoor days many have reported being victims of ivy poisoning.

Some old-timers say the plant is especially virulent this year. Whatever the reason, this plant does spoil many outdoor good times for people during the camping and picnicking season.

Poison ivy is so easily identified that there is no reason why the smallest toddler cannot be taught to recognize it. The simple couplet quoted above is a fine dictum for all, old and young.

In western Michigan and Muskegon country there is just one plant for which poison ivy may be mistaken. That is the wafer ash or hop tree, which grows in the sandy duneland and takes on tree-like proportions with well developed woody trunk. This has a three-parted leaflet.

There is confusion in the minds of some people regarding the five-leafed ivy, Virginia creeper or woodbine, as it is variously called. Like poison ivy this is a vine and may have a shrubby character, frequently covering old fences and even running up tree trunks as does the poisonous kind. It climbs and twines about old buildings, walls and thickets. Later on it will be characterized by blue berries whereas the poison ivy has white waxy fruit. Both have inconspicuous flowers. Both turn brilliant red in the fall.

In the shrubby form the three leafed is known locally as "poison oak."

The white berries and scarlet foliage of the autumn are attractive lures to unwary woods-wanderers, but one must remember that this plant is a mean actor.

Do not take chances with plant poisoning. It can be very uncomfortable and lead to serious results.

Washing with water and a good naphtha soap upon returning from excursions into ivy-infested terrains is a good habit. Potassium permanganate or witch hazel extract will arrest irritation until a physician or pharmacist can be reached, if poisoning does take place. Old-timers will tell that crushing the leaves and stems of touch-me-not or jewelweed and applying them to exposed parts is good to counteract the effects of this annoying plant.

Control measures are helpful in reducing poison ivy. Spraying with a combination of ammate and 2,4-D has proved satisfactory in several parts of the state, and is recommended for use by private property holders.

Do not spoil summer outings because of poison ivy. Be woods-wise. Enjoy Michigan's summer days outdoors by knowing and avoiding poison ivy.

# STRAWBERRIES ARE RIPE

June days are strawberry days.

The oft-repeated saying of Dr. Boteler that "doubtless God could have made a better berry, but doubtless God never did" is on the lips of many woods-wanderers these days as they sample the delectable wildness of native strawberries.

Muskegon country is a veritable strawberry patch — if you know where to look for this wild fruit. Adaptable to field, marsh, roadside and uplands alike, these berries are tempting treats for fishermen, bird enthusiasts, hikers and flower lovers as well.

The most common native species of Michigan is Fragaria virginiana and it is widely distributed throughout the entire state. This native of America was introduced into England in the seventeenth century and was coveted because of its fragrance and aroma which greatly excelled the native European species of the Continent.

John Burroughs, one of America's saints of the out-of-doors, says, "We have two kinds of strawberries, the wood berry and the field berry." Of the first he says, "It is wild as a partridge and found along open places in the woods and along the borders, growing beside stumps and rocks. It is small, cone-shaped, dark red, shiny and pimply. It looks woody and tastes so."

Of the field berry he says, "Some are round and stick close to the hull; some are long and pointed with tapering necks."

Of all haunts of the wild strawberry, the daisy meadow is the favorite in Burroughs' day and in our own. Indeed, daisies and strawberries go together. "Nature fills her dish with berries, then covers them with the white and yellow of milk and cream, thus suggesting a combination we are quick to follow."

North, south, east and west of Muskegon, throughout western Michigan, hidden under the green, toothed, three-parted leaves, are Nature's treasures, blood-red, juicy, romantic and delicate to the taste, to be had only for the searching. "The strawberry, in the main, repeats the form of the human heart, and perhaps of all the small fruits known to man, none other is so deeply and fondly cherished, or hailed with such universal delight as this lowly, but youth-renewing berry."

# SUMMER USUALLY MEANS JOY

Summer came this week and today is Midsummer Day. Midsummer Day is not generally observed in this country, but in Europe and many other areas it is an important occasion for celebration.

There are many myths and legends which have accompanied Midsummer Day through the centuries, and most of them deal with elements in nature — the plants and animals as well as supernatural beings, elves, witches and their kind.

The day, June 24, is also St. John's Day and this has its influence on the observance of Midsummer Day. This is the day when the common yellow-blossomed plant known as St. Johnswort traditionally starts to bloom.

Mostly Midsummer is a day of joy and happiness, but one activity I recently learned about is very distasteful. On the island of Trinidad, June 24 is the day natives "harvest" or slaughter the young oilbirds.

In the original account of the oilbird, Von Humboldt, the German naturalist, traveler and statesman, told how the natives of Venezuela collected the young at the peak of their fatness and boiled them down to produce oil for cooking and lighting. This exploitation greatly depleted the population of oilbirds to near extinction.

The birds on Trinidad were subject to the same slaughter until recently when the small colony at Springhill Estate in the Arima Valley came under the protection of the Asa Wright Nature Centre. Eight other colonies of oilbirds are breeding in caves in the mountains or on the seacoast. There are estimates of from 1,000 to 1,500 adults on the island. It is hoped that two other colonies may have protection, one at Oropuche and the other at Aripo. As of today, the others are unprotected and will doubtless be despoiled of their young.

The oilbirds are among the stranger birds of the world. They have a resemblance to our nighthawks and whip-poor-wills but differ from them in many ways. They feed only at night and then chiefly upon the fruits of various forest trees, particularly the palms and laurels, both of which are rich in oil. In the night flights they snatch the fruit off the trees and swallow them whole. The pulp is digested and the seeds are expelled. The birds are attracted to these aromatic trees by their acute sense of smell.

Their entire life is spent in darkness or semilight. The colonial nests are hidden in rocky caves or grottos which are almost inaccessible to humans. To visit the Springhill or Dunstan Cave birds we took a difficult trail through the jungle, climbed a rocky wall and crossed a swiftly flowing mountain stream, the bed of which was inches deep and slippery with the discarded seeds of the digested fruit.

The ladder across the stream led to the cave's entrance from which in darkness we heard the noisy uproar of the birds. Amid a variety of screams, clucks and snarls and other unbirdlike commotion, three of the large birds flew directly at us, others took wing the other way seeking a back exit. These were followed by many others, but right at the front on a high ledge, three remained — parents with their young.

The nests, used year after year, are mounds of regurgitated fruit which forms a paste that hardens as it dries.

Staring at us, and very protectively colored in their rich browns, black and white spots, this family reminded us of a trio of owls with their large eyes and round heads. In flight they are like huge nighthawks. They are 18 inches long with a wingspread of three and a half feet.

This family stayed quietly on the nest, with the youngster between the parents and their stare changed to a glare as our party stood below to view them. Nearing Midsummer Day, when in the past the nests have been raided, perhaps they were overly protective of their offspring. The hissing and snarling continued as many of the birds flew through the grotto, doubtless hoping to drive us out. Our observation was as short as possible for the commotion was disturbing.

## MIDSUMMER CELEBRATION

Summer came this week and this weekend comes the old celebration of midsummer. It is not an American holiday, but wherever there are tradition-loving Englishmen or Scandinavians, there will be some recognition of it. Here the Vasa Lodge at its center on Scenic Drive, annually takes note of the day with a Summer-Pole (similar to a May-Pole) and holds a festival on the Sunday nearest midsummer.

One of the traditions brought from Sweden is to decorate with seven different kinds of flowers, using especially those of blue and yellow, the colors of the flag which is displayed on the summer-pole. There is no problem this year finding the flowers. Nature has provided them all.

St. Johnswort (Hypericum) is a very important plant for midsummer. Its common name for the saint, the husband of Mary, is given because it is believed to flower on June 24, St. Joseph's Day. This year it did not wait to flaunt its golden flowers, but was in full bloom throughout western Michigan, from the state line to Ludington, by the last day of spring.

Few plants are thought to be endowed with as much magic as this one. In fact, its scientific name, Hypericum, comes from the Greek meaning "having power over spirits." One of the purposes of celebrating midsummer is to protect against the evil influences that surround one for the coming season. This plant was hung in homes for a special blessing on Midsummer Eve and also burned as a fumigant in midsummer bonfires to insure protection.

It has close association with witches, and in the old days to step on it was to incur the wrath of these hags. The following night the culprit would be ridden on a broomstick all night and dumped unceremoniously in his bed at daybreak, tired, exhausted and unhappy. Beware, because there is so much St. Johnswort about, should you be afield, you can scarcely miss treading on it.

Medicinally it was used for blood ailments for, according to the Doctrine of Signatures, the tiny reddish dots on the leaves indicate its efficacy.

Yarrow (Achillea) is another of the plants in full bloom now which is often a part of the midsummer bouquet. This comes in three colors, white, pink and yellow; the last, a garden variety. As with St. Johnswort, much magical lore surrounds this and has been handed down from the Middle Ages. It is used both for medicines and formerly for charms. Because of the highly dissected leaf, it is called thousand-leaf. Few wild plants have as many common names as this one, which is a tribute to its popularity and wide use. A few are: milfoil (meaning thousand-leaf,) devil's hops, old man's pepper, staunchweed and nosebleed. Several of these indicate its medical uses.

Achillea comes from a myth that the famous hero, Achilles, was dipped at birth in a protecting potion, but since his nurse held him by his heels, they were unprotected. This plant healed him when he was shot in the heel in battle and so was used in early days by military men and knights to cure wounds.

It grows abundantly in fields, pastures, hedgerows and roadsides, even in vacant city lots and along railroads.

Because the plant was ruled by Venus it was used as a lovecharm. Next to Midsummer its most popular use is at Halloween when, if a green leaf is worn, it will insure the fidelity of one's mate and loved one's true affection all year.

Vetch, introduced into Muskegon country just before the turn of the century, furnishes the blue of the Midsummer celebration. This was brought here through the efforts of N. B. Lawson, one-time mayor of Muskegon, to use as a sand-binder, as he had seen it used in Italy. It was effective and has spread throughout western Michigan and brings beauty to the summer season.

Other plants which make up the midsummer bouquet of wild flowers are the wild rose (June's own flower,) the ox-eye or white daisy, coreopsis, moth mullein, pentstemon, loosestrife and mallow. Queen Anne's lace, knapweed and chicory come later in July.

The Germans and English tell us that on Midsummer Eve the king of the elves and fairies, Oberon, turns into a rabbit and visits gardens. Also on this eve, the fungous circles known as "fairies' rings" are formed by the dancing of these sprites.

Whether or not you celebrate Midsummer in the Old Way, at least make it a point to welcome the coming of summer by getting out in the country, on the by-ways preferably, and revel in the floral beauty that summer brings.

## INSECTS A PART OF NATURE

"Bugs! Who needs 'em?" is a common remark when the conversation turns to insects.

Insects (which is the proper name for "bugs") are the predominant type of animal life in the world today. By that we mean that there are more kinds of them and more individuals than any other faunal group.

Generalities are bad, and it is worth considering that there are many insects which we can cultivate and befriend in our yards and gardens.

Six of these friendly ones are the praying mantis, ladybird beetle (ladybug,) caterpillar hunter, burying beetle, dragonfly and lacewing fly.

The first of these insects is the praying mantis. Given this name because of the kneeling aspect with folded, upraised forelegs, it could also be called "preying," for it feeds voraciously on other insects. Its green color is very protective when it hides among the leaves of garden plants and snaps up harmful insects.

In the past few years these insects have increased considerably in the West Michigan area. Part of this is due to the placing of egg cases in yards and gardens by avid plant lovers.

Another common insect, the ladybug, needs no introduction to anyone,

I'm sure. These insects have been around since the colonists came to America from England. They occurred in masses on the hop vines, where through the growing season they ate aphids and other injurious creatures. Then, in the fall when the vines had been harvested, they were set afire, and all were eager for the ladybugs to escape before they were destroyed.

Right now the beetles are congregating in large numbers on the beaches preparing to hibernate. In the Middle Ages, this beneficial insect was dedicated to the Virgin Mary and the name Our Lady's Beetle was later shortened to ladybug.

There are about 350 different kinds of these insects in America and most of them are useful. One kind is given the credit for saving California's citrus industry when it was attacked by San Jose scale.

Although there are many advertisements to buy these beetles, the local population is really sufficient to care for most gardens.

Two other beetles, whose work in our yards may go unnoticed, are the caterpillar hunter and the burying beetle. The first of these is also called the bombardier bug or skunk beetle. It is a handsome, irridescent insect, an inch in length, with an orange border around its glistening, bluish-green sheath wings. They feed voraciously on larvae of tent and gypsy moths. Often seen on the beaches running along seeking prey, they are agile and sprightly, and if picked up, squirt an acrid, ill-smelling fluid which gives them the name "skunk."

The burying beetle is another beauty with his reddish-orange spots on a dark, bluish-black background. They feed on the carcasses of birds, small mammals, frogs and snakes. Digging under the object as it feeds, it sinks down into the ground and is finally buried.

If you are fortunate enough to have a pool — garden or swimming — then you undoubtedly play host to dragonflies. Dragonflies are not only beautiful insects, but they are highly beneficial. Like butterflies they fly by day. They have two pairs of net-veined, transparent wings and large eyes which cover most of the head, which bears a pair of very short, bristle-like antennae.

These lovely creatures were the dread of our childhood days. They were called "the devil's darning-needle" and we were cautioned if we told a lie, they would "sew our mouths shut." Probably this tale aided in keeping us on "the straight and narrow way."

Later we liked their other name, "mosquito hawk," better, for by then we had learned of the benefit of their voracious appetites in devouring the pesky prey on the wing.

116

Dragonfly larvae are strange, grotesque-looking creatures, given the classical name of "nymphs," because they are completely aquatic. They have gluttonous appetites and although usually eating small water creatures, scuds, fairy shrimps and other crustacea, the larger ones sometimes turn their attention to taking small fish, minnows and fingerlings. They can be annoying and destructive if they invade a rearing pond. Seldom does this happen. Dragonflies winter in the larval stage as nymphs.

These insects are swift, direct fliers in pursuit of their victims taken aerially. When they alight and are at rest their wings are outstretched. This position distinguishes them from their smaller, but equally attractive and beneficial cousins, the damselflies, which close their wings over the body.

Both of these insects are welcome visitors to any yard or garden. They can be easily attracted by standing water, a pond, pool, basin or even a bird bath.

Hawking about one's premises these large insects with patterned wings and streamlined, graceful bodies not only bring beauty and activity but reduce the mosquito, midge, fly and gnat population.

## JULY

### WRENS REARING FAMILIES

As June is the "home month" of the birds, so July is the "month of young birds," for nestlings are now deserting their cradles to begin life by themselves.

Probably no young birds, with the possible exception of the robins, are watched with such genuine interest by human friends as the offspring of Sir Christopher and Jenny Wren.

Almost every human household has its nesting box of favorite wrens which have been watched since the arrival of the mother and father birds the latter part of April and early May. Through all the periods in their domestic life, including the selection of the nesting site, building of the nest, laying of the first egg, completion of the clutch, days of waiting during incubation, emergence from the first egg, coming of brothers and sisters, their development into fledglings and now their departure, these feathered neighbors have been closely observed.

To most bird lovers, wren family affairs are now taking on the most interesting phase for their human landlords. With the exit of the first brood, a new clutch of eggs soon will appear to keep the tiny mother and father birds busy with an ever-increasing family.

Wrens are among the native birds which raise more than one brood of young during their annual stay in Michigan, revealing one of the secrets of their early season activity. I have known of one pair of wrens which filled six nesting boxes and occupied five of them during the same season, rearing five families of youngsters. Is it any wonder that wrens are among the best known of our native birds when they carry on their family life so extensively?

The young birds of the species, as of many others, require continual feeding during the early days of their emergence from the nest, making it indeed a full time task for the parents. Food from daybreak to sunset is the rule in the wren household, and it is thus these birds prove most valuable to their human friends. Their rent is settled in the capture of insect pests, their chief article of diet. Unable to soar after their prey, as many insectivorous birds do, these tiny creatures usually hunt close to the ground where their brownish, finely-barred feathers offer excellent protection among the grasses, leaves and weeds. They search everywhere among brush, in woodpiles and about trees for their food and are among the most valued of bird friends because of the great host of insects they destroy.

They also repay for their lodging with a cheerful, bubbling song, one of the most joyous and happy among the musical bird notes. Song is not the extent of wren sounds, however, for few birds are more conversational than these little feathered busy-bodies about the dooryards. They chatter excitedly when disturbed, scold like veritable shrews when annoyed and twitter confidentially when pleased. But none needs be told about "wren talk" for it is everyday gossip in almost everyone's back yard.

Wrens, especially the little Jennies, are excellent housekeepers, tending their nests carefully and constantly, keeping them free from vermin, dirt and untidy debris.

Several years ago a pair of house wrens built a strange nest here in Muskegon. The house was perched on a gas pipe about twenty feet high, and for several years had been the home of nesting wrens. The landlord has had many pleasant hours watching the activities of the parent birds, and their young, as they emerged from the house and played about the clematis vine which climbs about the pole.

The landlord saw something shine and glitter in the beak of the wren as it made one trip into the box. It appeared to be a safety pin, and the landlord reminded himself to watch for it when the bird house was cleaned the following spring.

When the house was cleaned the next spring they found the safety pin and five others, three open and two closed. But that was not all — for these birds had sought out other metal items in the neighborhood and had a real collection of "scrap."

The cleaning process revealed four paper clips, 28 bobby pins, eleven hair pins, one garter slide, 27 small nails, one fish hook, one screw eye, 38 staples and 39 miscellaneous pieces of wire, a total of 156 pieces of metal in addition to the conventional twigs, plant fiber, string and cotton.

This strange assortment of nesting material did not hinder the successful incubation and rearing of a bird family. The landlord recalled that the usual happy group of birdlings emerged from this boxful just as for the many years before when the normal twigs, grass and weeds were stuffed into the box.

Much of the time Jennie is a demure, affectionate and mild little creature. But do not misjudge her, for in an instant she can fly into a fury and give her husband such a scolding he may seek the seclusion of a cock nest for escape. Sometimes both of the pair seem to have a rash disposition and a sense of perversion, as did one pair which took advantage of the absence of another pair of parents in the same yard to forcibly eject their neighbors' children from the other nest. This most unneighborly act led to an open feud which resulted in the death of all the young.

As wrens frequently return to the same nesting site year after year, it was a relief to the human landlords the following year when only one of the pugnacious pairs reappeared to take possession, living in domestic peace and establishing friendly relations with new neighbors.

## BIRD-WATCHERS AREN'T LAZY

No one ever accuses bird-watchers of being lazy. They are thought of as early-risers, pursuing birds at the crack of dawn with eyes maybe only half-open.

There comes a time when even the most ardent birder wants to remain in bed. That day came for me recently when I decided to let the birds introduce themselves. It was at my Montcalm County cottage at Crystal.

Shortly after midnight, when I put down my book and turned off the bedlight, an old friend called out, "whip-poor-will, whip-poor-will, whip-whip-will, will." I aimed to keep track of the number of his calls, but sleep took over.

Five a.m. and one of the most welcome calls of all drifted in from the hayfield to the east of the grove. The whistle of the quail, "bob white, bob white, bob white," delighted me. I seldom hear them in Muskegon, so it was especially welcome. Then, there was the "coo" of the mourning dove, which isn't their name, but gives them away and gives them their title.

From then on the calls came fast and furiously as though each wanted to answer the roll call first. There was the chick-a-dee, a very persistent caller. The chipping sparrow kept up its constant chirp from dawn to dark, giving us no chance to overlook it.

Before daylight a couple of killdeer flew over the cottage screaming loudly and emphatically.

Three flycatchers were insistent in their demands that we hear them: the pewee, phoebe, and chebec (least flycatcher) could all be distinguished.

The towhee or chewink let its whereabouts be known. The catbird's "meow" let me know it was still nesting in the shrubbery and thicket near the old bee tree. There was a cuckoo calling after daylight, and I hoped it was eating tent caterpillers from the cherry saplings.

The red-eyed vireo from a tall beech was giving its "sermon," which gives it the name of "preacher-bird." And, not to be outdone professionally, the ovenbird, a ground-living warbler, called out its "teacher-teacher-teacher-teacher," from which it gets the nickname "teacher-bird."

By now the jays and flickers were busy about their day's work and were calling back and forth through the grove.

Just then, a squirrel jumped from the towering maple on the roof and hurried along the ridge pole. It was time to get up. The bird chorus was now in full tune, not only the "name-calling birds," but all of them.

Coming downstairs for morning coffee, I flung open the back door, and an old friend greeted me. From the alfalfa field just to the north came the happiest of all summer songs — "bobolink, bobolink, bobolink — link-link." An old friend indeed, Robert of Lincoln, common in childhood in mid-Michigan, but rare on the sandy duneland shores of Lake Michigan.

It had been a long time since I had "birded in bed," but it was a choice experience, for besides a very respectable list of others identified by their calls there were sixteen who introduced themselves by name.

## COUNTRYSIDE AGLOW WITH FLOWERS

July is the month of field flowers. Since July 4, when the fields were filled with the national colors — red hawkweed, blue vetch and white daisies, more and more flowers have bloomed to add to the floral carpet throughout rural Michigan.

Now roadsides, country lanes, city lots, marshlands and the dunes are ablaze with bright flowers. Trumpet vine, perennial peas, turk's cap and wood lilies, butterfly weed, silkweed, puccoon and prickly pear. To the woods-wanderer and road-walker the scented blooms of paler shades are the essence of midsummer. Bouncing bet, soapwort or graveyard pink is a common weed in the Muskegon area now. Its fragrance permeates the

July air like an exotic perfume. The hawkmoths or hummingbird moths know the secret of its aroma and visit it frequently during the late afternoon and early evening.

Many of the state's highways are lined with the two sweet clovers which are so very attractive to bees. To many it is a surprise to discover the exquisite fragrance of the common milkweed blossom. These round, rosy flower heads have a very distinctive scent which is sometimes carried half a mile on the gentle summer breeze. The monarch butterflies seek these out both to feed upon and to lay their eggs, for this is the favorite food plant of their larvae.

Bergamot's spicy aroma is another scent that July is sure to offer. Bees are so partial to this plant that the wild species is commonly known as bee balm and the red garden cultivar also masquerades by this name.

Evening lychnis is a summer flower that makes the evening air almost sickly sweet with its heavy scent. Contrasting with this strong night perfume is the dainty, delicate perfume of the blossoming linden or basswood tree which is at its best on a sunny summer day.

Most of the lovely, fragrant blossoms are pale or white and are at their best at night. Many of the white flowers depend upon insects to pollinate them and the heavy sweetness helps to direct the searchers to its quarry. These pale and ghostly blooms are certainly more noticeable to the night hiker when he is not distracted by the brilliance of the trumpet vine and butterfly weed.

It is brilliance by day and fragrance at night that are July's gifts to the outdoor wanderer and highway traveler.

## PRIMROSE A NIGHT BEAUTY

Not all of nature's beauties are revealed under the blazing sun of midday. Some of her choicest loveliness is kept for the night wanderer.

The evening primrose is one of midsummer's lovely blossoms and to see it at its best one should seek it on a summer night, when its lemon-scented fragrance reveals its hiding place.

The flowers are large and showy and of the purest yellow arranged on an erect and leafy stalk. The green lance-shaped leaves, arranged alternately, appear as stair steps inviting insects to dine; but most of the insect guests entertained by this plant depend upon their wings.

Most prominent of the evening primrose's nocturnal visitors are the night-flying moths, also children of the dusky hours when most flowers are asleep. Chief among these is the Isabella tiger-moth, better known in its youthful stage as the woolly bear caterpillar.

The evening primrose is gracious and even generous to these insects, for it is upon them that it depends for transportation of the golden pollen from flower to flower. The pollen is loosely connected by cobwebby threads from the stamens of the bloom, and it is these that are carried away by the insects to aid in cross-fertilization of the species.

Sometimes when blossoms are not fertilized by moths and insects during the night, they remain open in the morning hours awaiting the services of some friendly bumblebee.

Historically, the evening primrose is important to botanists, because it was one of these plants upon which Hugo DeVries, Dutch botanist, experimented in development of the mutation theory.

Several species of this plant are common in Michigan fields and along roadsides. Sundrops, a cousin, is partial to dry, sunny fields.

Though bedraggled and disheveled-looking by day, the evening primrose is a charming delight for the nature lover who walks the fields by night.

## INDIAN PIPES ON FOREST TRAILS

Few flowers are found now in the forests and wooded dunes of western Michigan, although the fields and highways are ablaze with blooms.

However, the dark, deep shadows of wooded trails during these midsummer days offer a few unusual blossoms to the flower hunter. Evergreen trails are now at their best and at this season they take on a pallid, damp loveliness not seen in the lushness of early spring.

The trails of the Muskegon State Park are among the more interesting at present.

Besides the lovely greens of club mosses, ferns, mosses and the understory of leafy shrubs, there are myriads of brilliant mushrooms and related fungous growths which add interest to a trek.

Three flowering plants sure to attract the attention of the careful observer are the Indian pipe, the pinesap and beechdrops. All three of these plants are unusual in that they do not possess the familiar green foliage commonly seen with blossoming plants.

They more closely resemble fungi. In fact, like those lower plants, due to the absence of leaf-green (chlorophyll), they cannot manufacture their own food material and therefore are dependent upon types of plants for their very existence. The Indian pipe is a saprophyte living on dead organic matter, but both the pinesap and beechdrops are partially parasitic, receiving nourishment from other living plants.

Of the three, the Indian pipe is best known and most conspicuous. It appears as a waxy translucent pipe standing several inches above the carpet of brown leaves or greening moss. It is known as the corpse plant, ice plant and ghost flower, and tends to produce an eerie effect when first seen.

No other flower symbolizes the spirit of the quietness and solitude of the forest as well as this one. Cool, clammy and waxy white, it stands like a ghost bloom in the dimly lighted woods.

Picked and taken from its place it turns black and wilts shortly. It is protected in many places and is not satisfactory as a cut flower.

In the olden days a lotion was made of it for the eye, and in some parts of the country today it is still used as a medicine. It was also known as "fit plant," and was used medicinally in the treatment of convulsions.

Indians looked upon these plants as omens of bad luck, believing disaster befell any habitation near which they grew because of an evil manitou which lived in the pallid blossom.

Being a member of the heath family this strange July bloom is a close relative of the trailing arbutus, harbinger of spring.

Bad luck to the Indian in bygone days who found the flower, but good luck today to any blossom-loving woods-wanderer who comes upon a clump of these delicate pipes on the forest trail.

## PRICKLY PEAR IN BLOOM

In July, Michigan's deserts "blossom like a rose" and now sand swept areas in western Michigan are gorgeous with the blooms of the state's only cactus, the prickly pear.

This plant is widely distributed throughout the New World and is found in scattered places from Massachusetts and Washington on the north to Peru in the south. It is not necessary to travel to the more remote desert regions of the United States to find this cactus in its natural home for it is rather common in the duneland and sandy stretches of this county.

Right now the prickly pear or Indian fig, as it is called in some parts of its range, is ornamented with beautiful chalices of golden yellow, and against the slabs of green stem, this plant vies with all in beauty.

This cactus is among the highly specialized of Michigan's plants and has adapted itself particularly to the arid conditions under which it lives. The green slabs which are so conspicuous a part of the plant are not the leaves as one might suppose, but rather enlargements of the stem and are used for both the manufacture and storage of food. The leaves are represented only by multitudes of tiny spines.

Even these, however, have not made the cactus immune to raids of persons seeking to commercialize its beauty. The exploitation of Michigan's wild flowers should be stopped. Each season more of the wildings are going, and now cactus is added to the list which includes arbutus, bittersweet, columbine, dogwood and lady's slippers, formerly sold here each year.

At present it is the blossom that attracts the attention of humans as well as insects. These yellow or reddish orange solitary blooms, sometimes three inches across, lend a dash of color to the sandy stretches, which when seen in the glaring sunshine of a hot July day, give a picture of summer never to be forgotten.

As the sun sets in the evening the gorgeous golden chalice closes, folding its petals again and again on successive nights to reopen in the brilliance of the noonday sun and welcome vagrant bees in search of nectar.

Our species is an eastern form, smaller than some of the western varieties and possesses a fruit quite inferior to the Mexican importations, although it is edible and tasty, giving the plant the name of Indian fig.

This plant, Michigan's chief representative of the cactus clan, is found in the dry sandy sections of Allegan, Ottawa, Newaygo, Oceana and Muskegon counties and in a few other districts. Another species of the same genus, Opuntia, has been reported from sections of the Upper Peninsula where it is believed to have been associated with Indian ceremonials years ago.

## BEACH GYPSIES

Birds as well as bathers are crowding the beaches during these warm summer days.

They are early arrivals, usually before seven o'clock. Then, during the middle of the day many of them desert to return again about dusk after many of the picnics and beach roasts are over.

Birds follow food, and these beach gypsies are no exception. They soon discover the remains of outdoor meals and come for the crumbs.

The usual number of herring gulls is about the breakwater arms and toward night fly out to the west ends. Black terns are the common ones that harass fishermen and tease for handouts along both sides of the channel. Morning and evening, the observant is sure to see the graceful flight of the great blue heron winging its way along the shore. About six o'clock these large waders frequently fish along Lake Michigan and in the shallows of Muskegon Lake.

"Runners," the plovers and sandpipers, are becoming more evident now than previously during early summer. Several kinds are busy each day running and scampering about close to the waves.

Martins, swallows and swifts are abundant as they feast on insects flying above the water. These birds congregate at the time of insect hatches and take their toll of caddis, mayflies, stone flies, gnats and midges. Mosquitoes also fall prey to them.

Robins and mourning doves are less frequent visitors to the beach scene, but during the past week some have been daily diners at Pere Marquette Park.

The blackbird family is omnivorous, and the picnic diet seems to agree with them, for birds usually seen far from water are now common at Lake Michigan. Cowbirds, grackles, blackbirds and an occasional oriole visit garbage cans and seek leftovers.

Redwings are regular beach combers and appear every hour of the day. Young and old are frequenters of the sandy shores.

Blue jays do not hesitate to join in the fun, and the tracks of the crow reveal the daily, or nightly wanderings of these birds.

House sparrows, with an occasional chipping and song sparrow, are counted as picnickers these days.

Nearly every day a pair of kingbirds feast on scraps near the concession stand.

OAK PRUNER AT WORK

Many people in western Michigan are bewildered by the difficulty they have in keeping yards and lawns neat under their favorite oak trees. Daily, leafy twigs and even good-sized branches are found strewn about the premises.

This litter is the work of a long-horned beetle, commonly known as the oak twig pruner and familiar to scientists as Elaphidion villosum.

It is the larval stage of this insect which does the damage, and if one will carefully examine the fallen twig, he will often discover the culprit in the soft inner part.

The adult beetle, only about three-fourths of an inch long, is characterized by its long antennae or feelers which give it the name "long-horn." There are many beetles of this group, most of which are plant-eaters. The general color is dark brown, and the insect is covered with a grayish down.

The eggs are laid about the plant and then, when the young larvae reach their maximum growth, they girdle the twig which has been their home and it falls to the ground. In this fallen twig they complete their development and, after a period of pupation, change into the adult beetle and emerge from the dead twig ready to carry on the cycle of oak pruner.

Because of the living insect in the fallen twigs the only successful way to combat these injurious insects is to gather the fallen parts and burn them. This is almost a daily task if one is to be conscientious in it. Then also the success of the undertaking depends a good bit on one's neighbors for the adult insects are winged and easily can spread from place to place.

Muskegon and environs have been particularly infested with this insect pest this season, and the fallen twigs resulting from the larval activity of the oak pruner can be seen in all parts of the city and county. Forest and woodland trees also harbor these insects, and to people living near wooded sections, it becomes even a greater problem.

SAND CHERRIES RIPE

Sand cherries are ripe in Michigan duneland, and there is a good crop this year.

Last year there was hardly a cupful to be found on any full-grown plant throughout the Muskegon area, but things are different this year. Thanks to the affable weather in April, bees were able to do their proper work this year. The fruit set well and with intermittent rains and hot sunny days, the bountiful cherries are full of juice and hang heavily from the bushes.

By some, these cherries are called "sugar plums," but this is a misnomer, for they are true cherries. They are about the color of the cultivated black sweets but are on the tart side and smaller.

Sand cherries are members of the fore-dune association and are found among the marram grass and sand reeds. Both of these plants with their fibrous roots have helped to establish and stabilize the sand so that shrubs, such as the numerous willows and sand cherries, can take root. This fore-dune society is between the beach and cottonwood zones.

In April the scraggly shrubs were loaded with beautiful, fragrant white blossoms. That is the crucial time for the plant. If the bees cannot visit them and do their work of pollination, there is little fruit in July and August. A very wet April can ruin the crop.

If one is to gather fruit from the wild, it is important to get permission from the owner of the land. I was fortunate this week in finding good picking and in fifteen minutes had two quarts, which is enough to make jelly. Later, I may gather three or four more quarts for juice to use this fall.

As from all of nature's larder, it is important not to take more than one can use and to remember that some wildlife also depends on these native fruits.

In fact, I was delighted to see a mother oriole feeding her family of three youngsters from a bush of berries. They were perched in a nearby cottonwood, and she made regular trips to the bush to "show how it's done."

The orioles and I were not the only two cherry pickers. A red squirrel, chipmunk and gopher all visited those near me. Noisy jays and a pair of pheasants were about the ripening cherries, too.

These sand cherries belong to the most fragile of the duneland area and because of this have suffered most from those four-wheelers and snowmobiles whose drivers are careless and like to "take the bumps."

"The bumps" are often formed by sand accumulated around these shrubs and running over them does great damage.

If the sand cherry, which grows in few places besides the Great Lakes dunes, is to survive, great care must be taken.

## MICHIGAN'S BEAUTIFUL ROADSIDES

They are "weeds" to many of us, albeit pretty weeds. To the colonists, early settlers and pioneers they were so important that their seeds, roots and cuttings were brought from "the Old Country" to be used in the New World.

Uncounted miles of Michigan's highways and byways are now beautified by these two — chicory and soapwort — valuable plants of a day gone by.

The chicory has again come into its own. With the high prices of coffee, chicory has again been used to flavor it. In fact, one recent brand even shows pictures of the two plants, making no apologies for the addition.

The South never gave up the use of the chicory in the popular breakfast beverage. When in a Louisiana coffee house for breakfast, the waitress asked after our order of "coffee," "What kind? Morning, evening or southern?" I wasn't sure, so she explained. "Morning is real coffee; evening, decaffeinated, and southern is with chicory." I took southern. That was in 1968, and since then I've had this plant in my herb patch.

If you, too, want to include it in your garden, don't try to transplant it. Gather seeds and sow them in the spring and fall, and before long your harvest of roots will surprise you.

Chicory has been growing wild in Michigan since before the Civil War. The first was recorded in 1860 and since then it has spread to every county.

The blue dandelion-like flowers have given it a variety of common names: succory, blue sailors, ragged sailors, and blue dandelion.

The flowering season is July to frost. The individual flower heads last only a day and sometimes just a few hours, the shortest of any common wildflower.

Not only are the blossoms a beautiful cerulean blue, but they are very attractive to goldfinches.

The other familiar plant brought over for colonial gardens is soapwort, commonly known as bouncing bet.

The plant belongs to the pink family and has the characteristic sweet, spicy fragrance of the others. So old and familiar is it that it has a variety of names: old maid's pink, London pride, lady-by-the-gate and hedge pink.

Having escaped from the early colonial gardens and being brought westward with the pioneers, it is very widespread in the United States.

It reached Michigan in 1839 and as the name suggests, it was used as a cleansing agent. The juice of the roots, stems and leaves when crushed and put in water make a lather for washing.

In parts of the south this plant has never been discarded, and today more housewives are experimenting with it as a "natural cleansing agent."

This plant can easily (some say too easily) be grown from the seed, but should be planted in a spot in the yard where it can run wild.

I like this plant because it invites the delicate hummingbird moth to feast in its blossoms. At twilight the scent of the spicy flowers and the sight of the delicate moths feeding are a never-to-be-forgotten summer pleasure.

Goldfinches are happy these days.

One of their favorite plants has gone to seed providing them both with food and nesting material.

At present these little "wild canaries" may be seen wherever there is a patch of old man's beard, goat's beard, or vegetable oyster.

All of these names apply to plants which are described by children as "giant dandelions" or "granddaddy dandies" because the seeding head looks like an overgrown dandelion although it is brownish instead of the usual and more familiar grayish white.

Frequently observers will notice these seeded heads are bowed down and the stem is bent at a sharp angle. This is where a dainty little goldfinch had a summer picnic eating the large pointed seeds. He was more tidy than many human picnickers and carried the remains, in this case a soft downy seed umbrella home — to line a baby's cradle.

Goldfinches are among the later of the native birds to nest. Sometimes called thistlebirds, they wait for the thistles to go to seed before they build so they can utilize the films of thistledown, it is said. In this section they are partial to the other plant, old man's beard, and will fly a long distance to find it.

Goldfinches are useful birds in yards and gardens because they eat great numbers of weed seeds and their growing nestlings require their constant attention. These birds in a garden are a real asset to anyone.

As winter feeding increases, goldfinches remain during the cold months and make delightful winter companions. They tend to flock during the winter. It is not unusual to have twenty or thirty clustered about a tubular feeder which will only accommodate a modest dozen. They are not patient birds and will frequently crowd a nearby branch, vociferously urging the eaters to hurry. They soon become impatient and push the lucky ones off the perch and help themselves. For many bird-watchers, this is part of the fun of winter feeding.

The families can be easily identified because the male is a jaunty little bright gold bird with black cap and accents of white and black. The youngsters, however, look like mother and are olive green with a slightly yellowish tinge and the beginning of light wing bars.

The young ones often follow the parents with outspread fluttering wings and a teasing, impatient call. They would much rather be fed than learn to search for their own food, but the adults are insistent and stern teachers.

The adult birds seldom abandon youngsters when they have reached this stage but they do leave them alone for varying periods. Humans should not pick up the young birds and should not hang out the winter feeding tube in summer.

## YOUNG BIRDS ON THEIR OWN

The last two weeks of July present a great variety of activities among Muskegon bird residents.

Many young birds are able to care for themselves by July if their parents are among the early nesters, but some still choose to remain close to mother as an extra source of refreshment. With persistent coaxing even a harsh bird mother may be persuaded to supply the desired berry or insect as the menu dictates.

Goldfinches and cedar waxwings have just started their family cares as they are late nesters. Grackles, on the other hand are among the first to cast off family responsibilities. Being one-brooded and arriving very early in the season, by July their well-grown youngsters are feeding with the adults in family groups.

By now they have joined together and grackles may be seen in large flocks along the roadside, by beaches, near grain fields and in parks. One of their chief delights, after they have satisfied their appetites, seems to be to annoy other birds not as fortunate as they in having an early nesting program. They are always poking about curiously and snooping in nests, hollow trees, fence posts and the like.

Red-winged blackbirds also are already joining together in bands to forage before they take their southern flight. They belong in the same family with grackles, but confine their activities chiefly to swamps, cat-tail marshes bordering ponds, lakes and streams.

A different type of bird which is flocking before the end of the month is the swallow. They come together, forming roosts, often in marshes, and by late afternoon telephone wires will be lined with them over weedy waterways where insects are abundant.

In addition to the nesting of the late breeders and the flocking of the early ones, some birds have retired to the deep woodlands to molt.

Still another group are those which are gypsying from the south on a vacation into the northern states. These are the herons and egrets and in recent years egrets have been found wandering in western Michigan and in southern counties in increasing numbers.

After the last week in July, birds will be less conspicuous and are rarely heard in full song because they are preparing for the southern flight.

July is a high point in the bird activity of Michigan, and many bird-watchers will be in the field during the hot mid-summer days.

## COWBIRDS HAVE FEW ADMIRERS

Few birders take the time to admire the cowbird.

There are many reasons for this attitude, especially in Michigan where this bird represents a major problem for the endangered Kirtland's warbler. In fact, a control program has been set up in the warbler's area to destroy the cowbird and reduce the competition for nesting areas.

The cowbird is one of Michigan's few brood parasites. It does not build a nest of its own, but instead lays its eggs in the nests of smaller birds. They are left to be incubated, hatched and raised by the foster parents.

It is not unusual this time of the year to see a small bird (warbler, vireo or chipping sparrow) being followed by a large, awkward, youngster brownish-grey in color. Only once in a half century of birding have I seen an adult cowbird feeding a young one. This week I saw another unusual episode in the life of a young cowbird.

On the bird table in the yard I saw a young cowbird all by itself. There was apparently no parent anywhere. It called and called repeatedly to attract the attention of a parent to feed it. It even went through the wing-fluttering appeal for food. No parent appeared.

I thought perhaps it was being trained by its parents to seek food for itself. A family of jays came, and after stuffing their babies full of feed, off they flew. The youngster watched and appealed for food. Then, grackles came and again the begging behavior was displayed. The grackles paid little or no attention, in fact, they showed slight aggression.

The little cowbird was becoming very hungry and very insistent to each bird that came to feed.

Starlings, robins, mourning doves and catbirds came and the little cowbird stayed on — crying and fluttering. This went on for most of two hours, and I was beginning to wonder about feeding it. Apparently, its foster parents had deserted it. Perhaps they thought it could feed itself — or were worn out with its care.

Then a rollicking band of house sparrows — male, female, and a host of juveniles — came to feed. They surrounded the cowbird and began picking and pecking at the food. The young cowbird watched them. First it turned its head one way to eye them, then to the other. It cried and fluttered, but no one looked its way.

The cowbird noticed their eating and for the first time stopped crying and fluttering. It bent its head and picked up a seed. It shook its head, eyed the sparrows and tried another seed. Then it settled down with the sparrows and enjoyed a picnic lunch. The sparrows soon flew away and left the cowbird, still enjoying its meal. It has since been patronizing my feeding table for several days, always by itself.

Cowbirds are omnivorous feeders, eating both seeds and other plant products along with insects and animal food. The old name of this bird, in the early days of the west, was buffalo bird, because it followed the animals snapping up insects from around the animals or even from their backs.

With the coming of cattle ranches to the west, replacing buffalo, the birds quickly adapted to the new animals and followed them similarly. So their name became cowbird.

Our species is the brown-headed, and seldom are others seen here. In the west there is another, larger one — the bronzed — which is distinguished by its red eye. Last week I observed this bird in its courting display in Madera Canyon, Arizona.

At first it was the routine behavior we are familiar with in the brown-headed, but as we watched a somewhat larger bird flew straight up two or three feet in front of the hens. It hovered momentarily and then came down. It repeated the aerial stunt over and over. On the ground its ruff was raised about its neck. We were fascinated with this behavior, but the hens he wished to attract were unimpressed and kept on with their feeding.

Brown-headed cowbirds are said to parasitize 200 species of birds while the screaming cowbird victimizes only the non-parasitic bay-winged cowbird. In tropical America the giant cowbird, twice the size of our species, drops its eggs in the pendant nest of the cornbird and yellow-tail, both birds of the Icteridae (oriole) family.

## QUEEN ANNE'S LACE, PRETTY PEST

Michigan fields and roadsides are now abloom with wild flowers and most conspicuous among them is the wild carrot, more aesthetically known as "Queen Anne's lace."

A veritable Jekyll and Hyde among plants is this one. It is considered a "pernicious weed" by farmers and a beautiful flower by others who seek it especially to use in floral arrangements for porch and summer table. It lends itself particularly to combining with other summer flowers and its lace graces many bouquets. It is a popular altar flower in rural sections during August.

Many years ago the wild carrot was seldom seen in fields and along highways of Michigan, but it has multiplied rapidly until now few counties, if any, are free from it. So rapidly does it spread that one twenty acre field which had three blooming plants was entirely filled in three years. Many seeds are formed on the flower head and these are easily scattered. The root is strong and sturdy, characteristic of the parsnip family to which it belongs.

The wild carrot is a European emigrant. Its exact date of entry into Michigan is not known but, like the house sparrow and starling, it has adapted itself so well that it is growing to pest proportions in some localities.

Other common names for the plant are bee's nest plant and bird's nest. Bees are frequently found in the flower head and the latter name is suggested by the concave form of the umbel when it has started to set seed. Queen Anne's lace is by far the most attractive name and the blossoms do remind one of dainty little lace doilies spread in the summer sunshine to dry after laundering.

The central floret in the cluster is often purple, indicating the royal household to which it belongs.

In the early days of America, wild carrot was considered a medicinal herb and in some rural sections today the seeds and roots still are used as a stimulant, diuretic and carminative.

Being listed by most states as a "noxious weed," Queen Anne's lace can be gathered plentifully and used either decoratively or medicinally and no one will object. Farmers welcome any measures which help decrease its growth.

THE MILKWEED ZOO

The milkweed may be just a common pest to the gardener, a weed to be hurriedly disposed of before it scatters its myriads of filmy seed-laden parachutes, but to the nature lover the milkweed is a whole zoo.

The collector of insects need not stray far from the patch of milkweeds in his backyard to find representatives of many groups. Many species are seen and many strange phenomena of insect life are enacted on the stalk of a single milkweed plant.

The best known and probably the most conspicuous of the milkweed's numerous guests is the large, tawny and black monarch butterfly. These insects are seen hovering above the plants because it is here they lay their eggs, thereby providing for the young caterpillars an abundance of their favorite diet of tender milkweed leaves. During July and August these caterpillars can be found in various stages of growth upon the leaves and stems of the plant. Likewise, the chrysalis of this species frequently is formed on the food plant and often these beautiful green, gold-dotted pupae are observed hanging from the mid vein of a leaf.

A relative of the butterfly which frequents the same plant is the caterpillar of the harlequin moth. This youngster is clothed in downy tufted fur of yellow, black and white.

Among the beetles which are invariably found upon this food plant are the common milkweed beetle, the tortoise beetle and a close relative of the potato beetle. The first named is the most evident and is colored red with black spots. It is easily identified by the elongated feelers or horns.

Bees and flies visit the milkweeds frequently, especially after the blossoms begin to appear. Doubtless they are attracted by the large, showy, fragrant blooms. Among the most interesting of these visitors is the "cuckoo." This insect lacks pollen-gathering apparatus but lives in the nests of other bees and imitates their habits, thus gaining not only habitation and food but also protection.

Milkweeds are very popular with ants at this season of year for just now the ants are utilizing the milkweeds as pasture grounds for their "cows," green plant lice or aphids which they keep under observation and from which they obtain a supply of sweet liquid. This insect "herding" is a favorite ant pastime in July and August, and many milkweed plants can be found upon which this strange insect association is going on. The ants profit by the device and the aphids appear unharmed. They get plenty to eat and biological rumor has it that the ants are so solicitous of the welfare of their "cows" that they are known to transfer them to fresh pastures when the old one becomes a bit lean.

# JULY DAYS GREAT FOR BUTTERFLIES

Late July days are butterfly days.

Many people who are not usually attracted to insects find themselves noticing the jewels of the insect world in midsummer — the butterflies, or flutterbys, as Europeans call them.

As June is the time of the great night-flying moths, now is the time for the display of the daytime splendor of the butterflies. With the blossoming of acres of field and garden flowers at their best, butterflies come into their own.

Probably the best known and most conspicuous of the butterflies is the monarch or milkweed butterfly. Since 1952 when they were first tagged here as a part of the Migratory Insect Research Project sponsored by the Royal Museum and University at Toronto, they have received much publicity and are to the insects what the robin is to the birds.

The monarch's first appearance is watched and recorded annually. During the summer they are tagged and recorded. This international project involves Canada, the United States and Mexico — where monarchs spend the winter.

The monarchs are among our larger butterflies and, because of their bright orange-red and black coloring, are very eye-catching. The swallowtails are probably the next best known. There are several of these in the area of which the tiger, spice bush, black and zebra are especially handsome. Some of their larvae feed on the plants of the carrot family and so gardens sometimes play host to them as do fields of wild carrot or Queen Anne's lace.

The mourning cloak and red and white admirals have been about since early spring, for unlike the migrating monarchs these remain and hibernate.

The viceroy is sometimes confused with the monarch because of similar coloration. However, the viceroy is smaller and has a conspicuous black cross bar on the hind wing. Its larvae feed on poplar and willow.

The fritillaries are handsome, medium-sized insects. They are bedecked with orange and red above and light spots and silvery specks on the hindwings which glisten like sequins in the sunlight. Their caterpillars like to feed on violets, golden rods and other members of the daisy family.

The anglewings, as the name implies, are easily recognized as a group but not so as to species. There are the comma, the question mark, hunter's and painted lady. Another striking insect is the buckeye, whose eggs and larvae are found on plantain, stonecrops and gerardia.

The yellows and whites are sometimes called puddle butterflies because in midsummer they gather about little pools in large flocks. There are several species of these, the alfalfa, cabbage and common sulphur being popular.

The nymphs and satyrs are a group unto themselves and as the name suggests, they like woodland openings and thickets.

The blues and coppers are small butterflies that make up in beauty what they lack in size. The American copper is bright-colored and about the size of a penny. The blues are more common in the West, but we have a choice one in the spring azure which is a precious reward for an early spring walk in the woods.

Of the seven thousand species of moths and butterflies in North America, Michigan has its fair share. July is the month to make the acquaintance of these living jewels.

# AUGUST

## MOLTING TIME ARRIVES

August is the silent month for birds. Many visitors will ask when they are here during the next three weeks, "Where are the Michigan birds we hear so much about?"

The answer is simple, but perhaps not very satisfactory for the bird-watcher who is here for only a short time. The birds are here, but because August is the month when many of the common so-called "song birds" are molting, they are comparatively quiet, and retire to deep woods and swamplands. During this period, which is difficult for birds, they lose their feathers which are replaced with new ones. Their general vitality may be low, just as one's pet canary or parakeet is sometimes "dumpy" during the molting time. The birds call as little attention to themselves as possible now, lest they become easy prey for their enemies.

But, by the end of the month they will be emerging from their hide-outs and will be in full fall plumage, some of them with a change of color.

*        *

If one is to get the most enjoyment from birds this month, try the shores, beaches and waterways of the state. This is an excellent time to get better acquainted with the water birds — heron, rails, ducks, teals, sandpipers, plovers, terns, gulls and bittern.

Marshes and swamps of August also yield surprises in the plant world, which make them a worthwhile hunting place. Bladderwort, pitcher plant and sundew are three of the carnivorous plants which prey upon insects. Several of the wild orchids are rewards of bog-trotters. The grasspink, arethusa, ladies' tresses, rattlesnake plantain and the fringed orchid belong in this group.

Pickerel weed, lady's thumb, swamp silkweed, turtlehead, arrowhead and the two lobelias, red and blue, are among the water-loving plants which bloom in August.

*          *

In the streams and lakes are the water lilies, the white or water nymph and the yellow or spatterdock, both of which are common on Michigan waterways. The rare American lotus is found in only a few places in the state.

*          *

August is the month of youngsters among mammals. Many parents are accompanied by the new ones now. Raccoons, skunks, chipmunks, squirrels, rabbits, woodchucks, muskrats and beaver are only a few of the many that are now busy with the training and upbringing of these woodland babies.

Ferns and mosses are at their best. A wanderer on the sylvan paths this month sees many ferns and mosses fruiting. These plants do not have seeds, but rather spores, which are borne in a variety of devices called spore-cases. Some ferns have two kinds of fronds — the fertile which bear the spores, and the sterile which are purely vegetative.

There are many different kinds of ferns in the Muskegon State Park, and many of the paths show them to advantage. The mosses are numerous, and among those conspicuous now are the pigeon wheat or haircaps, the tree moss, cushion moss, apple moss, fern moss, woodsymnium and common bryun.

In addition to ferns and mosses, the club mosses, which are more closely related to the ferns than mosses are green and fruiting this month. Like the lotus these are all on Michigan's protected list. The ground cedar, ground pine, deerhorn and ground hemlock are four of the common ones.

*          *

Frogs, turtles, snakes and toads are all busy in August. Young turtles are often hatched this month. Snakes and turtles frequently are seen sunning themselves along streams, and on logs and stumps.

Butterflies are among the most conspicuous of the larger insects, and caddis hatches this month are the delight of the angler — especially the trout fisherman.

# INDIGO BUNTING SINGS

With the coming of August and the stilling of so many bird voices, the few that continue to carry on the aerial chorus are much appreciated. Of the lovelier musicians of this small choir is the indigo bunting, a member of the sparrow tribe.

Sometimes confused with the bluebird, which belongs to the thrush clan, this bird is widely distributed throughout the state of Michigan.

It is fond of a variety of habitats, so a tramp through the fields, woodlands or along streams is almost sure to reveal this delightful bird. It is especially partial to roadside shrubs and thickets and is often found along the borders of wooded tracts. Even the pasture and orchard are choice haunts of this bunting. Just now, with the trees in full foliage, it is usually the song of the indigo bird that betrays its whereabouts.

It is a habit of the male to choose a singing perch and there, day after day, to pour out its joyous, canary-like warble, frequently from the topmost branch of tree or shrub. Early morning, just as the first rays of the sun touch the tops of the trees, is a favorite time for this concert. The indigo bird does not discontinue its song later in the day, however, for even at the hottest hours of noon these gay songsters add charm and melody to the August days.

The plumage of the male gives this bunting its name. It appears a brilliant blue, darker on the head and breast and lighter on the rump. The wings and tail are brownish, edged with blue. With the exception of the blue grosbeak, not a common resident of Michigan, this bird is frequently spoken of as our "bluest" bird but certainly its song assures us it is blue only in color and not in disposition. The partner of this brilliant songster is a demure little lady, almost sparrow-like in her attire. She is an indifferent brown with obscure darker streaks on the sides and a dusky white underneath, ideally colored for protection as she broods on her nest.

The indigo bunting is known by a variety of common names throughout its range. Most of these refer to the coloring, its relation to the finches or its song. A few of them are indigo bird, blue canary, indigo finch, blue finch and blue summerbird.

Although this bird is so widely distributed it is probably less known than many of the inconspicuously colored members of its clan, because it arrives later in the spring after the foliage is well developed. This tends to obscure it and lends protection to the brightly plumaged male.

The indigo buntings are definitely summer residents, arriving here in the latter part of May and remaining to raise one or frequently two broods. Then early in the fall days they noiselessly slip away toward their winter home in Central America.

The nests are sparrowlike and are located in briars, bushes and shrubs, along streams, wooded borders and roadsides. The eggs reflect the color of the male and are pale bluish-white.

Not only is this bird desirable because of its beauty of plumage, its grace of flight and its strikingly musical song, but also because of its feeding habits which are altogether commendable. It feeds on a very small percentage of seeds, the major part of the diet consisting of injurious insects such as caterpillars, span worms, cutworms, beetles, chafers, aphids, cankerworms, web worms and many kinds of bugs. It does not usually attack fruit or grain, and it is highly desirable for the agriculturist and gardener to encourage and protect.

## REDSTART IS ACTIVE

Among the more conspicuous birds which are still active despite the summer lethargy in the bird world, is the American redstart, a member of the wood warbler family.

This tiny, gay, bright orange and black bird is known by a variety of descriptive names, such as fire-bird, fire-tail, redstart flycatcher and Halloween bird. Contrasted with the male's brilliant orange and black plumage, the female is gray and yellow.

Redstarts are abundant about the wooded dunes of Muskegon country and are partial to the edges and borders of the woods and forests. They also like stream edges.

They are typical of the wood warbler family in that they are restless and nervous in temperament and move in and out incessantly about the foliage of trees and bushes. After a night of heavy dew, the birds are often seen at the borders of woodlots high up in the topmost branches of the trees and shrubs where the first rays of the rising morning sun can reach them. Here they glean drowsy insects from the leaves and twigs. They are beneficial to the gardener and farmer because of the great numbers of insects which they devour during their stay in Michigan.

Arriving with the majority of the warblers on their northern trek in May, they remain in this section until about October when they are joined by many of the northern breeding species. Then, together, they set out for the south, many going into Mexico, Central America and even to South American countries.

Redstarts often mimic flycatchers in their method of snapping up unwary insects. Cabbage butterflies and small moths form a staple article of their diet.

Unlike their cousin the yellow warbler, redstarts seldom nest in city gardens.

## OVENBIRD HEARD

Few birds of Michigan are more frequently heard and less seen than the ovenbird. This bird reverses the old axiom regarding good children which "should be seen and not heard."

A trip into almost any woodlot of the state this month will reveal this bird. The woods-wanderer is usually first attracted by its ascending high pitched call which resembles the rapidly repeated word "teacher." As the notes are repeated they increase in speed, strength and volume. Because of this characteristic song the bird is commonly known in local sections of Michigan as the teacher-bird.

During the past week large numbers of these birds have been arriving in western Michigan, and a number have been reported dead from accidents during flight. Two were found with necks broken indicating that they had probably flown against some obstacle. Every year, especially at this season, large numbers of these small birds and their relatives lose their lives on the migratory flight.

The ovenbirds belong to the family of wood warblers and are therefore confined to the New World, as this is one of the famous American bird families. It is made up of a large number of species, most of which occur in the Lower Peninsula of Michigan as transients; but there are some, such as the yellow warbler, the redstart and the black-throated blue, which nest throughout the state. The ovenbird is one of these.

Like the rest of the warbler family it is a small bird with a ground color of grayish green with lighter underparts, but unlike the majority of them which are foliage or bark tenders, this bird has taken up a ground life, and is most frequently seen in the leaves, or stealing along a woodland path in search of insect food.

The grayish white breast is distinctly spotted in streaks and the crown is orange bordered with black. From this crown the bird is locally known as the golden-crowned thrush, the golden-crowned wagtail and the golden-crowned accenter. The habit of twitching the tail also contributes the name, wood wagtail.

Thrilling as it is to see this bird after one has repeatedly heard its calling, that does not begin to delight as does the discovery of the nest. It is from this remarkable structure that the name ovenbird is derived. The nest is a piece of art, as bird architecture goes. In the woodland, hidden away oftentimes in the driest part, on a carpet of dry, brown leaves there is sure to be tucked away a little dome-shaped bundle of rootlets, leaves, grasses and bark strips. When more closely examined through the side opening, as in a Dutch oven, there often will be found from four to six cream-white eggs spotted with reddish brown.

## TRY NIGHT HIKING

Long an advocate of night hiking, I have seldom been able to find companions for this brand of outdoor diversion. One recent night, however, two blowouts brought me a welcome opportunity to indulge my hobby, and not alone.

It can happen to the best of cars. When only three tires remain inflated, two alternatives are left: hiking or hitchhiking. Our party preferred hiking. It proved both interesting and pleasant.

We started out with the lights of the stalled car behind us and Arcturus shining brightly in the dark sky ahead. Along the roadsides could be heard the late summer insect orchestra, crickets, katydids, locusts, tree crickets and cicadas strumming their evening serenade.

Those who like the outdoors miss much by confining their nature rambles to the daylight hours. The sights of day give way to sounds and fragrances at night. Corn cockle and evening lychnis were scattering a delightful incense along a ditch. In the corners of a rail fence a magnificent stand of evening primroses was opening, inviting nocturnal insects. Nor did the invitation go unheeded, for while we watched, two long-tongued, night-flying moths of the Sphinx family paid a visit, followed by other hungry guests.

In a cornfield a dancing of wings showed two io moths fluttering in and out among the rows, seeking places to deposit the eggs that will perpetuate their species for another year. Along a swampy place fireflies were scintillating like fairy lanterns at a gay and rollicking party.

We almost stepped on a long, slender shape and were startled when it glided out of our path, shadowy and swift. It was a blue racer hunting in the darkness for its evening meal, an unwary mouse or rat.

Two bats flitted through the sky near a patch of woods, and we were sure the ancients had done well in naming them "flittermice." We hoped they were dining on their favorite fare, mosquitoes.

Far above the bats, cleaning the upper air of insect pests, nighthawks were circling and zooming over woods, fields and swamps alike. And from a distant woods a whip-poor-will, the nighthawk's country cousin, called in tireless rhythm.

Night hiking is a quiet pastime, but it will bring you sounds and smells you cannot hope to encounter in the daylight hours.

## SNAKES DO GOOD

Seldom do we start on an outdoor tramp with a group this time of year but someone asks with a note of suspicious alarm, "Will there be any snakes?"

The answer, "Probably not, but I wish there would," usually solicits a variety of responses, for most people are not eager to see these interesting creatures of the grass jungles.

Mrs. Howard Cleveland of Hart is a pleasant exception and in a letter she regrets the fact that so many boys and girls these days hunt out and kill snakes regardless of their kind and habits. She goes on to say, "I was brought up to believe snakes did as much good as harm, so why pick on them?"

This is exactly the attitude that boys and girls are developing in their camp and outdoor experiences. Of Michigan's sixteen species of serpents, only one, the rattlesnake, is harmful to man. The rest may be handled with immunity.

It is true some, such as the "blacksnake," prey partially upon birds and game, but most of the others are instrumental in keeping down the population of mice, rats, moles, gophers, grasshoppers, beetles, and other injurious insects. Many celery farmers pride themselves on their allies, the blue racers, which frequent their lowland.

The pilot snake and milk snake are both great mousers and for that reason are often found about houses, stone walls, barns, sheds, granaries, corncribs and similar outbuildings. The milk snake is misnamed because it does not feed on milk as was formerly erroneously believed.

Among Michigan's smaller snakes, the Dekay, red-bellied, green and ring-necked are beneficial because of the large numbers of insects which they devour. The grass or green snake especially does yeomen service in destroying grasshoppers.

It is not to be overlooked that snakes do eat frogs and toads and occasionally birds, but their destruction of harmful and injurious species puts the evidence in favor of the serpent. They do more good than harm and therefore are classed as man's friendly allies.

The best known of our western Michigan snakes are the garter and hog-nosed snakes. The garter or "streaked snake" is easily recognized as a medium-sized snake with three stripes of yellow, greenish or orange. It frequents a variety of places and favors stream or lake borders, thickets and moist uplands. It is harmless and interesting in captivity.

The hog-nosed snake is known by a variety of local names because of some of its behavior habits. It is called "puff adder," "blow snake" and "blower." When alarmed, it inflates its head and hisses menacingly. Also it flops over on its back with its belly exposed and "makes believe dead." So determined is it in this deception that if it is turned over, it will immediately flip over to play dead again. This species is satisfactorily handled in captivity and makes an entertaining "pet."

Michigan's largest snake is the pilot snake, sometimes called "black racer," which may reach a length of eight feet. The smallest is the red-bellied, which seldom exceeds ten inches.

Another snake which has a peculiar behavior is the fox snake. Its habit of rapidly vibrating its tail in the manner of a rattler has caused the death of many individuals of this species. They are frequently mistaken for rattlesnakes. The fox snake is harmless and very useful because of the large number of rodents which it destroys.

Michigan's one venomous reptile is the rattlesnake or massasauga. Dr. A. G. Ruthven in his "Herpetology of Michigan" says of this snake: "needless to say this snake should be avoided as it is distinctly venomous, but on the other hand most of the current stories about it must be discredited for it is doubtful if its bite is sufficiently noxious to kill a healthy adult. It is a sluggish snake, slow to bite, and usually gives warning with its rattle before striking. It is thus little to be feared. It prefers the vicinity of swamps, although not aquatic in its habits."

Contrary to popular belief, Michigan does not have the cottonmouth or the copperhead, two species which are commonly attributed to this state.

Snakes form a real part of Michigan's summer out-of-doors, and to the tramper or hiker who is willing to take a little time and search out these wildings there is much of fascination, of entertainment and of wisdom in store. Much is yet to be learned concerning the habits and life histories of these grass jungle wanderers. With snakes, as with human beings, the better we know them the more we come to appreciate them and see their good qualities.

"Will there be any snakes on the next hike?"

"We hope so."

## PRAYING MANTIS, A STRANGE VISITOR

A welcome visitor paid me a call.

It was during one of the severe thunderstorms of the past fortnight and I was watching it from my favorite rocking chair on the front porch.

On the ceiling of the porch I noticed a strange green stick about four inches long. I thought it unusual that it could remain there, so I started to investigate. No sooner had I gotten up than I saw it was no "stick," for it had been disturbed by my movement and turned its head.

Then I knew it was a praying mantis, for no other insect in all the world can turn its head like this. I was delighted, for this is the first one I have ever seen in the yard. It is true I had planted an egg case two or three years ago. Having seen none of the insects in all this time I assumed that the birds had found and destroyed the case, and that that was the end of the mantis here.

Now one was calling on me at a time when I had plenty of opportunity to get acquainted with it. Apparently it, too, had taken shelter on the porch while the thunderstorm continued.

This mantis was a lovely shade of leaf green and could easily hide and be overlooked in the yard and garden among all the foliage and shrubbery. I measured it and it was four inches, although most books give the maximum length as three and a half. Probably it has been eating extra well this season.

To me, among all the thousands of insects, the praying mantis has always held a special fascination. Although a member of the order to which the crickets, grasshoppers, walking sticks, locusts and katydids belong, it is different from all of them.

Three features set it apart from them, in fact from other insects in general. I have already mentioned that it can move its head, in a most uninsectlike manner. In addition, it has a hinge in the middle of its body which allows it to raise the front part which then has somewhat the appearance of a giraffe's long neck. The third feature is the unusual development of the front pair of legs. These are so long that they seem out of proportion to the rest of the body and are very strong and bend at the elbows. They are equipped with barbs inside to aid the insect in grasping its prey.

These insects are called praying mantis, because of the religious attitude some have imagined they assume with the front part raised. They might equally and, possibly more correctly, be called the preying mantis for they are among our important carnivorous insects.

The praying attitude which the insect simulates is its deception, for from this position it strikes out with one of its poised arms with lightning swiftness and brings the prey to its mouth. Struggle as it may, the victim seldom gets away, for the barbs are very efficient and hold the meal securely. My visitor feasted on a miller right over the doorway in fine view.

The mantis is not only a carnivore, but it is a cannibal as well. It would as quickly eat another mantis as any other insect. In fact, the female mantis eats her mate! I vote for preying, not praying, after this shocking act!

In spite of this, the mantis is a good mother and provides an excellent home for her young. I will admit it is best if she is not around when they hatch for her appetite might get the better of her. The little mantes do eat each other so only a few of the large number that escape the egg case survive. It is these egg masses, which are placed on twigs and about tree trunks, that are now sold throughout the country so that gardeners may have the services of these carnivorous insects to help rid their yards and gardens of injurious pests. It is for this purpose I placed such an egg case in our garden a couple of years ago. Here in the northern states the eggs do not usually hatch until late May or June. Scores of little mantes emerge from the mass and are subject to many hazards in addition to their own kind. Many are devoured by ants upon their emergence. As soon as an egg case is broken open, ants rush to it and stand by for a meal.

It is not until after one or two molts that the young have a hardened crust and get their elbow pinchers to working on such practice insects as gnats, midges and mosquitoes. Later they tackle large insects, sometimes bigger than themselves.

The mantis gives off a dark liquid, similar to the tobacco juice of its cousin, the grasshopper. In some sections of the rural south this is thought to be poisonous, but it is not. Along with the green protective coloration it is a security device to ward off enemies.

The mantis is man's friend. As far as is known they eat little that is useful to us. They keep down numbers of pests that would destroy our food crops and bring disease. They help to maintain the balance of nature. They do not bite or sting and as one of their devotees says, "They should never be killed — their life is already all too short."

My visitor stayed all afternoon and night (I looked at 2 A.M.) but at 6:30 the next morning she was gone.

## SPARROWS ANSWER S.O.S. CALL

Few bird species are more successful in Michigan than the English or house sparrow. There are many attributes which contribute to the success story, not the least of which is cooperation.

Wednesday a bronze grackle happened to alight on a large limb of a cottonwood tree near Lake Michigan. Upon the branch was situated an enormous sparrow nest. Last year a robin's nest was in this location, but early in the spring a male sparrow discovered the site and finally was able to persuade a mate to assist in reconditioning it. Now it is the home of the sparrows. Young recently have left the nest, and more eggs are being deposited in it this week.

No sooner had the blackbird arrived on the limb, about a foot from the nest, when the cock sparrow set up a persistent alarm call. No attempt was made to fly at the intruder or to dislodge him. Just this persistent cheeping continued. Finally we began to doubt the bravery and courage of this sparrow, who would allow a large bird to come so near the nest without more concern. The sparrow sat on a branch just above the big bird and watched it while he chirped loudly and incessantly.

The blackbird was embarrassed and turned its head first on one side and then on the other to get a better look at the sparrow. Neither of them moved.

Then a whirring of wings from the direction of a neighbor's garden, and eight sparrows flew noisily into the tree and alighted on a limb just in front of the grackle. Only one of these was a mature male, the others were either hens or juveniles. Perhaps they were the young previously hatched from the nest, banding together for the protection of their former home.

No sooner had the eight arrived than the first bird flew at the head of the intruder. That caused him to duck, but not to give ground. The helpers remained on the limb facing the enemy, and several of them joined in the alarm, now less loud but still persistent.

The grackle continued to eye the group and hopped sideways, one hop nearer the nest. Nothing happened. It took another hop to the edge of the nest. The sparrows did nothing, just watched. The owner of the nest was much concerned, but made no attack.

Emboldened by their passive resistance, the blackbird looked about and then hopped directly upon the rim of the nest. It was peering down cautiously into the depths when like a thunderbolt it was hit from three sides, knocked off the nest, and fell floundering down almost to the ground before it caught itself and was able to use its own wings.

Two males and one other sparrow had struck at it simultaneously as it stood on the nest.

The blackbird did not return but joined its mate in a nearby cottonwood tree. One by one the sparrows then flew away in the direction from which they came. The owner and one female remained and twittered conversationally as the others flew away.

Sparrows are cooperative, and apparently they answer the distress call of a neighbor, then await his direction for the fray.

SPARROWS PRAISED

House sparrows aren't all bad, contrary to what some think.

Not everyone has time to watch them and catch them at their good deeds. However, a hot day last week slowed me down enough so I sat on the porch and caught them at it.

I saw a couple of sparrow families very busy in my neighbor's garden and I hoped they were not damaging his crop, for we have all been very proud of this new garden. They weren't.

The whole group was concentrating on one row, the cabbages, and eating their fill of larvae of the cabbage butterflies. They spent half the morning there and I think did a pretty good job of it, for I could not find one when I went over to check up on them.

That same day I saw a commotion in my yard and discovered it was the "coming out day" for the ants. They were boiling up out of the hill all neatly equipped with their new wings. There were hundreds of them. Whether the sparrows saw me investigate, or did their own, I do not know, but it was only minutes until a small group descended and began feasting on the emerging ants. They made short work of them.

Then it was a matter of where next, for with their new little families they have to keep busy foraging.

It did not take long to find something to vary their diet of insects with plant seeds. They found a small patch of goat's beard, salsify, wild vegetable oyster — call it what you will — that giant "dandelion" that is very attractive this time of year. The gigantic seed head is a perfect sphere and the seeds are much larger than the dandelion's.

The sparrows ate many of the seeds and left the fluff. The wild crop will be reduced next year, because of their picnic, but I do not care for my neighbors do not like the plants in their lawns and it is one of the few wild ones I do not particularly enjoy eating. Perhaps it is because my first taste of them was very bitter. At any rate, the sparrows are welcome to them.

The sparrows were not the only foragers this week, for I, too, was afield in Nature's wild garden. I found three of my favorite tea plants ready for harvesting. They may be gathered from now until frost. They were sweet fern, goldenrod and sassafras. Tea is my favorite beverage and I like a variety, so the herbal teas from the native plants come in handy.

Sweet fern is really not a fern at all, but an attractive little sub-shrub that grows in dry sandy and woodland borders throughout the area. It has fragrant fern-like leaves from which it gets its common name. The foliage is the part used for the tea and is easily stripped from the twigs and stems by pulling gently down from the tip.

Never strip an entire plant. I find it is well to leave some foliage on each branch if the plants are small. This plant makes a very aromatic social tea, which has also been used medicinally as a tonic and to relieve diarrhea. A small lemon drop in the bottom of the cup enhances this tea.

I gathered a whole basket of goldenrod leaves, for if I could have only one native plant tea, this would be my choice. It is one that is easily collected for the plant is very abundant. Several species of goldenrod can be used, but the choicest one is the sweet-scented (Solidago odora).

It is conspicuous from August to October and can be harvested during this time. The tea has a lovely golden color and a most aromatic agreeable taste.

It is sold commercially as "Blue Mountain Tea" and in addition to its social use, it has many medical ones. It is often used to disguise the objectionable taste of medicine.

Then, there is the old standby, sassafras. Usually it is the bark of the roots and larger stems that is used, but I like the less pungent and milder taste of the leaves and green bark, so I gather some now.

Early settlers administered a cup of sassafras tea in the spring to "thin the blood" and it has been used traditionally to flavor candy and beverages such as root beer. I gather the leaves for tea, but more especially I like to dry and pulverize them to thicken soups, stews and gravies. This is the filé, so popular in Creole cooking, which gives it one of its ethnic qualities. Spiced sassafras tea served hot with a cinnamon stick to stir in a few drops of honey is a delicious fall drink.

The sumac fruit was not yet ready for harvesting, but should be watched. Serviceberries were ripe and I found the birds had left some on the woodland trees. The sand cherries are a poor crop this year and I had trouble finding a pint and had to tramp far and wide in the dunes for them. I did not get enough for my usual supply of jell and juice. August is the usual harvest time for these, although some are available earlier.

There are a few cautions I should pass on to neophyte foragers. First, of course, pick only those plants you can unquestionably identify. Be particularly careful of poison ivy for its white waxy berries are very attractive now, but do not pick them. Birds eat them and scatter the seeds about indiscriminately. The blue berries of the Virginia creeper (five-leaved ivy) should not be eaten.

Beautiful as the Queen Anne's lace (wild carrot) is along the highway and in fields now, gather it only for aesthetic uses — bouquets, dried arrangements, pressing and coloring. Do not pick it for culinary use and do not gather any other white-flowered plant (umbel) that looks like it. Some of the area's very toxic and poisonous plants are "look-alikes" for it, including poison hemlock, the plant given to Socrates.

The sparrows and I have been very busy foraging since August came, and perhaps you would enjoy it too, if you like herbal tea, wild fruits and different greens for salads.


BIRDS PREPARE TO LEAVE


Nighthawks, along with chimney swifts and hummingbirds, are the last birds to arrive in spring, bringing up the rear of the migration. Bearing out the old adage, "the first shall be last and the last shall be first," these birds prepare to leave as soon as August comes.

All over the blueberry marshes in the Upper Peninsula and in much of Northern Michigan these birds are gathering in family groups, combining with other families and hawking their way over the lowland snapping up insects, their favorite diet item.

The name is a strange misnomer, for these familiar birds are neither hawks nor night fliers. They feed mostly at dusk and just after dawn. Of course, during the past weeks they have been busy during all hours keeping food in the gaping mouths of their offspring.

Nighthawks have taken well to city life and even in these modern days of popular suburban living, they have not deserted the core city. In many cases it seems as though the higher the skyscraper, the better they like it, especially if it happens to have a flat graveled roof. It is these flat roofs with a topping of gravel that they choose for nesting sites. Since they do not build nests, but merely pull or scrape a few pebbles together among which they deposit the twin eggs, they act as though these roofs were provided for them.

Over the past years, the Federal Building has had its share of these nests. Just last year the birds discovered Mercy Hospital and raised a family there. Their young are dark and light speckled and are very protectively colored among the pebbles.

Nighthawks are birds that can be counted on downtown and seen by the most casual observer looking skyward. They are easily identified by a white spot on the wing which from below looks almost like a hole.

Like the young, adult nighthawks have a perfect natural camouflage, for their plumage — mottled brown, gray, black and white fits into the background unnoticed until the bird moves. They are excellent parents and care for the young unceasingly until they are able to fly from their high-rise home.

The nighthawk is first cousin to the rural woods-loving whip-poor-will, the chuck-will's-widow, the poor-will and the pauraque. They all belong to the goatsucker tribe. This name was given them in the past because they were seen about farm animals. Much of the time they were thought to milk the goats. Actually, they were snatching up their favorite food — insects from the stables, barnyards and even from the animals themselves. Few birds are better insect traps than the nighthawks and their relatives.

After the young are able to fly and search for their own food the parents lead them to places of abundant food, which at this time of year is over wetlands and marshes where insects are hatching. This is a perfect training ground for the young. As more and more families arrive, it is not uncommon to see great flocks of nighthawks swooping low over the plants.

A spectacular display is annually put on by these birds in the area of the Tahquamenon River. In August it is almost impossible to visit this region without seeing numbers of these fascinating birds. They are now on vacation from their domestic urban duties and are enjoying a little wilderness scene before they leave for the south.

Because of their constant insect-hawking, these birds and their goatsucker cousins are among the highly beneficial ones that serve us in ridding the summer of annoying pests.

A trip to the mall, the city hall, courthouse or museum in Muskegon before mid-month is sure to reward one with a glimpse of these avian urbanites.

## HAWK MIGRATION IN FULL FLIGHT

Some August day when the wind is from the east, go to P. J. Hoffmaster State Park, climb the Dune Stairway and view the passing of the hawks. It is a never-to-be-forgotten experience, one which you may never see again.

These majestic birds are all protected by state law because of the large number of rodents and insect pests they eat.

It is a bit ironic that we now view this beautiful procession from the same area where, in the 1930s, more than 600 hawks were killed in order to determine their feeding habits. It was the study of these sacrificial birds, however, that made possible the legislation which now protects the passing thousands.

The hawks belong in three groups: the accipiters, the buteos and the falcons. Each of these has distinguishing characteristics which set them apart from the others. The accipiters are ten to twenty inches long, with short, rounded wings and long tails. They fly with short, rapid wing beats and glides. These are mostly hawks of the woods and include sharp-shinned, Cooper's and goshawk.

The buteos, with their broad tail and heavy body, are the soaring hawks. In size they range from the small broad-winged hawk (thirteen inches) to the rough-legged hawk (twenty inches). Others include the red-tailed and the red-shouldered hawk.

153

The marsh hawk is seen over wetlands and is easily identified in either the gray or brown phase by the white rump. This trait cannot be seen during migration, however, when it often soars at high altitudes.

Falcons are streamlined with pointed wings and longish tails. They are built for rapid flight, rather than soaring. The three passing here are the peregrine, formerly called duck hawk, the merlin (pigeon hawk) and the kestrel (sparrow hawk). During the summer these birds are often seen sitting on telephone wires along the road.

During the August migration, flocks of one species may be spotted, but more often they are mixed. A bonus which an observer may sometimes see includes an osprey or even an eagle.

While song birds are scarce in August, do not overlook this opportunity to see the hawk parade.

## BIRD CHORUS STILLS

Blossoming flowers turning the marshes and swamps into wild gardens; the bird chorus giving way to the insect symphony; nature's patch overloaded with wild berries of many kinds; warm, sunny, lazy days for fishing; beaches thronging with sun worshippers and bathers; roadside tables filled with picnickers — that's August!

Insects come into their heyday now. It is they that make the late summer chorus one of the joys of August evenings outside. The cicada is the harbinger of sultry days and its strident wail from a nearby shade tree tells that warm summer is really here. Some insects are already congregating for migration and hibernation.

Snapping turtles are hatching and salamanders are changing into their mature form to live on land. Toads and frogs are abundant as tadpoles change into "four-legged land animals" and overrun the swampy lowlands.

Gulls and terns begin to return from the northern nesting grounds, and almost daily the local population of these birds is augmented by their arrival.

Mid-month brings ripening chokecherries and elderberries to the kitchen for jelly, just as the early days provided the cook with blackberries, dewberries and blueberries. August is a bountiful month both to birds and humans.

Ragweed victims suffer most this month, but more and more spraying and persistent cutting has helped to relieve many and to remove this plant menace from many sections of the state. Never before in our travels about

Michigan in midsummer have we noticed so much attention given to weed control and this should presage well for hay fever victims.

Evening hikes are pleasant during this last month of summer. In addition to the usual summer constellations, the Milky Way and Northern Lights frequently put on phenomenal displays in August.

Day and night, August is summer. So, make the most of it in Outdoor Michigan — the Water Wonderland.

CICADA NOISY NOW

That shrill, monotonous hum making one even warmer than the thermometer's rise is the cicada, harbinger of sultry weather.

It is commonly known as the locust or harvestfly and spells August and hot weather to out-door-wise folk.

The noisy insect is the male, and as musicians the cicadas are instrumentalists rather than vocalists. They play upon two minute drums located under the wings close to the body. They are played by muscular action causing friction.

The cicada is not closely related to the grasshoppers or crickets as the common name "locust" might imply, but rather they are "true bugs." Michigan's cicada is rather closely akin to the proverbial "seventeen year locust" of periodic occurrence.

These insects spend most of their life as larvae underground sucking the juices of plants and particularly attacking tree roots. Seldom do they cause injury. The larval period may be from two years in some species to as much as 13 in others. The life span of the adult insect as contrasted to this is short, seldom more than a week. The females are silent while the males make tree tops their concert platforms. Often the monotonous wailing comes to a sudden stop. This frequently indicates that one of the cicada's enemies has caught it. This pursuer is the "cicada killer," one of the thread-waisted wasps. These wasps prey unceasingly upon cicadas with which they provision their nests.

This wasp and several species of birds keep the cicadas in check, and as a rule little harm is done by the hummers.

An indicator of late sultry summer weather, cicadas would be greatly missed should they all be destroyed.

# AUGUST IS BLUEBERRY MONTH

August to the early Michigan Indian of this region was min-gisiss, the huckleberry moon, and with the modern cultivation of blueberries, we could well call it "blueberry month."

Many berry-pickers and woods-wanderers use these two terms interchangeably, but actually the two berries are not the same. They are closely related in the heath family. I get many calls in August asking the distinguishing characteristics of the two, and although there are many apparent differences, it is the seeds that count.

If the fruit has more than ten seeds — count them the next time you bite one of those big luscious berries from a local plantation — it is a blueberry. On the other hand, if you bite down on not more than ten "nutlets" — seeds to you and me — you are eating a huckleberry. These are larger and harder than the seeds of the blueberries.

The heath family to which both of these belong is a large group and starts the early parade of wild flowers here with the blooming of the lovely fragrant trailing arbutus. This is the "mayflower" of New England and is the theme of poetry, song and legend. It is protected in Michigan and is still found in numerous situations in Muskegon country. Indians called it "beaver's ear" because of the size and shape of the leaf.

There are other ways of telling the blueberry from the huckleberry. If the berries are dark blue to black without a bloom, they are huckleberries (Gaylussacia). True blueberries (Vaccinium) are more blue than black.

To further possible confusion, there are high and low bush blueberries. The high are usually preferred for food. So near alike are these cousins that when gathering them in the wild, few pickers make any distinction, and they are combined for use in pies, jellies, pancakes and muffins. As with the commercially grown fruits, wild ones may be dried, frozen or canned.

Wildlife, both birds and mammals and even turtles like them. Two different times I have shared a blueberry swamp in the Upper Peninsula with a black bear. Box turtles are especially partial to them.

Blueberries go by many names including bilberry, whortleberry, deerberry and dangleberry. Crackleberry usually refers to huckleberries because of their hard seeds.

So whatever its name and wherever you gather it, it's the tastiest of August berries.

# AMBROSIA OR RAGWEED

The ragweed seems to be a Dr. Jekyl and Mr. Hyde among the plants if its scientific name can be believed.

To the botanist and kindred plant authorities, the plant enemy Muskegon country citizens have fought is known as "Ambrosia elatior."

"Ambrosia, indeed," mutters the hay fever victim. "Either that early botanist responsible for the naming of this weed did not know its propensities, or he had a distorted sense of humor."

The two ragweeds most widely distributed throughout Michigan and the major causes of late summer hay fever are the common ragweed and giant ragweed (A. trifida).

Both of these are found in Muskegon country, as they are in most counties of the Lower Peninsula.

Unlike many of the more disagreeable and pestiferous of the state's weeds, these two are natives of Michigan and were probably recorded in the first official list of the state's weeds assembled in 1839 by John Wright. There were only 17 weeds officially listed at that time. However, just 21 years later a revised list catalogued 25 more of which, according to "Some Important Weeds of Michigan," three of the most pernicious today were included: quack grass, Canada thistle and field bindweed.

Today there are more than 150 species listed as weeds and of that number, few are more annoying and injurious than ragweed.

Study and experimentation have shown that weed control can be effective, and so important is this to the welfare of the citizens of the state that Act 66, effective since August, 1919, provides for the annual cutting of noxious weeds before July 15 and levies a fine upon offenders.

Ragweeds are easily recognized by the much branched stem, the highly dissected and variable leaves, the spike-like racemes of greenish yellowish flowers, the rough and homely appearance and the bitter taste. The plant has two kinds of flowers, the staminate and pistillate. It is the staminate which produce the irritating pollen which causes hay fever, and the pistillate which produce the seeds. Both therefore are injurious and should be destroyed. It is important, if possible, to destroy the plant before the blossoms appear. Pulling or cutting before July 15 in Michigan will be effective in most cases.

Giant ragweed differs from the common species in its larger height and conspicuous three-nerved leaves, which are lobed rather than dissected. It is known also by the names of king head and horse cane and is found in moist soil, especially in river bottoms, and low, swampy cultivated grounds. It is frequently found about the margins of celery farms and along the Muskegon river flats.

Common ragweed is wider in its distribution and is very common in cultivated ground, roadsides, vacant lots and waste places. It springs up very quickly when land is left uncultivated. It prefers drier soils than the giant form and is one of the first plants to come in as a part of the ruderal association forming a green cover over exposed soil. Some people have commended it for this service.

This, however, along with the fact that from its seed a useful oil has been experimentally derived, does not yet outweigh the damage and injury it does, and does not justify its preservation.

Other names by which the common ragweed is known locally are Roman wormwood, hogweed and wild tansy, but by whatever name it is called, it is still one of the great plant enemies Michigan residents have to deal with.

No, it is not Ambrosia to the hay fever sufferers nor to the allergic workers in August.

## MICHIGAN'S INLAND LAKES

One of the finest ways we can think of to spend the lingering days of summer with one's family is at one of Michigan's thousands of small inland lakes.

My favorite has always been Crystal Lake in Montcalm County. I still look forward to a day or so at the end of August on this one. It is typical of many throughout the state.

A rowboat or canoe is my favorite mode of negotiating these lakes. There should be someone along who is interested in fishing, for there are sunfish, bluegills, rock bass, crappies and perch among the submerged weeds. Still-fishing is fun here. Trolling is even more so, because there is always the chance of a bass, pike or walleye hitting your offering.

Try picking a lily pad from the sluggish end of the lake. There are two kinds — the round pads of the white lily and the more oval-shaped ones of the yellow. Moose are fond of the yellow ones. Look at the community of creatures on the underside of the lily pad. There are snails and their eggs, flatworms, redworms, beetle eggs, leeches and their egg cases, and the larvae of water insects. Water spiders and beetles may be nearby.

On the surface of the water are the backswimmers, water boatmen, skaters, whirligig beetles and diving ones. Perhaps there will be a giant waterbug searching for its prey — tadpoles and young frogs. Water scorpions are also predators feeding on eggs found in the water.

On top of the lily pads may be frogs of several kinds and on the blossoms look for damsel and dragon flies, or even small moths and butterflies. The reeds and rushes which extend above the pads also have their share of these creatures. Turtles are about, both in the water and on sunning spots like logs and stumps.

Take some time to study the plants, while you're at it. Besides the water lilies there are pickerel weeds, though most of their blue blossoms are gone by late August. The lady's thumb with its bright pink-to-red floral head sticks up from the water's surface. There are common pondweeds, chara, elodea, and water milfoil. The insect-catching and eating bladderwort is fascinating. This yellow-flowered plant has small bladders that trap insects and tiny crustacea and then "digest" them for its nitrogen needs.

Cattails along with other grasses, sometimes cover large areas of the lake's edges. This is where many of the birds may be found. Heron, bittern, rails, coots, and gallinules are some that are common. There are also loons, grebes, redwings, marsh wrens and yellowthroats that frequent these habitats.

Flying low across the water in search of their favorite insect prey are the swallows and martins. Watch for flycatchers, kingfishers, and hawks on dead trees and stubs near the shore.

Ducks and teals are now accompanied by their young and often swim among the lily pads. Crows and jays are sure to spot your boat and let the whole world know you are there.

In addition to the turtles, there may be water snakes, and if you are lucky, you may catch sight of a muskrat or two and beavers busily constructing a winter lodge.

The small inland lakes of Michigan offer a whole world of their own these last days of August, with their special flora and fauna. It is all there for anyone who takes a "day off" to get acquainted.

HATE TO CLEAN FISH?

How often have you heard someone say, "I love to fish, but I hate to clean them?"

There was a simple rule in our family which has stood me in good stead all these years. Dad was not a stern man. He was a wonderful fishing pal over the years. On my first fishing trip with him (aged 7) I learned that rule. "You catch 'em and keep 'em, you clean 'em!" I caught fish on that first trip, and I cleaned them. He was very patient as he taught me the best way, and gave me a "wonderful" fish knife.

This rule proved to be good conservation advice, also, for you gauged your catch by the number you wanted to clean for immediate or future use. Just because they were biting well, you didn't overload the boat.

To me, my fishing trip is not complete until that last fish is cleaned and cared for.

As a youngster, many times I thought I was too tired to finish the job, but Dad stood by, and I did it.

I, too, love to fish, but I don't hate to clean them — thanks to a disciplining Dad in my early days.

# Fall

Autumn is an Indian,
Copper brown with bright accessories.
Autumn is an Indian,
Who stalks Summer as a brave his chosen squaw.
Autumn is an Indian,
Who flees before the paleface, Winter.

# SEPTEMBER

## FROST LEGEND PUNCTURED

Jack Frost is much overrated as an artist.

Already red leaves have appeared throughout the woodlots, fields and stream borders, and no frost has touched.

Autumn coloring is the result of a complex chemical change that goes on within the green leaves and is more closely related to food manufacture (photosynthesis) than frost.

There is a regular succession of coloration for various plants, just as there is a succession of bloom from the skunk cabbage of early spring to the witch hazel of the year's end.

In each group of plants: herbs, vines, shrubs and trees, there is a leader that signals "time to change." Already these flags are up and the parade of the colors has begun.

First in mid-August the red leaves appeared on the pigweed or lamb's quarters, a familiar weed of barnyard and vacant lot. This was the first indication that changes were at hand. By the way, this is one of the wild plants that makes good greens and wild herb salads.

Next we saw red creeping up a cottonwood and flying out like a crimson banner in late August breeze. This was the five fingers of the woodbine or Virginia creeper, the first of the vines to don its autumnal dress. It's ruddy and bright now.

Then a little trip into the rural area, and like a red army the dwarf sumac bushes were marching up a hill. Yes, they signal the shrubs it's time to turn.

Any direction from Greater Muskegon the pepperidges are showing color — red, of course. This tree, also known as the tupelo, or sour and/or black gum is a favorite wherever it is found. Even without their color they are easy to recognize. They are undecided trees; their branches cannot make up their minds which way to grow — so — they grow every way. They grow up, down and at angles from the bole. Besides, a fine description of their twigs was given by my friend. She said, "They look like tightly braided hair that's come undone."

So — pigweed, woodbine, sumac and pepperidge are communicating with us. We get the message — Autumn is almost here!

## SEAGULLS BRIGHTEN BEACHES

Visiting the beach these days, one is inclined to hear, "See all those seagulls." Then an impertinent birder is apt to say, "What kind are they?" That brings on more words and a closer look, for many casual observers do not realize how many kinds of gulls there are.

Since early August the permanent group of gulls at the beach has been continually augmented by others. In mid-August there was a group of three hundred and only recently that had increased to an estimated one thousand.

So far, those there are mostly the lakes' common one, the herring gull. Intermingled in the flock, but sometimes in their own little group, are the ring-billeds.

It pays for the birder to keep an eye on these changing flocks, for last week there was a real thrill as a large all white one was flying over the congregated herring gulls on the beach. It was a majestic bird, seldom seen here at this time of year and on continued observation was identified as the glaucous gull.

The glaucous gull is larger than either the herring gull or its somewhat smaller cousin, the ring-billed, both of which have a gray mantle in maturity. Often this time of year one sees numbers of large grayish brown gulls, which are erroneously thought to be females, but are actually the young, and these juveniles may be either sex and are sometimes larger than their parents.

Another gull which is regularly seen here spring and fall as a transient is the Bonaparte's. This is a small bird with a black head and flashing white wing tips. In the winter plumage, the black head is reduced to mere dark spots near and behind the eye. Large flocks of these birds, numbering two or three thousand in years past, were common in the Edgewater section of Muskegon Lake in April. However, recently these large flocks have not been seen, but some groups are always accounted for on our lakes. They prefer Muskegon Lake to Lake Michigan. Contrasting with this small dainty gull visitor that comes spring and fall is a giant — the great black-backed gull. The name helps to identify this big fellow, who has a heavy black mantle over the back and wings. These large birds are highly predatory, especially in nesting areas and are usually seen here singly or in small numbers associated with the herring gull flocks in winter and early spring.

Another gull, which is an irregular visitor here, is the Franklin's gull. This one, about the size of the Bonaparte's, can be distinguished from it by the darker wing tips edged with white. The Franklin's is less a gull of the coasts than a prairie species and prefers field insects to fish.

Other gulls, which are listed on Michigan Audubon's Field Check List are the Iceland and little gull, making a total of eight. Strays from the Arctic, Atlantic and Pacific Coasts may occasionally show up in the state and always cause the alerting of the hotline to birders throughout the Midwest.

Western species, which in some cases are counterparts of our birds, include the glaucous-winged, western, California, Heerman's, Sabine, and kittiwake. The wide-ranging herring and ring-billeds are also found in the Pacific Coast.

Gulls are world-wide in distribution and in addition to many of our familiar ones, I was delighted to find four new ones in England and Scotland. These were the lesser black-backed, the black-headed, little and common gulls. These were seen primarily at the ports, about the estuaries, especially of the Dee, at Solway Firth and on the canals of the Chester Ring.

In Trinidad I had the good fortune of adding the laughing gull to the herring and ring-billeds which were there. Islands are usually good places to observe gulls, because many of them provide nesting places for them, as do the islands of upper Lakes Michigan and Huron. As far as we know, gulls are found in every state of our Union except the Island State of Hawaii. To many, it seems unbelievable that with so many islands and the enormous coastline, there are no gulls. Any gull seen there is considered a "stray visitant or accidental." "Hawaii's Birds" published by the State's Audubon Society, does not list a single gull in the index.

There is, however, a gull cousin, that is well worth the trip to the Islands for any birder to see. That is the white tern, or as the Islanders call it, "the fairy tern." It is an exquisite little bird, pure snow-white with a black ring around the dark blue eye. The black bill is blue at the base. I saw it on Oahu, but it is common on the Northwest Chain, and throughout the Tropical Pacific.

Human residents, who like many of the birds, migrate south and west for the winter, would do well to visit the local beaches before they depart, and review the gulls here so that they may have a basic group to add to as they meet new ones on their travels.

Gulls are among the very beneficial birds along the shore as they are the original "white wings" cleaning up the beaches and scavenging about city landfills. Another place to see gulls and their tern cousins is at the Muskegon Wastewater area where large numbers often congregate.

Visitors to Salt Lake City have seen the beautiful monument that the grateful Mormons erected to the gulls for saving the crops from insects during three seasons in the early history of Utah. This was the first monument ever erected to birds in appreciation for their intervention in human affairs.

Gulls are mostly birds of the coastal areas. Take this opportunity to visit the beaches and become acquainted with these spectacular birds, symbol of our ports and waterways.

## ANIMAL TALES READ ON BEACHES

One does not have to wait for winter and the soft carpet of new-fallen snow to read the wanderings of wildlife.

Now that most of the beaches are deserted by humans, the animals have taken over, and their tales can be read daily. Since many of these authors are nocturnal, their stories are best read in the early morning.

I find the beach at Pere Marquette Park a convenient library. Each morning there are tracks and stories found around the south arm of the breakwater. One morning recently there was evidence of much activity during the night and early morning hours. Squirrel, gopher, chipmunk, opossum, rabbit, rat and mouse trails were along the beach. Several of these were concentrated in clumps of grasses where apparently the animals had been eating seeds and insects.

Squirrel and rabbit tracks led down to the water's edge where they may have taken a drink and explored piles of driftwood and water weeds, doubtless finding food.

The tracks of domestic dogs and cats were also about, but no signs of tragedy were seen this particular morning, so any encounters must have been amicable.

Birds had also visited the beach. In fact, some were still about searching endlessly for food. Sanderlings and other small peeps scampered along the breakwater. Frequently they would come wheeling into the beach and search a while before going back to snap up insects from the cement.

I was pleased to find large heron tracks, for I had not seen my favorite blue heron this summer. Of course, there were crow and grackle tracks, for they are common picnickers all summer, even when swimmers and sun-bathers are there.

A fair-sized flock of gulls has taken over where the guards were stationed and their wanderings were interwoven in every direction. Sandpipers and plovers were still about and their dainty trails led all along the waterline from one pile of water weeds to the next.

My favorite, the ruddy turnstone, also was there. Not having any stones to upturn, he was busy with small sticks and weed piles.

Even sparrows and starlings make trips to the beach. The sparrows favor the grass clumps, but the starlings are everywhere.

Birds and beasts are not the only authors writing on the sand. Insect tracks and trails are everywhere. The large beetles, caterpillar hunter, bombardier, stag, and june bug were the most conspicuous; but there were tiger beetles, grasshoppers, crickets, spiders and harvestmen (daddy-long-legs) as well. Ant hills and ant-lion pits also showed considerable activity around them. There were tracks around sand spiders' holes indicating they had eaten well.

Each morning the stories are different, just like the daily news in the paper. No two days are alike. One reads comedies and tragedies in this sand-writing.

## RARE BIRD (CARACARA) HERE

The more experienced the bird watcher, the bigger the thrill when a rare bird is sighted.

George Wickstrom, a veteran bird-watcher, had such an experience a few years ago in the Muskegon State Park. Anticipating a view of migrating hawks, he visited the park at about ten in the morning.

In the distance he saw a flock of starlings harassing a large, hawk-like bird. As it drew closer he thought it might be an osprey, but soon the field marks proved it to be a caracara — a very unusual bird for Michigan.

Later Wickstrom had a very good view of the bird when it perched in a dead cottonwood tree and displayed its long legs, red face, eagle-like beak and long neck. These are unmistakably the marks of a caracara. In its native south and southwest home it is frequently called the "Mexican buzzard," and is commonly seen on the ground feeding on carrion.

It left the state park paralleling the channel between Muskegon Lake and Lake Michigan and then was seen flying south across the channel.

This is the first record of a caracara seen in Michigan and was reported to Dr. Robert W. Storer at the Museum of Zoology in Ann Arbor.

## DUNE GRAPES ARE PLENTIFUL

Paw Paw may be the grape capital, but one does not have to go there for grapes. The dunes are full of them. That's where I have been — completing the sand cherry harvest and starting on the grapes.

Oh, I have some "tame" grapes in my yard, but they are such a temptation to neighborhood children that I have long since given up hopes for a harvest there. I may get a handful if I'm lucky, so I just take to the dunes and the wild ones.

Muskegon area duneland yields three kinds of wild grapes and they are all good for jelly, jam, conserve and other delicacies — juice and wine.

The three common ones here are the frost grape, the summer grape, and the fox or river-bank grape. Each of these has its preferred habitat in the sandy dune zones. The frost grapes, which I gathered Monday, like the cottonwood zone. The fruits are small, shiny black berries, on well-crowded stems this year.

The summer grapes are found all the way from the pine association to the climax forest, and their leaves are more deeply lobed than the others, and the fruits are larger, medium-sized black berries with a bloom.

The fox or river-bank, as the name suggests, likes the moist margins of swales or of the duneland pools and ponds. Their fruit is blue, rather than black, but does have a bloom. They are intermediate in size.

These are all good bird and wildlife food, and no one should be greedy enough to take all and leave none for the birds.

The sand cherries have been nice, large and juicy this year, and there were still a few for the picking over the past weekend. They are found primarily in the foredune and cottonwood zones, and I regret to say, they have suffered greatly in the last few years from dune buggies and snowmobiles. Perhaps, of all the duneland plants, they have been most affected.

Yes, I know cherries and grapes take sugar and that can lids are hard to get, so dry them. The Indians and early settlers did and liked them that way.

It is an easy process and fun to do. The sun drying days are almost over for the season now for it takes a few days in the 80's to do it hastily. A slow oven at 140-150 degrees is "perfect" and the drying can be accomplished in about six hours.

Trays should be not more than two or three berries or cherries deep. For the cherries, stems and pits should be removed; for the grapes just remove the stems. Dip the grapes in hot water; wash the cherries, dry with paper and drain off excess juice.

When done, grapes should be dark brown and leathery (like currants or small raisins — which they are), and cherries should be sticky and pliable. Cool at room temperature over night before storing. Small amounts dried at a time are most successful. Watch for hot dry days in Indian summer if you want to sun dry. Air drying can also be done inside — but takes longer than oven-drying.

This week I hope to gather wild elderberries — they, too, dry well and make delicious pancakes and muffins for winter menus.

You will be rewarded on these foraging trips with choice glimpses of birds and other wildlife sharing the harvest with you.

## COLORS HELP AVOID POISONING

Late summer and early autumn days attract children to wander about outside where bright colored berries and other fruits entice them.

Every year there are cases of poisoning from eating these wild fruits.

With the recent emphasis on survival foods, more persons are taking an interest in wild edibles and children hear this and often experiment unknowingly.

There is a basic test of edibility which we use in experimenting with wild foods, but it takes sixteen hours to run it, and that can be too long for young children who have eaten poisonous plants.

The two plant products that are most attractive to children just now are wild berries and mushrooms. Young children out of the home and in school for the first time should be cautioned against eating things along the way.

Scientists have discovered a "color code" which really is a help in determining edible plants. Most BLUE and BLACK berries are edible; RED berries are edible sometimes; and WHITE berries are almost never edible. Eating ANY wild fruits in large quantities is dangerous and eating them to the exclusion of other food is risky.

Let us take a look at the color code. Blue berries include all the blue — and huckleberries and their relatives; elderberries, grapes, viburnums and clintonia.

Red berries which should be avoided are nightshade (also known as bittersweet) and pokeberries (red to deep purple). The nightshade is a relative of the potato and tomato and as the fruit matures, it has less toxic quality than when green or in the ripening stage when it is most dangerous. The toxic principle is solanin, and because tomatoes also have this, at one time they were considered poisonous and shunned for eating except as love charms when they were called "love apples."

As in the case with bittersweet, the pokeberries (also known as scoke, pigeonberry, inkberry) are less dangerous when mature. The roots are poisonous. The leaves and stems, when young, are often eaten as greens, for the cooking destroys the active principle, phytolaccin.

Bittersweet and pokeberries cause the most concern to parents in the early fall. Barberries are sometimes eaten by children, but as a rule they are pithy and not tasty, so only a few are tried, and they present little problem. The berries of tartarian honeysuckle, as the barberries, can be overlooked as a dangerous source. Red spells danger for some of the fall-fruiting plants, but not for all.

Most of the other red berries as our code suggests not only are not dangerous but are edible. In the woods the scarlet berries of jack-in-the-pulpit may cause a burning in the mouth, but it is the core that is poisonous. Eaten in small quantities and cooked, they are harmless and called Indian Turnips. The cranberries, both bog and high-bush, and wild cherries are edible, as are the red-berried elders, which ripen earlier in the year.

This red, white and blue code is easy to remember and the most important of all to learn is that WHITE fruits should be avoided. This is especially true this time of year for two of the very poisonous plants are now producing — the poison ivy and poison sumac. Both of these have white berries which sometimes are very attractive. The fact that birds and some other creatures feed on them does not indicate they are edible for humans. Some of the worse cases of ivy poisoning about which I know came from gathering the berries and using them in "fall arrangements" of dried plants, grasses and wild fruits. Avoid all white-fruited plants and teach children to do this.

Another suggestion regarding poisonous plants is to avoid eating those with milky juices unless positively identified. Do not eat wild plants that resemble melons, parsnips or cucumbers, and avoid all mushrooms unless you "know them as a friend." There are enough friendly ones abundant now, so no one needs take a chance. Fairy rings, shaggy manes, puffballs, stumpies and corals are among the "fool-proof" ones now.

170

# SOLIDAGO, MALIGNED, BEAUTIFUL

Goldenrods wave from every vacant field, woodland border and thicket edge. They are the batons that bring the full symphony of autumn into key and happy harmony.

Perhaps no plant has been more maligned than this beautiful harbinger of autumn. Condemned as a "hayfever plant" for years, scientists have now cleared it of the accusation. Very few are affected by the insect-borne pollen of the goldenrods. It is windblown pollen, such as the ragweed and its relatives, that cause discomfort for so many. The whole problem is an interesting study in human behavior and association, for patients have been shown goldenrod when the pollen had been removed and the mere sight of it caused sneezing. Be that as it may, our interests in the goldenrods are elsewhere now.

To most folk "goldenrod is goldenrod," but not so to the observing woods-wanderer. There are goldenrods and goldenrods — 100 different species of them on the continent and at least a third of them (36) are found in Michigan. We cannot go into all the different kinds, and since their properties are much the same we will just lump them together. There are, however, among the common ones the early, blue-stemmed, Canada, sweet, field, stiff-stemmed, wreath, rock, alpine, dwarf, beach or seaside and most interesting of all, the white goldenrod, properly named "silver-rod."

Goldenrods belong in the daisy family and are perennial. The species are distinguished by their flowers, position and arrangement, leaves, stems, manner of growth and habitat.

The generic name, Solidago from Latin, means to strengthen or draw out and refers to their reputed medicinal qualities. Herbalists, the Indians and early settlers used the goldenrods medicinally and also for dye. They were thought to be astringent, styptic, carminative, aromatic and a mild stimulant. The leaves were frequently used to disguise the unpleasant taste of disagreeable herb medicines. Goldenrod is especially good when the hot infusion is poured over a lemon drop in the cup.

Another important use of goldenrod over the years has been as a dye plant. With different mordants, more than a half dozen colors and tints can be achieved. In this the blossoms, leaves and roots may all be used in the dyer's pot. The species especially sought after for this purpose is Solidago nemoralis, a low-growing plant commonly called gray or field goldenrod, or very pointedly, "dyer's weed." The rich deep yellow of the usually one-sided panicle of blooms contrasts with the gray, often cottony, stem and the grayish green leaves. It grows in fairly dry, open waste and sterile places and blooms from July to November.

For Blue Mountain Tea the favorite species is S. odora, or sweet goldenrod. It cannot be mistaken for any of the others for it gives off a sweet anise-like scent, and the graceful panicle is formed by the golden florets all being on one side. The bright green, lance-shaped leaves are recognized by minute dark dots. This plant likes dry soil. Other kinds of goldenrods may also be used, but this one makes choice tea.

A favorite of mine is the dainty wreath or blue-stemmed goldenrod. It likes shady roadsides, moist woods and thickets and can be distinguished by its bluish stem, which is unbranched, and its golden clusters of tiny florets. It bends gracefully like a wreath and one is tempted to pick it and make a golden crown.

In rich woodlots and thicket borders the zigzag is easily seen. It has broader leaves than most and the angled stem gives it the common name, white goldenrod, but I prefer the name silver-rod for its creamy white blooms.

Perhaps the real beauty of the whole tribe is the early, plume or yellow-top. Its beautiful, spreading, recurved, branching panicle comes early and is often dried for winter decorations and flower arrangements. It prefers dry rocky soil and is generally both the first and the last of our goldenrods to bloom.

Right now the goldenrods are attracting myriads of insects, particularly the butterflies, and they are also attracting me. Now I am afield gathering the leaves of the goldenrods and drying them for tea. This is part of my own celebration of our country's bicentennial, for the tea made from goldenrod played a part in this country's history.

It was the tea of this plant, along with other native brews, that replaced the imported teas thrown overboard at the Boston Tea Party. Of those used, this is one that has survived for the two centuries, and today in many of the health stores it is marketed as Blue Mountain Tea. In my estimation it is one of the choice native teas — it is sweet and aromatic and has little of the medicinal taste some object to in others.

Just strip the leaves from the stalks and dry them, either in the sun or a slow oven — the top of a gas refrigerator is perfect — and then store them in an air-tight container, preferably not metal.

Then all year you can treat yourself and friends to a cup of bicentennial tea and think back to the glory of Michigan's autumn when you gathered it.

# WILD FOODS AWAIT

Autumn brings Indian Summer, following the first snow, Squaw Winter, but we did not wait for these to get out in the woods and fields for our Indian harvest.

September is Manominiki-gisiss, Moon of Wild Rice Gathering, to our Indians. So along the Muskegon River (named from the Indians) we harvested a little wild rice. The crop was poor and underdeveloped here this year and the birds had come in early for the harvest. Even a few kernels, however, satisfy me because there is such an abundance of the other things I look for.

The tea plants are favorites of mine and there is just no end to them, this or any year. Besides the goldenrod leaves, popular tea leaves are those of wild mints, strawberry, blackberry and blueberry. For medicinal teas and tisanes the joe pye weed, boneset, vervain and ironwort are now abundant.

Wild fruits were also dried and used by the Michigan Indians and some of them were included in their popular food, pemmican. Wild grapes, elderberries, chokecherries, high bush cranberries, haws, rose hips, crackleberries, and earlier, serviceberries or shad were all used. Several of these, including the sand cherries of our dunes, I use for jellies and conserves.

This is also the time to gather the ruddy fruits of the staghorn sumac, for their tart flavor gave the redman his own special brew of "lemonade."

Bark and twigs of sassafras and spice bush are grist for the food mill of the woods-wanderer these days, and used as seasoning in place of expensive cinnamon and cloves release pennies for high priced staples.

Tramping the woods and fields is good exercise, helps the energy crisis and brings in natural foods. Maybe a return to the Indian way of life would not be too bad — at least for a day.

# DUNE GRASSES

Grasses are as important to the dunes as trees are to the forest.

They hold the shifting sands in place by their fibrous and running rootstalks and stabilize the young dunes so that other vegetation may get a start.

Without the help of the grasses in the Lake Michigan dunes, the sands would be as shifting as the Sahara. The shifting dunes at Silver Lake are an example of live hills where the grass has not been allowed to take hold.

This is the prime time of the whole year to see the grasses at their best as many of them are now flowering and setting seed for another season. Of the dozen or more grasses common to our sandy stretches, there are three everyone should know and they're easily recognized right now.

They are rye grass, which resembles the cultivated cereal, sand reed grass, tall, graceful with a magnificent plume, and the marram grass, smaller with a yellowish-green tinge and a more dense, solid flowering tip.

All of these can be seen through the 200 miles of Michigan duneland from the Indiana border to the Straits. Excellent examples of all are at Muskegon State and Hoffmaster State Parks. A trip to either will repay one with beauty and an appreciation of these useful plants.

The rye grass is often used by the highway department and other road-builders when they wish to protect the shoulders from erosion. It, along with the others, is characteristic of the fore-dune association and occasionally is found growing even on the wave-washed beach. Here it cannot survive for long because of the constant wave action dislodging the roots. The spike is easy to recognize and is very different from the other two. Each seed bears a long bristle as it matures.

To many, the sand reed grass is the most beautiful of the three. It grows in clumps and attains a height of eight feet in favorable situations. The spreading cluster which now bears the seeds adds grace and distinction to the plant. There are few outdoor sights right now that are lovelier than a large clump of this tall grass high on a dune ridge with a blue sky behind it. The delicacy of the composition will tempt any camera fan, artist or just plain dune-treader.

Growing along with the sand reed is the marram grass — the true "dune grass." Its name "Ammophila arenaria" means "sand-lover," and what could be more suggestive of the duneland? It, along with the sand grass, has a long rootstock sometimes creeping a hundred feet underground with small clumps of fibrous roots along the system, entwining to hold the sand. This can best be seen where the waves have eroded a section of the beach, and the bank has fallen, thereby revealing the large tortuous root system of these grasses. This plant is used in many parts of the world to stabilize shifting soil.

# SAND DUNES BLOOM

There is no month quite like September in the dunes. The sandy stretches are attractive and full of wildlife all during the year, but somehow the attraction is never stronger than in September, just before the fall equinox.

It is when there are "miles" of swallows and martins strung along wires that pass through the dunes. These insect-eaters have been assembling since July, and all through August their numbers have been augmented. Now, any day may be the last that we see them. As the nights grow cold, and insects scarce, they have to take off for warmer climes.

For several weeks the nighthawks have been circling and calling, sometimes low and sometimes high, over the sand hills. They stage regular "dances," sometimes, as they pirouette in mid-air.

On the ground are the killdeer with their lively youngsters. Occasionally other plovers and sandpipers wander from the beach into the little temporary pools that are a part of duneland.

The cottonwoods abound with flickers and blue jays. Right now the blue jays, along with other birds, are busy harvesting sand cherries. One pair had their three youngsters with them in one bush. In less than half an hour they had it completely "picked."

The blue jays and woodpeckers are gathering acorns and hiding them. Kingbirds are not uncommon in duneland these days, and with an east wind, a variety of hawks will fly over. They are worth watching for.

# NEW BIRDS IN MICHIGAN

Amid all the talk of endangered species and disappearing birds it is good to know that some new ones are finding their way into Michigan.

In recent years there has been an increasing number of southern and western species that have visited this state, and some have liked it well enough to stay. Mockingbirds, yellow-headed blackbirds, Brewer's blackbird, egrets, including the cattle, summer tanagers, blue grosbeaks and dickcissels are some that have been reported by Michigan birders.

Now the house finches, natives of the south and west, are here and it is important to know about their appearance in Michigan. Individuals have been spotted here and there, mostly in southeastern counties for some time. Several have been recorded here recently (1983).

Twenty of these visitors have already been color-banded and there is an attempt being made by members of the Michigan Audubon Society to map the range of the house finches here.

These birds, belonging to the finch family, along with the buntings, native sparrows, grosbeaks and crossbills, are cousins of the goldfinch and the purple finch, well known here as patrons of feeding stations. House finches are often mistaken for the more common purple finches by the casual observer. A closer look, however, will help to distinguish them. The house finch is only slightly smaller than the purple and the male has less red color but it is usually much brighter than is the purple. Look especially for dark spotted-stripes on the underparts and sides. These the purple finch does not have. It is more difficult to distinguish between the hens of the two species, however the house finch does not have the dark cheek patch and mustache of the purple female. According to Peterson this south-western species was released in New York about 1940 and by 1980 had spread as far as Illinois, Wisconsin, Michigan, Tennessee and Georgia. The call of the house finch is similar to the house sparrow and the warbling song is somewhat harsher and less musical than the purple's.

California visitors will be familiar with these bright-colored little finches because they are that state's very common bird. They are found in nearly all habitats, especially in urban and suburban areas as well as desert, woodland, forest, chaparral, gardens, ranches and savannah. Only the highest mountains are without them.

My introduction to them was when they nested in a large palm tree in my yard and made regular trips to the fig tree in the backyard to eat insects from the fallen figs and even a taste of the fruit itself. Later they nested in the eaves much as house sparrows do here. The parents lined the young up on a wire and carried food to them after they had left the nest. Finches are devoted parents and tend carefully to the young.

To assist the Michigan Audubon Society area birders are asked to keep records of any house finches seen. Four questions are especially asked: (1) How many males (colored)? (2) How many brown-streaked birds? (3) What is the date and time of sighting? (4) Is there a nest in the vicinity?

In addition to these questions, record any color-banding. Report what the colors are, whether on right or left leg and which on top and bottom. This color-banding facilitates recognizing individuals and helps to map their movements.

If a house finch is found dead, directions advise, "Straighten it gently, place in plastic bag, attach twistem and place in freezer." Give any information about cause of death and location as well as name, address and phone number of finder. Send to Bird Division at University of Michigan, Ann Arbor, Michigan.

This project is in the charge of Ellie Cox, 18310 Sutherland, Detroit, Michigan 48219, who can supply additional information. To assist be sure and check all finches and sparrows that visit your feeding station this fall and winter and familiarize yourself with the appearance of house finches.

# OCTOBER

## ASTERS STAR NOW

From Michaelmas Day, September 29, all through the month of October it is the asters that star in the floral parade. In fact, the word "aster" means "star," and it is these various constellations of flowery stars amid the green autumnal grasses that lend a special enchantment to this season.

There are 250 species of wild asters throughout the world and Michigan has its share with more than 25 different kinds. Because they readily hybridize even in nature, it is difficult to keep them all properly named and to distinguish the close relatives.

September's floral wealth is in goldenrods and October's in asters. A noted horticulturist in Lyons, France, liking both these plants, attempted hybridizing them and about 1910 he created the now familiar Solidaster (taking its name from the Solidago [goldenrod] and Aster). As might be expected, this flower has golden flowers, pale yellow ray flowers and darker colored disk florets. It is a popular cultivated perennial plant, a favorite in British and other European gardens.

To enjoy asters, which are Michaelmas daisies in Europe, one should be privileged to cruise the British canals through the heart of rural England, as I did on Michaelmas Day 1978. Mile after mile the banks were strewn with these dainty plants in full flower. It was fun to greet familiar faces of asters I thought of as American. There were the New York, New England, white-wreathed, heath, calico, smooth, flat-topped and showy to name a few. There were many others whose names I had to find in a British flower book. British lists include more than a hundred species and hybrids and they are beloved as garden plants as well as wildings. In nursery catalogs they call them Michaelmas daisies, because that day marks the blooming of many. I like one English gardener's comment and truthfulness: "Almost any of the wild asters, if accorded the cultural treatment given garden forms, would equal the beauty of the named varieties."

This should be an inspiration to us here in western Michigan to get outside and enjoy the beauty of these floral asters as one after another come into their ascendency, much like the heavenly stars. Their colors range from white, through all shades of yellow — from the palest of pinks to deep rose and almost maroon — from light blue through the gamut of blues and lavenders to purple. Their sizes also vary from less than a quarter of an inch across, to the blue purple giants two inches wide. Like many of the daisy (Composite) family to which they belong, they possess flat floral heads made up of two kinds of florets, ray and disk, after the manner of the ox-eye daisy or brown-eyed susan. The plants are much branched and the flower heads seldom single.

The earliest of our asters to bloom is a large, cordate-leafed one which comes in the summer woodlots with a few large floral heads of dull pinkish white called Marguerite's aster. A few asters bloom during August and September. But it is after Michaelmas Day that these little "wild daisies" really come into their own. It is a bit ironic that the beautiful garden flower, commonly known as "China aster" is not a true aster, only a distant relative.

These plants are named primarily from their structure, leaves, stems and flowers, and manner of growth. Rather than try to remember the characteristics of all our two dozen, it is well to consult a good field guide and even take it on the aster-viewing excursion in order to name them on the spot. If this is not possible, in most areas a sample can be gathered and taken home for identification and naming.

If the name Michaelmas daisy is too long, and aster too common, to suit one's taste try the old traditional name of "starwort," which is most suitable.

## MUSHROOMS THROUGHOUT AREA

The first week of autumn has brought out a great variety of fall mushrooms.

Already I have had tasty helpings of inky caps, fairy rings, field parasols, shaggy manes and best of all, blue-noses. Others I have dried and frozen.

With the exception of the shaggy manes, all of these were found on my lot. In addition to the ones already mentioned, I found "little wheels," bird's nests, and several others, about a dozen in all.

179

If I could find all those different kinds without leaving the city limits, imagine what the fields, woodlots and parks are now displaying.

Meinert County Park is a favorite place of mine to see the fall fungi in full array. This is a great area to learn to identify mushrooms and puffballs.

With all these popping up like magic overnight, many people are eager to try some new and different ones. There is just one rule for these gourmets: Do not eat anything you cannot identify beyond a shadow of a doubt.

There are edible mushrooms appearing at every season of the year. From April with the morels to Thanksgiving with stumpies and oysters, there is a parade of delectable fungi that can satisfy the most demanding tastes.

Here are a few suggestions that will make mushroom eating a pleasurable experience for you this fall:

Beware of the red ones. Some are edible, but unless you are an expert, pass them up. Don't overeat of any kind. Do not gather and cook any that are over ripe or wormy. Don't mix different kinds in cooking, and never consume inky caps, shaggy manes and alcohol at the same meal. There are good scientific reasons for each of these rules.

I have left the most important item for last. This regards the dangerous group, the Amanitas. They can be deceptive because they are beautiful parasols and most alluring, but they can be deadly.

Look for three things, a ring around the stipe (stem) and a bulbous base sitting in a cup underground. Notice it is important to dig this fungus out of the ground in order to fully identify it. For that reason never break a parasol off above ground.

Never place these mushrooms in a basket with ones to be eaten. Also be sure to wash your hands carefully after touching them. Caution is the key word in handling these mushrooms. It is best to leave them alone if you plan on gathering the edible ones.

Now a few less gloomy suggestions. Puffballs and corals are two safe groups, as are the toothed mushrooms. Some can be bitter and tough, but generally they are easy to recognize and present few problems.

As with all mushrooms, the fresh, young ones are the most desirable and a modest serving of each is best.

STUMPY MUSHROOMS IN ABUNDANCE

Moisture and mushrooms go together. In spite of — or possibly because of — the driest September on record, there is a bumper crop of the late summer mushroom — the "stumpy."

To be sure, there is a shortage of many other kinds of common fungi usually found around here this time of year. But few people care because of the abundance of stumpies.

"Stumpy" is the name commonly given to at least two types of mushrooms found in this area. Scientifically, they belong to the two genera, Armillaria and Collybia. It is easy to distinguish between the two. The Armillaria, often called the honey fungus, has a collar on the stem, while the others do not.

Of the honeys, there are two distinct forms, according to Dr. Alexander Smith, authority on American fungi and author of the book, "A Mushroom Hunter's Field Guide." The first grows in large clusters in oak-hickory wood lots and the caps are strong honey yellow to ocher from the margin inward. These typically grow from stumps, logs, buried wood and sometimes living trees. They are the earlier of the two and usually appear before the leaves turn color.

The second kind come later as the leaves fall and even after the trees are bare. They favor evergreens as well as hardwoods and the cap is dark brown to almost black, brownish gray toward the margin and often scaly. The first form is more common in this area and many have been garnered recently.

While stumpies are abundant here, other species of early autumn mushrooms are scarce. The boleti, a group which has thick caps with pores underneath instead of gills, are seldom seen now. They are colorful and many are edible. Caution must be shown toward the "lurid bolete," which has a brilliant red to maroon pore surface and whose yellow flesh turns blue when bruised or cut. This is a poisonous species and like the gilled Amanitas with the three "signs of danger" — a ring, bulb and cup — should be avoided. Just recently in the wooded hills at Big Blue Lake we found both the poisonous fly Amanita with its bright red-orange cap and white warts and the beautiful but deadly all white "destroying angel." Do not pick or even touch these fungi if you are out on a search for edible ones. Another "bad actor" is the death cap, whose cap may appear greenish. Do not depend on color for these, look for the danger signs.

Two other types of fungi which will be common after some fall rains are the corals and puffballs. Both of these are easily recognized by their form and, for the most part, can be eaten. The giant puffball is a great delicacy. A one-foot diameter puffball was discovered along the Muskegon River in 1977.

In spite of the dry weather during September, some shaggy manes appeared, but moisture will bring more. They are good eating but must be used before the gills turn black. Canning is the favorite way for preserving stumpies although some like to freeze or dry them.

There are many mushroom-hunters in Greater Muskegon and all brandish the motto, "Know Your Mushroom." Beginners should not mix different kinds of fungi and I recommend carrying several sacks in the field to collect different kinds in order to keep unknowns separate for identification. For area pickers, Dr. Smith's book is a favorite. As for beginners who may not wish to pursue the hobby in depth, the Golden Guide, "Non-Flowering Plants," has an excellent section on fungi, giving colored plates of the most common kinds, indicating their edibility status.

Few outdoor hobbies can be more rewarding this time of year than "fungi-foraging for fun."

## WASTEWATER SITE IS FOR BIRDERS

Birders have their special days when they seek out their bird friends and enjoy their bird-watching hobby. The day of the Christmas Bird Count, the Valentine Bird Watch and the Big Day in May are all important in this area.

But in recent years another "special day" has developed. That is Columbus Day, October 12.

This is an appropriate day to associate with birds. According to historical tradition it was a flock of migrating birds that held the Santa Maria on course and made it possible for Columbus to quell the dissatisfaction of his near-mutinous crew. When the birds were seen, the crew knew land could not be far away and so was willing to continue the voyage. They dropped anchor at the Caribbean Island of San Salvador.

Since the creation of the Wastewater System it has been a prize place for birding, and over the past few years October 12, Columbus Day, has become a special bird day. Just as for the 487 years since Columbus was guided by migrating birds, the flocks have continued to move on this day.

Birders at the Wastewater System had a real treat, not only for the species present, but for numbers of individuals as well.

The birds could be heard long before one viewed them. They were in the air, on the lagoons, and in the fields. Accurate counting was impossible, but estimates were made of the hundreds of waterfowl there. Close to five hundred Canada geese were seen, approximately 150 blues and 50 snows or wavies.

To name and number all the ducks would be a real task. Suffice it to say that there were fifteen species, including 75 of my favorite, the little ruddy duck. Among the ducks, the real thrill was seeing several white-winged scoters that are a treat to birders here.

In addition to the geese, ducks, teal and other waterfowl, the shorebirds were abundant with at least ten to a dozen different kinds in a great range of sizes. This offered a fine opportunity for beginning birders because of the chance for comparison and contrast in identifying them.

Water birds were not the only visitors to the Wastewater, as a huge flock of about one thousand tree swallows was winging in and out, snapping up insects before continuing on a southern flight. Several species of the blackbird family made up large assemblies. Crows and blue jays were associating with the visitors.

Among the other land birds that are often a reward at the Wastewater were pipits, which have been making semiannual stop-overs here between their northern and southern homes.

These are only some of the prizes that await birders at this fine site. But do not count too strongly on ducks any longer, since the hunting season has opened. If you do plan a non-hunting trip, go in the afternoon.

In addition to the many birds of passage at the Wastewater, many are seeing flocks of them in their yards and gardens where they are getting last minute snacks before leaving. Among these, hummingbirds have been visiting fuchsias that have escaped the frosts and are still inviting them.

By the end of the month these dainty little birds will be gone, joining their southern cousins for the winter.

Robins also have been about lawns and parkways in small bands and before long will disappear. Hermit thrushes were passing through and I was delighted to have one hop right up on my doorstep. Could it have been the same one that ate here last spring on its way north?

It was not banded so I shall never know.

White-throats and white-crowned sparrows have been feeding in combination groups the past weeks as they journey southward.

October is the month I see the most bluebirds of the year. When they gather in family groups and join with others, old orchards generally tempt them, and I count on a trip into the rural sections of the county to catch a last view of these charming little thrushes.

# HAWKS MIGRATE TO SOUTH

Geese and ducks are not the only birds that fly south in autumn.

Hawks have been drifting southward over the dunes and along Lake Michigan's shoreline since August. All of Michigan's hawks and some of their relatives — ospreys, eagles, and a very rare caracara — have been a part of this migration.

Every year many bird watchers go farther afield to see these beauties. Some go to Hawk Mountain in Pennsylvania. It was my privilege to view it one weekend at a fantastic spot — Pt. Pelee Provincial Park near Leamington, Ontario.

Our party was thrilled with the sharp-shinned hawk which harassed flocks of blue jays and blackbirds and frightened the warblers, kinglets and other small birds in the bushes.

It was a treat for us to see the many red-shouldered hawks, because they are less common in Michigan than they used to be. They are magnificent birds and along with their cousins, the red-tails, staged a never ending aerial show for us.

Along the boardwalk in the marsh were marsh hawks, both brown and gray. The broadwings vied with the other buteos in aerial maneuvers and were abundant. In addition to the sharpies, there were occasional Cooper's and a few goshawks. All three of these hawks are beautiful to watch in the air and are swift, direct and darting in their flight. Some of us thought they might even steal our caps in their energetic dives.

To many, the most beautiful of all are the falcons — the peregrine, merlin, and kestrel. Formerly in the U.S. these were called duck hawk, pigeon and sparrow hawks, respectively. But now the older falconry names, along with falcon hunting, have been restored.

Twenty-five states have now met Federal standards governing this ancient sport of taking game with trained birds of prey. At present there are less than two thousand active falconers in the states and about a score in Michigan.

Other hawks besides the true falcons are used in the sport, but the rare peregrine, merlin and kestrel are the favorites. The peregrine in recent years has suffered greatly from pollution problems and is endangered. But that is another story.

Hawks are still moving southward, and if you can't view them at Hawk Mountain or Pt. Pelee, do not overlook our two state parks, Muskegon and P. J. Hoffmaster. They are fine viewing areas.

Halloween means black cats, bats and owls, in addition to all the ghosts, witches and phantoms that are about.

It will be too dark to see black cats, and the bats are already hibernating for the cold months. So if you are looking for wildlife to help celebrate this autumn holiday, owls are your best bet.

Michigan has eleven different kinds of owls, three of them belonging to the Upper Peninsula. There are, however, eight kinds in Muskegon country. The three in the U.P. are the great gray, hawk owl and the boreal.

There is the snowy owl, a winter visitor, which comes into this area annually during the months of ice and snow. These beautiful, pale, majestic birds are frequently seen along the Muskegon waterfront and on the Causeway. From Halloween onward into November is the time to watch for them.

They are more often seen than their darker relatives because they do their hunting and feeding by day. My earliest record of the arrival of this owl at the Causeway is November 1.

More common than the snowy owl, but seen less often because of nocturnal habits, is the great horned owl, so named because of its large, upstanding ear tufts. This, the largest of our common owls, often nests in the old remnants left by crows, hawks, and even eagles. It is an early nester, sometimes laying eggs in February.

Perhaps as common as the great horned owl, and more often seen or heard in town, is the screech owl. This small owl, about the size of a robin, sometimes takes up residence in a bird house, while other tenants are south. Usually they nest in hollow trees. Their quavering whistle is a series of short notes.

During last year's severe winter, numbers of these small owls were found in fireplaces throughout the area. They probably had been warming themselves by the chimney and had fallen in. When there were no fires, most of the little visitors were removed without harm. Screech owls have two color phases — gray and brown.

Two other eared owls found here are the long-eared and short-eared. The long-eared is more often found in wooded areas whereas the other is partial to open country and marshland.

The three earless owls are the barred, the barn and the saw-whet. The largest of these, the barred owl, is a bird of the woodland and it also likes river bottoms. It is commonly called the "hoot owl." These owls are fairly plentiful throughout western Michigan.

Barn owls, on the other hand, are uncommon here. Next to the snowy, they are our lightest colored owl and can be distinguished from all others by their heart-shaped face, small eyes and long legs. As the name suggests, they like buildings for nesting. They also nest in trees.

My favorite is the tiny saw-whet, about the size of a cardinal. They often argue with chickadees, but the "chicks" are the aggressors. They like evergreens and are sometimes found resting during the day. Their small size and nocturnal habits make them difficult to see.

In case you don't see an owl on Halloween, don't worry. Many stay around the Muskegon area all winter.

## HALLOWEEN PLANTS AND ANIMALS

With the coming of October's end and All Hallows' Eve (Halloween), thoughts center about the dark days and long evenings.

Many plants and animals have become a part of the celebration that has grown up over the centuries. Most of our customs of today pertaining to this time of year go back to the ancient Druids and Romans.

Among the animals which have become part of our Halloween are the bat, the black cat, owl and crow. All of these are either black creatures or like the darkness — and some are both black and lovers of night.

It is this somber aspect that has made them a part of the Halloween celebration along with other attributes which have been given them during the ages. All of these animals were considered the familiars of witches and warlocks and since they played a large role on All Hallows' Eve, attention was given to their friends.

Here in our area these creatures, owls, bats, black cats and crows are no more active in late October than at other times. In fact, usually by this time our bats are safely hung up for the winter in their favorite nooks and crannies. Crows have been flocking for some time and winging their way to their winter roosts. They are active by day, not by night.

Owls still are active and about, and it was my surprise the other day to discover a long-eared owl sitting in my maple and being "cussed out" by an impudent jay. This was the first time in years I had the good fortune to see one of these fellows in broad daylight. The great horned, screech and barred owls are common and are frequently heard on the outskirts of the city as well as in wooded and rural areas.

Soon the snowy owl from the north will be putting in its appearance, but it is a day-flier and plays no part in Halloween lore.

The black cats can be counted on day and night.

As familiar as these animals are, the plants of Halloween, apples, pumpkins, corn and nuts are also common. These go back to the Romans, whose festival of harvest honored Pomona, the goddess of fruit. Apples at that time were endowed with the ability to tell one's future, and so were used in many ceremonies and games. Nuts, likewise, were able to foretell lovers' affections.

## ARACHNIDS THE WEB-SPINNERS

Spiders are not the favorite creatures of most humans.

I like them, and probably one reason is that in early childhood my gentle Quaker grandmother taught me the couplet: "If you wish to live and thrive/Let the spiders run alive."

In those long-gone days before various anti-insect sprays and chemicals, spiders were the first line of defense against harmful, often disease-spreading "bugs."

It has been determined that these small creatures actually eat more insects than all other animals put together. Birds, too? Yes. When we consider that there are 30,000 named species of spiders, representing only a quarter of the world's spider population, as compared to about 8,600 bird species, we get some conception of the creature's work. It takes more insects to satisfy a bird, but there are many more millions of spiders.

This month spiders will be conspicuous because many of them are hunting winter quarters in garages, outbuildings, and even inside houses. The average life of a spider is just one or two seasons, although tarantulas have lived from 25 to 30 years.

Spiders are wrongly called "insects" or "bugs." They belong to another group of animals, technically the arachnids. Although they differ from insects in many ways, chiefly it is their two-parted body and eight legs that distinguish them easily. Mites and harvestmen (daddy-long-legs) are their close cousins.

Spiders are particularly active right now in woodlots, yards, gardens, along stream borders, thickets and lake shores as they prepare for winter.

Unlike many insects, many spiders live through the winter and some even care for their egg sacs during the long cold weeks that are coming.

The arachnids are the civil engineers and weavers among all the small animals. They build bridges, dams, tents, tunnels, caves, trap-doors and folding-doors, pits, highways and funnels. As for weaving, they construct sheets, curtains, draperies, nets, single threads and filmy hide-outs.

Often on a bright autumn morning the lawn and yard will look like a miniature encampment as hundreds of newly spun tents or sheets will be embroidered with dew. These are the masterpieces of the common grass spiders and some idea of their numbers can be estimated by the size of the "encampment." Grass spiders are very beneficial and keep down the insects in yard and garden all during the year. Many of them hide out in fallen leaves and weed patches during the winter.

Cobwebs are signs of spider friends that have taken up residence inside, where they have corner-curtains and draperies to catch unwary insects. Often spiders have a little den at the side of the web and if frightened will drop to the floor and scurry off to safety. Sometimes if caught, one will "play possum," curling up its legs and remaining very still, until the captor, thinking it dead, tosses it carelessly aside. With surprising alacrity it "comes to life" and scurries off for a corner.

House and grass spiders, like most of our spiders are harmless, but two poisonous ones are known from Michigan. Neither of these is common and both are seldom seen. They are the black widow and the brown recluse. Both of these are southern species which have extended their ranges northward. The widow is most often found outside in trash, dumps and outhouses, while the rare recluse is partial to houses about the floor and behind furniture. There are no present records of the recluse in this western Michigan area.

Among the better known spiders here is the beautiful gold and black argiope, a large orb-weaver often found in fall gardens, where it has been a valuable helper all year.

Crab or flower spiders are also well known to the gardener. These very colorful little ones often hide in flowers and are protected by their markings.

Jumping spiders sometimes charge out at their prey from the arm of lawn furniture or from patio cement. These are pretty little black and white creatures that merit a second look.

A favorite arachnid here for dune-wanderers is the sand spider which burrows a tunnel and then installs a folding door that protects it from sifting sand. This large one is sand colored and can be found by locating its open hole in duneland. It is sometimes called a trapdoor spider.

Ballooning spiders are my favorites during early fall. These may be of several species. Tiny spiderlings ascend fence posts, tall grasses, saplings or even low branches on tall trees, release a bit of silk, and as it lengthens, it is caught by a breeze. The small ones are pulled from the perch and float off to a new area. A battalion of these minute balloonists in full flight is one of the exciting sights of these early autumn days.

Spiders are not confined to land; they also live in water as the fishing-spider proves. Waterlily pads are a favorite hide-out for this net-spinning fisherman.

The spiders' silk has been used a great deal in scientific instruments and is still important in the industrial field. The webs are also used in art and crafts and web prints are popular in modern decor.

A Spider Museum, the only one in the world, is at Powhatan, Virginia. A visit there is never-to-be-forgotten for an unbelievable appreciation of these small creatures is gained as one views the exhibits, meets living spiders, hears illustrated lectures and takes the exciting walk down Spider Trail at a leisurely pace in the relaxing atmosphere of a spider's world.

Look kindly on these little creatures this fall, as both they and we prepare for the long cold white weeks ahead.

## WILD FOODS

Hunters and fishermen are not the only ones about the woods and waters these days. October brings the foragers out also.

While the others bring in the main course, the forager can provide the side dishes: the vegetable, greens, salad, condiments, pastries, beverages, and fruits and nuts for the making of desserts.

As for nuts, the acorns and beechnuts are a poor crop for gathering this year. Insects have infested these trees so that much of the fruit is inedible. Black walnuts and hickory nuts offer a better harvest.

Roots are available and there is a great variety to be found. Among those which can be cooked as vegetables are Jerusalem artichoke, wild salsify or vegetable oyster, evening primrose and chicory. Both dandelion and chicory roots dried can be used as substitutes for coffee.

Greens for salads and cooking are plantain, watercress, chickweed, purslane, sorrel and mint, which can also be used for jelly, syrup, vinegar and sauce.

Sassafras and sumac, both given their names by the Indians, are traditional, along with mint, for making tea. Rose hips also are a favorite for this. Goldenrod leaves make a choice beverage.

Flours from wild things, including cattails, grasses, acorns, and amaranth seeds can be made, but are better as an addition to commercial brands than as the main ingredient. Foraging and preparing enough for a batch of bread or biscuits would be a real task. Fruits and nuts are among the pleasant rewards of fall foraging and these can be used in a variety of ways. Jellies, jams, conserves, syrups and pickles are only a few of the suggestions for them.

The recent warm days and moist nights have been a special boon to the forager. A fine crop of choice, edible fungi has developed.

The stumpies and corals have been available during September. The recent weather has increased the number of fairy rings (Scotch bonnets) and hydnums in area fields and woods.

The bonnets, found in a ring or arcs in grassy places, lawns and parkways, have greatly increased this month. Choice in the woodlots and along nature trails are the lovely white-toothed fungi, known variously as bear's beard or hair, satyr's beard, Medusa's head and bear's head. These range in size from two or three inches to large clumps a foot or more across.

I consider this quartet fool-proof, and for the beginning mushroom hunter they are easy to identify. Any good book on edible fungi will give field characteristics and recipes for these choice four.

"October's bright blue weather" of the poet is exactly the time for the foragers to go afield, for not since spring has the harvest been as bountiful.


TWO SPECIES GONE?

When a plant or animal species is removed from the Endangered List it may be good or bad.

When the species in question has succeeded in holding its own for an adequate period of time, shows promise of increasing with the expectation of stabilizing the population, after careful investigation it is removed from the list. This is good.

There is another side to the coin and that is bad. When a given species has been listed and studied over a period of several years and there is not only no sign of increase or holding its own, nor even observing one individual, it is concluded the species disappeared and it is removed from the Endangered List.

This is a depressing experience for us all, for no species should be allowed to become extinct, since each has its own peculiar niche in the web of life.

Two Great Lakes fish have recently been proposed for removal from the list because they are now presumed extinct according to Ray Arnett of the Fish, Wildlife and Parks Service.

The blue pike and longjaw cisco once helped to support substantial commercial fisheries. No specimen of either species has been found since the late 1960s.

Once common in the eastern Great Lakes and Niagara River, this subspecies of walleye was abundant and very plentiful in the late 1800s. By 1915 the catch showed extreme fluctuation in population and by 1958 the commercial fishery collapsed.

At least four factors are viewed as contributing to the blue pike's disappearance. Scientists attribute it in part to overfishing, predation by and competition with introduced species, to oxygen depletion in western Lake Erie and possibly hybridization with the walleye may account for its final disappearance.

The longjaw ciscoe was common in Lakes Michigan, Huron and Erie. Along with other deepwater ciscoes, they supported a substantial fishery business until about 1950. They were highly esteemed as smoked fish and were popular in this area.

They were taken with gill nets set in water from 100 to 300 feet deep. As the ciscoes decreased in abundance, the gill nets decreased in mesh size which caused additional depletion. Habitat degradation, particularly in Lake Erie, predation by sea lampreys, competition with alewives and smelt are elements that are thought to have further reduced these fish. Again hybridization may have played a part in their demise.

The longjaw ciscoe was listed as endangered in 1967 and the blue pike in 1970. Since no specimens of either fish were found, there was little that could be done under the ESA (Endangered Species Act).

In 1977 the Blue Pike Recovery Team contacted all fish and game agencies in the United States to determine if this fish existed in their waters. All replies were negative, so it was concluded extinct by the team and recommended for removal from the list.

Before the removal of these species, the Service requests any information anyone may have on any blue pike or longjaw ciscoe populations that exist. Address information to the U.S. Fish and Wildlife Service, Federal Building, Fort Snelling, Twin Cities, Minn. 55111.

## JIZZ, THE GIST OF BIRD WATCHING

Identification is the first step in bird watching, just as an introduction is the first step in making a new human friend.

Fieldmarks are generally accepted features which distinguish one species from another, but these are not always easy to determine as any experienced birder can testify. They may be color markings on the plumage, the beak, feet, legs, tail, song, flight pattern, other forms of locomotion, size, feeding habit, ad infinitum. The field guidebook tells you what to look for, but seeing it is not always that easy.

In Britain they do it differently and even have a word for it. I was watching with a birdman at the Caerlaverock Wildfowl Trust near Dumfries, Scotland. We viewed thousands of barnacle geese, which had arrived overnight from Greenland and Spitzbergen. Suddenly, he pointed to one bird in the great flock of barnacles. "Look, it's a brent — see how different its JIZZ is."

"Jizz?" I mutteringly queried.

"Yes, you know, jizz — don't bother with fieldmarks yet."

I didn't know.

"We don't have that word in the States."

"You don't? How strange. It's so important and so useful, you know."

I still didn't know.

Then I hesitantly asked, "What is it?"

At once, he became academic, almost pedantic. "Jizz is the characteristic impression of a given animal or plant species."

"Oh, the total of all its attributes — the whole bird," I summarized.

"Yes, yes — that's it exactly — jizz!" He went on, "Individual fieldmarks may change — but jizz, never. Take that brent, there are dark-bellied and light-bellied birds and some in between. Marks change, jizz is the same."

He was right. I could see the brent did have jizz different from the host of barnacles all around it. Then I thought of the great black-backed gull and the glaucous, for in addition to their size and plumage, their jizz is different from the herring gulls, with which they associate.

Blackbirds, grackles, redwings, cowbirds and starlings and no two of them act or are alike — each has its own jizz.

I like the word and could see its usefulness, so when I got home, I looked it up. Not a single one of my American dictionaries included it. Just English slang, I thought.

Then I called Hackley Public Library. "Please, will you check your latest edition of the Oxford English Dictionary for "jizz — j-i-z-z?"

The answer came shortly: "Origin unknown. 1922-present, the characteristic impression of a given animal or plant species." I'd heard that before at Caerlaverock.

## NOVEMBER

### EVERYTHING IS BROWN

After the brilliant colors and gold of October, November is fast becoming the brown month.

Everywhere one looks are various shades of brown — brown on the oaks, on the ground, among the grasses, weeds and in the ghosts of both wild and garden flowers.

Brown tree limbs and brown bird nests, brown in the marsh, the fields and the woodland. Uplands and lowlands, brown. Even occasionally the water in one's favorite lake or stream looks brown this month.

This is a month for those who like to hike or just ramble outdoors, and many are the places that are inviting. Numerous summer secrets are revealed as one takes to his feet following trails, paths or goes just cross-country.

These are days when the leaflessness of the trees reveals a number of birds' nests that have gone unnoticed since early spring. One discovers the homes of neighbors he did not even know he had. It is fun to try to identify these pieces of bird architecture. In most cases it is all right to collect these nests, for although many birds return to the same area or site, they seldom return to the same nest. This is particularly true of the small song birds, but not of the birds of prey which frequently return, refurbish the nest and incubate again.

There are many items to consider in identifying nests, such as — size, inner and outer, location, height from ground, material, depth of cavity, thickness of wall and texture of materials.

While looking for nests one can become better acquainted with the trees. Watch for twig arrangement, opposite or alternate, location, color and form of winter buds, color and texture of the bark and the general shape of the tree. Each species has its own characteristics and then there are individual differences which one may discern.

194

Nuts may reward the search about the trees, if the squirrels, chipmunks and other wild ones have not harvested them first. It has been several years since I have beat them to the beechnuts, although this year I did find a small handful and they were tasty. Hickory nuts, walnuts and butternuts are easier to find.

Cocoons are other November treasures one can find. I hope the woodpeckers are slow in discovering them, for once they locate them, they have a good meal, and there is no lovely June moth left to emerge.

Speaking of bird-life, that of November compares very favorably with the March population. Most of the insect-eaters have left and the seed-eaters are still about, along with the omnivorous feeders and birds of prey.

Already some of the winter visitors have arrived and by the end of the month, if we get a snow storm or two, they will be looking for a handout. Juncos, nuthatches, creepers and finches are here. The snowy owl is usually seen before mid-November.

Now is the time to start inviting the birds to your table if you plan on entertaining them this season. Start with a minimum of feed and then in-crease it as the natural food diminishes. Many birds establish their routes fairly early in the fall so that by the time winter is here they have their grub line staked out.

In spite of some warm, sunny Indian summer days in November several of the "seven sleepers" have already bedded down for the long winter sleep. Bats and jumping mice are among the early ones to "go to bed." Chipmunks are spending more time in their hide-outs and some of these days will be your last glimpse of the chippies until late February when they clean the burrow. Woodchucks do not wait for really cold weather. Most of them are snoozing away by now and do not look for them on February 2. Wait until April.

Bears, raccoons and skunks are lighter sleepers and most of them stay up late.

Snakes, frogs, toads and salamanders are cold-blooded, and they are in winter quarters.

Among the browns of November do not overlook the mushrooms. While there are fungi of many colors, it is the various browns of the stumpies, the Scotch bonnets, puffballs and inky caps that still offer good eating.

Since darkness comes early now, one should not overlook the beauty of the November sky. The autumn constellations, especially Orion, the Hunter, are brilliant now, and shine out to tell us fall is here and winter is on the way.

November may be the brown month — but for those who enjoy the out-of-doors, it's a bright brown.

## MONARCH MIGRANTS

Where do butterflies go in winter?

Most of them die and leave pupae to carry on the population in the spring while a few, such as the mourning cloak, tortoise shell and admirals, hibernate in hollow logs, woodpiles, cracks and crevices or in outbuildings.

There is one, the monarch or milkweed, that migrates.

Bird banders are very busy during the last few weeks of summer and into early fall, but so are the butterfly banders.

Banding butterflies is different from banding birds since they wear tags instead of bands. The tags are put on the butterfly's right forewing about a third of the way from the body.

Since the early 1950's monarchs have been tagged in Muskegon, which is only one of approximately three hundred stations in the Internation Monarch Study Project. Records are sent to Dr. F. A. Urquhart, director of the program which includes Canada, Mexico and the United States.

Only a limited number of research associates are now incorporated in the project with taggers working under them. A biology class at Muskegon High School and several elementary school classes have tagged many area insects.

Butterfly trees are discovered in the region each fall. The annual count of tagged insects is approximately two hundred.

A highlight of the season one year was our trip to Pt. Pelee, Ontario, where along with thousands of birds funneling down from Canada, butterflies are known to do the same. They were moving when we were there and fifty were tagged on the trip, forty at the Point.

Monarchs have been recovered in Mexico and associates are now working there to assist in the study.

Anyone finding a "tagged butterfly" should follow instructions on the small tag and send it or the number to the Department of Zoology, University, Toronto, Canada. Only five returns have been reported here and those were all tagged in Michigan.

Dr. Urquhart, director and author of the book "The Monarch Butterfly" is now working on another volume which will include the results of the work since 1960.

The Muskegon station along with the work of the late Mr. Harry F. Stiles and Margaret Drake Elliott received recognition in the first volume and will be brought up to date in the new one.

Monarch tagging will continue into November, closing for the fall season about Thanksgiving Day.

## WINTER PREPARATION

Everywhere one looks today there are preparations for winter.

Birds are heading south while northern ones are arriving here; insects are hibernating and going into quiescent stages and they, too, are migrating; blossoms give place to seeds and are scattered far and wide, and trees are dropping their leaves. All of these are sure signs of getting ready for winter.

I'm always interested in lesser folk, so recently I was pleased to discover more than the usual number of snails in my yard and garden.

Most gardeners do not welcome snails, but I rather like them. My attention has been especially drawn to them during the past few weeks because each morning I have found one or more crushed in the little walk joining our neighbor's yard. I thought someone was carelessly stepping on them — and, of course, I blamed my husband.

Only last week I found out what was happening. These garden snails (land forms instead of the commoner water snails) were on their nightly rambles, much as their cousins, the slugs, and came to the walk which is almost a foot lower than the grassy approach. Arriving here under full snail speed, they did not realize they were on the brink of disaster and crashed down upon the cement walk. With their shells broken most of them were dead when I found them. A little safety board slanted against the bank to the walk helped and some have successfully used it.

This increased activity of the snails away from the garden itself has apparently been brought about by the cooler weather and their attempt to find secure winter quarters where they will be safe during the cold months.

Snails eat succulent leaves including garden plants and other soft vegetable matter. They are strange creatures in that their mouths are really in their feet and their tongues rasp away eating their food as they travel along at a snail's pace. As with silkworms, sometimes if there are many of them feeding at once, one can even hear them eat.

197

They are also wondrous because their eyes are on stalks which prove very convenient since they can put them both out at once, or one, then the other. They work on the principle of the finger of a glove turned inside out. The snail can vary the length of the stalk as needed.

Actually, snails might be said to have invented the mobile home for they carry their house on their backs. Where they go, it goes. An empty snail shell is a sad thing for it indicates the owner is dead.

Snails not only eat, but are eaten. In France and French cuisine they are very popular and a great delicacy, as escargot. In fact, one of the favorite momentoes to bring back from a Parisian tour is a set of snail forks, exquisitely designed and fashioned. Florida snails are the favorite diet of two birds seen by our southern travelers during their winter stay. The limpkin and everglade kite prefer snails to most other items. The limpkin is a fairly large bittern-like bird with a peculiar loud ringing call which gives it the name "crying bird." The biology of the everglade kite is so closely associated with the snail that when marshes dry up in drought years or are drained, the snails are exterminated and the kites leave. In recent years so much construction, with its attendant drainage, has been done that this kite has been listed as an endangered species and fortunate, indeed, is the Florida visitor who sees one of these majestic birds.

Speaking of Florida snails, the Muskegon County Museum has the finest collection of land snail shells in the Midwest. These were collected in Florida and arranged in matched sets to show variation in form and color. The collection is mounted in a table case and was the gift of a Chicago benefactor who summered in the White Lake area. I might add, there were no monstrous foreign snails from Florida in the collection. I cannot help but wish we had one to add to the display.

My garden snails were seeking a winter home and apparently were aiming for a pile of leaves that had been in the front yard overlong. Probably, like myself, they had decided my husband was going to leave the debris there all winter. They bury themselves under objects or burrow into soft humus and retire into leaf piles. Once they have chosen their wintering places they make a door of mucous and lime, sometimes two or three, across the entrance to the shell with just a minute pore to admit air. Then they sleep the winter away. Yes, the leaf pile will have to stay, for I investigated and there are snails already put up for the winter. I say "they" because snails are not male or female — they are both.

# WITCH HAZEL GLORIFIES AUTUMN

One of the shrubs that is adding so much brilliance to the "glory of autumn" is the witch hazel.

Its deep, intense sulphur yellow leaves are at their height now and against the brilliance of the sumac and sassafras, other bright autumnal shrubs, the hazel offers a golden contrasting note.

Soon, however, the leaves will drop from the witch hazel and then there will be revealed its secret — autumn blossoming flowers, scraggly like ragged urchins, up and down the stems. These, too, are of a yellow hue. For that reason they are seen only by close and knowing observers during these days when the leaves are gay. Toward the top of the bushes and the tips of the twigs, already the attractive little blooms are revealing themselves.

The normal blooming season of this plant is October and November, and frequently the golden blossoms persist into December. Although the flowers are formed before the leaves drop, they are usually obscured by the foliage and it is not until the fallen leaves have left the outline of the shrub that the attractive decoration is really appreciated. The golden flowers are four parted in structure, regular in form and massed together in crowded clusters at the axil of the leaf. Open seed pods also will be found on the twigs. These open forcefully and black seeds are shot out for a considerable distance. This is nature's way of making sure that the new little witch hazels will not be hampered by too much mothering.

The witch hazel takes the name "witch" from the unconventional time in which it blooms. A witch in the olden days was one who did things in an unconventional way. Hazel is a misnomer for this plant because it does not belong in the true hazel family at all. It was given this name in colonial days by the English settlers who thought it resembled the hazel of England. The leaf is the only part of the plant which even remotely resembles the English species.

However, not only the name remained attached to the plant, but also some of the old superstitions brought by these colonists have persisted about it.

Chief among these is the power ascribed to it as a divining rod. In this capacity it has been used to locate wells of water, salt and oil as well as mineral veins in various parts of the country. Many people are still firm believers in this method of locating hidden treasures and to this day witch hazel is much sought after in some parts. A more beneficial use for the housewife, at least, is the medicinal value of the shrub as a soothing extract.

From now on until late November this delightful flowering shrub can be seen throughout the country and western Michigan in wooded ravines, moist woodlands, along streams and in the dunes area, blossoming as the last bloom of the year.

## TUMBLEWEEDS, A DRIVING HAZARD

"Tumbleweeds crossing — drive slowly" is not a sign that motorists have seen along with those of "cattle crossing" and "deer runway." Drivers in western Michigan at this season of the year are about convinced such a sign would be useful near large fields of tumbleweeds, for on windy nights these bounce along the highway and blow against windshields, producing a real road hazard.

The two most common of the western Michigan tumbleweeds belong to the pigweed family and are widely distributed throughout the waste areas and sandy stretches. Of the two, the most conspicuous is often times deeply colored, a rich reddish purple, and where it grows in abundance produces a beautiful note in the autumn coloring. Others of the weeds are greenish to almost white.

These tumbleweeds, along with another common one known as "tumbling mustard," are round and produce many interlacing branches with few leaves and rather inconspicuous flowers and seeds which are dry and brittle. At maturity the main stem of the plant customarily breaks off near the ground and with a gust of wind the plant is off on its autumnal mission of scattering seeds. This it does far and wide. Of all the methods of seed dissemination provided by nature to care for the propagation of young plants, none seems more effective and more successful than the method of the tumbleweeds. Sometimes the whole plant is uprooted; then the whole thing will be blown about whimsically.

In the western states, across the plains and prairies these plants are much more abundant than in Michigan, and there they may be seen blowing for miles and finally resting along a fence or other obstruction, sometimes as high as the fence itself. In one section of South Dakota numerous plants, large as a bushel basket, had been utilized by an ingenious plainsman to fill the space between the two strings of barbed wire along the posts. He had fastened the plants by the root or stem to the top wire, and the bulk of the interlacing branches formed an almost solid filler for the space between the wires. This natural fence served for several miles and was undoubtedly much cheaper than extra lines of wire.

## METEORS PRESENT SHOW

With the time change and darkness coming earlier, the night sky gets more attention in late fall and winter than at other times. Once the constellation, Orion, the Hunter, starts across the sky from east to west, followed by his two dogs, Sirius and Procyon (stars), many eyes will turn upward and many will become star-watchers.

An unusual daytime display recently attracted much attention to celestial bodies. I'm a night sky-watcher, so I missed it. It was identified as a "meteor in a ball of fire," according to R. Newton Mayall, astronomer and author. "Slow, bright meteors are called fireballs. Frequently, their trail remains visible for some time. Fireballs that explode are called boldies."

Meteors themselves, often called shooting stars, are common. In fact, there are few starlit nights when some of these cannot be seen. Most of them turn to vapor and dust before they reach the earth. It is estimated that meteoritic material entering the earth's atmosphere daily exceeds several tons. However, the ones reaching the ground make up less than a ton.

There are also big ones, like the one causing the great crater in Arizona. The ground fragments are meteorites, usually heavy for their size and composed of iron, although they may contain rock with other minerals such as cobalt or nickel.

Now, if you missed the unusual daytime sighting, but still want to see meteors, don't despair. There should be another shower coming up later this month. Annually, for about seven days, near mid-November, the Leonids will be showing off. Named for the constellation, Leo, they appear at a rate of twenty an hour. They are best seen from midnight to early morning.

If you missed the Perseids in August and the Orionids in October, this is your next best chance before the end of the year.

I was lucky in August and had three good nights with the Perseids, so I will try for the Leonids next week. Star-gazing can be fun.

## MICHIGAN HAS CRANBERRIES

As Thanksgiving comes this year, once again turkeys can be seen in Michigan woods, for the efforts of the conservation department have been successful, and these majestic birds are reestablished in several areas of the state.

Not since late in the 1890's have these birds been a part of our state's wildlife picture, but now it is not unusual to see them in the Allegan and Benzie areas, and from these they have spread out extensively so now they occur as far north as Baldwin and wherever the terrain will support them.

*      *

Nothing is more typical of the American Thanksgiving dinner as an accompaniment to the turkey than cranberries. And, cranberries are also a part of the Michigan outdoor scene, for our state is fortunate in having two types of the low cranberries as well as the high bush type.

Few realize that Michigan, along with the New England States and Wisconsin, is a large producer of cranberries. The Great Lakes area is second to New England in the production of cranberries. This year was a good season for these tart red berries and word from the "berry bogs" of Roscommon and Crawford counties as well as the Upper Peninsula tell us there will be a good supply for the winter holidays.

*      *

The Michigan cranberries are related and in the same family as the blueberries for which the state is so well known. The name comes from the word "crane" and was given because in the early days cranes ate large quantities of these berries and fed conspicuously in the berry bogs. Also the stem of the fruit often persists on the berry and gives the impression of a bird's head with the protruding beak. At any rate the "e" has been dropped and the berry is familiar to all under its common name. Throughout the United States, generally, there are two types of low bush cranberries — the large, or American, and the small. Michigan is fortunate in having both of these and many of both kinds have been harvested this past season.

All types of Michigan cranberries grow on creeping, trailing, more or less prostrate vine-like shrubs and are partial to sphagnum bogs and lowlands where they form a conspicuous ground cover in which pitcher plants, sundews and cottony sedge grow plentifully.

The flowers, which are typical of the heath family to which the blueberries and cranberries belong, bloom in May through July, and the fruit occurs and ripens from August and September through the fall. The fruit often remains on the plant the following season, so it is not unusual to find blossoms, green and ripe berries all on the plant at the same time.

Cranberries are widely distributed in Michigan and probably grow in every county wherever there is a sphagnum bog. In the northern counties, these are frequently several acres in extent and may be surrounded with arbor vitae and tamarack trees.

*               *

In addition to these two cranberries, which are used extensively at the holiday season, there is another plant which is familiar to many in the northern part of the state. This is the high bush cranberry or viburnum. It is a medium sized shrub and frequently grows along rivers and streams. Like the others it is widely distributed and found locally in nearly all Michigan counties. The fruits are high in Vitamin C and the berries are often used in jelly. Occasionally, the fruits are also cooked to take the place of the other cranberries. This plant is also called cranberry bush and cranberry tree. The plants are not as closely related as the common names would suggest. The viburnum is a shrub of the honeysuckle family, while the others are heaths. The Indians used all of these berries in preparation of their pemmican, a staple food which they carried on the trail. Pioneers dried large quantities of these and used them during the winter.

I am sure ours will not last the winter out, but it will be Michigan cranberries on our table this year, because James Curnalia, retired history teacher at Muskegon Senior High School, knows where the choicest ones grow in Roscommon County and was there this year for the plentiful harvest.

Turkey and Michigan cranberries — there's nothing like it for a real American Thanksgiving.

THE THANKSGIVING TABLE

As Thanksgiving draws near with its climax of the feast, we naturally think of the fields, woodlots and forests of America.

No meal of the entire year is more typically and truly American than this with its turkey, potatoes, squash, cranberry sauce and pumpkin pie. All of these original products of the American wilderness were the Indians' gifts to the white man.

At this time of year, no bird is more thought of than the turkey and it is satisfying to many bird-watchers and hunters alike, that the turkey is again a part of the Michigan wildlife scene.

The first mention of Michigan turkeys was made in a letter by Father Marquette in 1670. From that time until the latter part of the nineteenth century this majestic bird was a conspicuous part of the wilderness scene of Michigan. It was common throughout the state, but especially abundant in the southern two-thirds of the Lower Peninsula.

With the turn of the century, the turkey passed from the woods of our state, and it was not until the last few years that, through the efforts of the Michigan State Conservation Department and game men, it is once more possible to see these large wildfowl in Michigan's wild acres.

Although the first mention of the turkey was in 1670, the bird was found in Michigan's territory long before that, as finds of bones in an ash pit in the Lapeer area places the bird here in pre-Columbian times, two or three centuries before America's discovery by white men.

Few Michigan birds give a greater thrill to the bird-watcher or woods-wanderer than a flock of these majestic, beautifully colored fowl strolling about or feeding in the autumn woodland.

But the turkey is only a part of the great American feast on Thanksgiving. Potatoes, likewise, are American. Although they are called "Irish," that is a grave mistake, for they came to us from South and Central American Indians where they were known as "batato" (sweet potato) and "papa" for the white.

The Incan words were corrupted into the popular term we use, "potato." Actually, the origin and early history of the potato is lost in antiquity, but after the coming of the white man it was carried to England, where it was shunned by Englishmen as fit only for cattle but taken over as a healthful food in Ireland. From there it came back to America by way of New England.

Then there is the squash, a truly Indian word coming from the Algonquin "askott asquash" and a real American, ancient Peruvian plant. It is believed these were cultivated by Central American Indians long before Columbian times and some authorities assert that there have been no "new types" since then. Ancient ceramics, clay tiles, depict many kinds which are still common in our garden and markets. Gourds, along with pumpkins, belong in the same family with the squashes.

Along with the turkey, potatoes, squash and pumpkin, we should not overlook the cranberry, for that is found in our own Michigan wetlands.

As we enjoy this year's Thanksgiving feast, may we be a little more thankful for our own natural resources which have made possible this day and this particular All-American meal, and may we review our determination to preserve the resources with which our country has been so greatly blessed.

# RARE FALCON HERE

While hunters were afield for deer and game birds and fishermen luring salmon, west Michigan birders were after a far greater trophy — the sight of a gyrfalcon at the Muskegon Wastewater System, during the past weekend.

This rare and exciting bird was seen Friday, and soon the word went out over the Birder's Hot Line to other areas in western Michigan. The prize bird conveniently remained over the weekend so that Saturday delegations came from Grand Rapids, Grand Haven and other communities to see it.

This excitement was all caused by the arrival of this unusual falcon, because as far as records show, this is its first appearance here. In fact, it is seldom seen in Michigan, although last winter one did spend several weeks at Sault Ste. Marie in the Upper Peninsula.

"Michigan Bird Life" in 1912 lists the gyrfalcon on the "hypothetical list," mentioning no authentic specimen, but commenting that in "Birds of Keweenaw Point" (1857), Dr. S. Kneeland says, "I have heard of a white falcon of large size (five feet in wing spread) which was shot on the point; this, I think, must have been a gyrfalcon." Checklist of "Birds of Michigan" (Zimmerman and Van Tyne-1959) adds that there is one record: Chippewa County, Sault Ste. Marie, a female collected January 21, 1932, by W. Welch and it is preserved in the University of Michigan Department of Zoology.

With last year's bird in the same area, this gives some indication of the rarity of the species in Michigan and the thrill of seeing one in the county.

The gyrfalcon is the largest of the North American falcons and is related to the tiny sparrow hawk (kestrel), the pigeon hawk (merlin), and the peregrine, all of which occur in Michigan.

They are distinguished from other hawks by their streamlined form, long pointed wings, large heads and tails that narrow toward the tip. They are the swiftest and most picturesque of the diurnal birds of prey. As might be expected, because of their speed, spirit, power, strongly taloned feet and powerful hooked beaks, they were favorites of the medieval falconers. It is from them that the "sport of kings" takes its name.

The rare gyrfalcon is a bird of the far north, breeding in Alaska, northern Canada, Greenland, Iceland, northern Scandinavia, Russia and Siberia. In North America in winter it wanders erratically southward to southern Canada and very rarely into the United States.

There are three color phases in the gyrfalcon and now they are considered one species. There is the dark phase, the white and an intermediate gray. Because of this, the light phase birds are sometimes confused with snowy owls and the dark, with immature peregrines; however, a careful study of field marks makes identification less confusing. It is the largest of the falcons, and more uniformly colored than the peregrine, and the dark cap and mustache are absent or indistinct. The somewhat slower wing beats of the gyrfalcon are almost gull-like.

Birders seeing the Wastewater bird were delighted to see it both in flight and perched, so that there was ample opportunity to observe it and iden- tify it as an immature bird. The feet of the adults are usually yellow, while those of the immatures are blue or grayish.

The appearance of this bird here in Muskegon County will mark November, 1979, as a red-letter month in many birders' journals, and for most who saw it, it was a "lifer" to be added to the ever-growing "life list."

Other November arrivals this past week in time for Thanksgiving were two snowy owls in the Causeway — Cobb plant area and a flock of twenty evening grosbeaks at Pere Marquette Park, bathing in a mud puddle at the corner of Indiana and Nelson Streets and feeding at neighborhood stations. Last year was poor here for evening grosbeaks, but perhaps these arrivals presage an invasion from the north. These birds, like other northerners, are inclined to be cyclic in their occurrence in the United States in winter. If they are on the way, better stock up on sunflower seeds, for they are gluttons.

BIRDS SETTLE DOWN TO ROUTINE

Bird life is settling down to the steady routine of winter months from which it will be disturbed only occasionally now with the invasion of north- ern species on the wings of arctic storms.

Most summer residents have left western Michigan and Muskegon coun- try for their winter vacationlands in the gulf states, Mexico, Central and South America. Florida draws a great number of migrant birds as it does humans during the months of the northern cold.

First of these summer favorites to leave and slip away almost unnoticed in early September were such winged insect eaters as the chimney swift, nighthawk and whip-poor-will. About the same time, hummingbirds disap- peared from gardens and parks and will not again be seen here until after mid-May. Among the last of the summer residents to leave is the woodcock, and sometimes these woodland elves remain until the middle of December if the ground is unfrozen so they can probe for worms, their favorite fare.

With the departure of this group of summer birds, the permanent residents receive more attention by the bird-watcher than they have had for months. These are the "old faithful" jays, nuthatches, chickadees, goldfinches, horned larks, red-headed woodpeckers, downies and hairies. The familiar gull flock about Muskegon Lake and the breakwater has been greatly augmented lately by the arrival of mature gulls and their brownish gray youngsters from the nesting grounds in northern Lake Michigan.

Added to these constant friends which are about for the twelve months, the group of winter visitors have moved into Muskegon and western Michigan for the next few months. Among the first to arrive this year were the kinglets, ruby and golden-crowned, the red-breasted nuthatch, and brown creepers. Many creepers have left. Two early arrivals this season were pine siskins and snowy owls, one of which was seen in late October, another in November. A great invasion of snowies is not expected this year. Contrasted with the early arrival of the great white owls was the late record for whistling swans which were observed on Muskegon Lake the third week of November.

As the weather becomes inclement and snow and ice storms become plentiful, the winter birds will be looking for lunch counters at the home yards of their friends. One Muskegon resident reported fourteen different species feeding at her station last year.

Few winter activities offer more interest to shut-ins, children and bird-watchers than the establishment of a bird lunch counter near one's window. Photographers often find good subjects near at hand through bird-feeding.

BIRDS NEED FOOD

November marks the time when friends of the birds should begin to think of winter-feeding. Now is the time to get out the feeding stations and look them over, repairing and perhaps even improving them.

The mild, sunny weather of the past month tends to make us forget that winter is not far away, and that soon the birds will be unable to find enough natural food. It is with the coming of winter with its ice, snow and sleet that the birds have come to depend upon their human friends.

Generally speaking, there are two classes of birds which may be aided by feeding stations. These are the insect-eaters and the seed-eaters. Few feeds that can be provided are more satisfactory to the insect-eaters than suet. There are many kinds of practical suet and meat scrap containers which these birds will patronize, but one of the most simple and equally effective is a mesh soap shaker which can be obtained at any variety store. These, filled with suet and hung conveniently in a tree, not only satisfy such birds as the downy and hairy woodpeckers, the chickadees and the nuthatches, but also satisfy the human host because of the many antics that are performed by the bird guests about it. This device also helps because it prohibits a large bird such as the blue jay from snatching and flying away with all the bounty.

The seed-eaters are not choosy, and a great variety of grains and seeds appeal to them. Cracked corn, millet, sunflower seeds, hemp, barley, oatmeal, grapenuts and raisins are just a few of the foods which satisfy these birds in winter. Corn on the cob tied to branches or stuck on nails in a post is sure to attract blue jays and cardinals.

Grit and water are just as essential for birds in winter. This is important to remember and to add these to the menu card.

Many of the winter birds are ground feeders such as the quail, pheasant, grouse, junco, snow bunting, redpoll and titlark, and for these it is well to keep a feeding area swept clean of snow. The grains and scraps can be scattered over this area, and grateful birds are sure to find it. It is important to select a spot from which hungry cats and similar bird enemies cannot easily pounce upon the visitors while they are feeding.

So, get out the last year's feeding station and renovate it, or select a choice place not too far out of range of your favorite window for your brand new station which you are initiating this season.

WINTER BIRDS HERE

Juncos have been arriving from their northern nesting grounds for several weeks. They have been feeding on weed seeds and grasses. Now flocks of them are coming, and it is time to supplement their natural food with handouts if you want them to be around this winter.

Most of the small, migratory summer residents have gone south and there is little chance of delaying them, but the winter visitors are on the way.

Chickadees, among the more delightful of patrons, are coming in from the forest and woodlots and visiting old feeder haunts. Jays, cardinals, and even woodpeckers are checking up on possibilities for lunch counters. By

Thanksgiving these will all have their feeding routes well established, and if you wish to be on their itinerary, now is the time to invite them.

Remember that the birds you can attract feed in three ways. Some are insect eaters, some are seed eaters, and others are omnivorous. It is important to supply food for all. Suet, meat scraps and peanut butter are suitable for the insect eaters. Most bird enthusiasts have their own favorite way of offering these delicacies.

The seed eaters take a wide variety of plant material — scratch feed, mixes, sunflower seed, and corn, both cracked and on the cob, are a few suggestions. The thistle seed, so popular for specialized feeders, is difficult to get this year because the crop from India is not coming into the United States. Canary seed may provide a successful substitute.

The omnivorous feeders will help themselves to both menus and will also thank you for table scraps, dried raisins, pumpkin, squash, melon seeds, and any other tidbits you wish to offer.

Hosts should also remember some birds are hesitant about eating off the snow-covered ground, so food should be scattered on a clearly swept area for them.

Some are bark tenders, and since most of these are insect eaters, bags of suet hung on the larger branches will entice them. There are many types of feeders and most bird-watchers have their own preferences.

Many like their lunch counters near windows where they may watch the antics of their favorites. In any case, if the feeder is not a wing type to adjust to wind direction, then it should be placed in a somewhat protected spot. This is important, for some are placed in such exposed locations that birds have to buffet the wind and are actually blown from the feeder.

There are many refinements to winter bird feeding which you learn as you continue the hobby. With time and study, it is possible to attract as many as twenty species.

Also remember that bringing large concentrations of small birds together for winter feeding can invite raptors, such as hawks and owls. But don't be disturbed if they appear. Blue jays are good scouts, and will sound the alarm if these large birds arrive. They also will police your premises for cats, dogs and other intruders.

## SNOW BUNTINGS COME

Winter is not here according to the calendar, but the arrival of hundreds of small white birds — snow buntings — from the north tells a different story. The buntings long have been considered the harbingers of winter, just as robins and bluebirds tell of spring.

Numerous reports from widely separated parts of the county told that these cherry little snowbirds arrived ahead of winter's blizzards and sleet storms.

Mid-November is early for these audacious, storm-loving little north-erners to arrive, but so numerous have been the reports of them, as well as of the snowy owls, about the county that indications point this year to an early migration of the winter visitant species.

It will be interesting to learn if the evening grosbecks return this season. Last year there were no reports of them in the county, but the year before there were many, and one bird was known to stay as late as April and was seen at the Causeway Memorial Park.

Snowbirds, or buntings, usually ride in on the blasts of winter just ahead of storms and blizzards. In their whirling, swirling flight, in large flocks of sometimes hundreds, they seem not unlike their namesakes, the snow flakes, as they eddy and twirl about on the air currents and frolic about windswept fields and vacant lots.

The snow buntings breed in the far north from Labrador and Hudson Bay northward and are seldom out of the sight of snow during their lives. They are arctic birds which visit us only in the winter. They are closely related to the beautiful bluebird and indigo bunting, which nest here in summer. Their general body shape is similar. The body, wings, and tail are predominantly white which contrasts attractively with the black and brown markings of the neck and head and back.

They are jolly little winter sprites, and no amount of cold or storm seems to disconcert them as long as they can find food. Their food is chiefly weed seeds for which they search unceasingly. Perched on a dried weed stalk above a snow drift, they are often seen pecking away, securing the tiny seeds which would annoy the gardener next year. They are very beneficial because of their feeding habits. On the snowy carpet, their light plumage protects them against predacious enemies.

Deserted meadows, vacant pastures and waste lots which offer an abun-dance of weed seeds are their favorite spots, but the grasses of Muskegon country's duneland also invite them when winter winds blow strongly, and lower plants are entirely blanketed by snow and sealed by ice.

These little winter visitors are "talkative," keeping up a persistent twit-ter while they feed. On the wing they have a sweet trilling whistle which is clear and bell-like, a lovely winter note.

They are gregarious, traveling at times congenially in flocks with horned larks, redpolls and longspurs.

With Indian summer scarcely past, the snowflakes are here.

## SWANS FOR A DAY

Traverse City is the Swan Capital of Michigan, but as in the old show, Muskegon was "Queen for a Day."

That day came in mid-November when thousands of swans stopped off here on their migratory flight. The real congregation was at the Wastewater System where an estimated five thousand were seen. Reports came from nearby lakes: Muskegon Lake had about 300; Black Lake 50 to 100; Bear Lake, Wolf Lake and others had their share. It was a swan weekend and it was the lucky birder who happened to see them from the warmth and comfort of home through the picture window. The real reward came, however, to those who willingly faced the snow flurries and slippery driving at the Wastewater to see "thousands," my largest sighting.

The beauty of the flight of these majestic birds is beyond description. One has to see them as they come winging in and alight on the water, accompanied by their characteristic calls.

These birds first thrilled me like this back in March, 1927, when on our honeymoon in Canada, Jack Miner took us from his Sanctuary over to nearby Lake Erie to see 1500. To me, a neophyte birder at that time, it was never forgotten.

Then a few years ago here a call came from Margie Botbyl that there was a big assembly of swans near Scottville in a farmer's field — of all things. It did not take us long to get there, and feeding in a cornfield were two to three thousand — now, right here in Muskegon County, this record invasion.

There are two species of swans in Michigan — the mute and whistling. The Traverse City ones, for the most part, are mutes, similar to the often seen "park swans" and the Old World swan of England. These are those commonly seen on the River Avon, both in England and Canada, and on the British Canals. These birds for years could be owned only by the Royal Family and selected guilds. There annually was a swan-dipping on the River Thames to mark the royal birds and separate those of the guilds.

Among the Muskegon visitors there were comparatively few mute swans. Most were the whistling swans, native to America and breeding in the Far North. The two species are easily distinguishable. The mute has

211

a yellow bill with a black knob at the base, whereas the whistling has a black bill; the mute holds its neck in a S-curve, while the other is straight. There are other helpful field marks. The immatures or cygnets of both species may be confusing because both have dusky pinkish bills.

The whistling call is muffled and musical and is often mistaken for that of Canada geese. The mute is usually silent, but does have a twanging note and will hiss or snort when disturbed. The mute often points its bill downward when swimming, while the whistling usually carries its level.

Mute swans tend to be non-migratory but where there are large concentrations, they leave the group and colonize, thus spreading their range.

America's whistling swans generally winter on the two coasts, ours going to the central Atlantic coast, seldom to Florida. A few may stay on the Great Lakes from time to time depending on weather conditions. This year Muskegon's Swan Festival came in mid-November and fortunate were those birders who attended.

# DECEMBER

## MUSKEGON COUNTRY FORESTS GREEN

Contrary to popular belief, although the verdure of the forests has disappeared, and dead, brown leaves carpet the floor of the woodland, Muskegon country forests are still green.

Many plants, which during the spring and summer months go unnoticed because of their evergreen habit, are more conspicuous now in early winter woodlands.

Of these, many belong to the floral family of heaths and are cousins of the trailing arbutus and huckleberry. As a rule, their leaves are roughly oval-shaped and thick. Some are protected with mats of hair or down on the undersurface, others have waxy coating and still others have rolled edges. All of these devices help prepare them for winter by reducing evaporation and regulating temperature.

The best known of these little evergreens are the arbutus and common wintergreen. In addition to these, the Muskegon State Park and similar places in duneland reveal prince's pine, shin leaf and pyrola. Some of these may still bear their fruits which are used by ground feeding birds.

Bearberry, a glossy green ground cover found especially in sandy stretches along the lake shore, is another member of this family which remains green all winter and furnishes food for wanderers with its bright red mealy berries.

Squawberry or partridgeberry is a plant which keeps green during the "long cold." In recent years this plant has become very popular as the foundation plant in "winter gardens," terraria and Wardian jars. The brilliant red berries persist all winter and are attractive against the fresh greenness of the foliage.

The club mosses also are favorites of the winter gardener. Several species of these grow in Muskegon country and western Michigan, but now care must be taken in gathering them because they are protected by law. It is illegal to gather, possess or vend them without the written permission from the owner of the property from which they are taken. This legislation became necessary and was supported by the Michigan Wildflower Association and Michigan United Conservation Clubs because great inroads had been made on these slow-growing plants by persons who gathered them carelessly and ruthlessly.

These mosses are known by a variety of names such as deer-horn moss, ground cedar, ground hemlock, ground pine and creeping Charley or Jennie. They are closely related to the ferns although called "mosses." They reproduce by means of small spores which are formed in cone-like receptacles on upright stalks.

Club mosses are found throughout the area although they are locally distributed. Where they are allowed to grow undisturbed, such as in the State Parks, they make the loveliest of green winter carpets. Care must be taken to preserve them here and elsewhere throughout the state.

## MICHIGAN'S OWN HOLLY

If planning porch boxes ornamented with Michigan holly and evergreens for this winter season, one better be sure he knows the source of the plants. Both the brilliant-berried shrub and the native conifers are on the state's protected list of plants.

Only twelve are specifically listed, but among those which are tempting to the autumn woods-wanderer are the climbing bittersweet, native holly, evergreens and club mosses. All of these in the past have been used extensively in decorative pieces and garlands for the holiday season.

Remember it is necessary to have written permission from the owner of the property from which the plants are taken or purchased. This is not always an easy matter, for in western Michigan swamps and marshes where holly grows, the owner may live miles away, in which case "better leave the pretty berries where they are for winter bird food."

The attractive berries of the swamp are delightfully gay and do add a colorful note to winter porch boxes. One is correct in calling this shrub a holly although with the coming of autumn its leaves fall to the ground. It belongs to the same floral family as the spiny American plant of the south and west and the European relative. Ours is a first cousin to these and all belong to the genus Ilex which indicates hollies.

Although locally the deciduous one is known as Michigan holly, in other parts of its range throughout northeastern United States it is called winterberry and black alder, and fever bush. This last name comes from its use in the early colonial days to assuage fevers. The berries also were used as a vermifuge and tonic.

The winterberry shrub is a lover of low, moist places, thriving in swamps and along well-watered ditches. The small, inconspicuous whitish flowers appear in May and early June and later give way to the attractive, bright, glossy red berries for which the plant is best known.

If one really wants winterberries, he will find them hardy and easily cultivated. They would make a delightfully attractive border planting, displaying their scarlet berries on black twigs against a background of a snowy garden or yard. An added bonus would be berries for all one's wants.

## CARDINALS ADD TO CHRISTMAS

The cardinal, the Bird of Christmas, comes into its own at this time of year. It is beloved by both rural and urban residents alike, as it visits feeding stations and remains during the long, cold months of winter. It is a bright, happy sight against the winter greenery amid ice and snow.

It is not surprising that it has become a favorite subject for holiday cards and has been used for years to bring America's season's greetings to friends and relatives the world around. The cardinal is our contribution to the aviary of Christmas, taking its place with the robin of Britain, the sparrows of Scandinavia and the doves of Italy.

It is a bird closely associated with humans, for it is easily attracted to feeding stations. It prefers the yard shrubbery and climbing vines of houses and outbuildings to the wilder places in woodland and forest. A bird of the suburbs, the cardinal moves in as soon as homes are established and landscaping done.

At the beginning of the century, the cardinal was considered a southern species; it has been consistently extending its range, until it is now at home in most of the states east of the Mississippi, from the gulf to the northern tier of the states. It is not common in Michigan's Upper Peninsula and is only scattered in locales north of the Muskegon-Saginaw line.

So popular has the cardinal been in the south in years past that it is the official state bird of seven states: Illinois, Indiana, Ohio, Kentucky, North Carolina, Virginia, and West Virginia. It was also the subject of two books a generation ago, "The Kentucky Cardinal" by J. L. Allen and "The Song of the Cardinal" by Gene Stratton Porter.

215

Cardinals found about here are non-migratory and spend the winter in the area, taking advantage of feeding stations whenever possible. They are omnivorous feeders and that makes it easier for them to subsist on a variety of food. They eat weed seeds when they are available, and buds if the snow is deep. In rural sections they visit grain and corn fields and glean the leftovers. When seeds cannot be obtained, they seek out the fruit on trees and shrubs and feast upon the persistent berries.

To encourage them to feeding stations, cracked corn and sunflower seeds are the ideal invitation. Few local stations are without these colorful birds at some time during the winter. In fact, so common are they in winter that they have appeared on the Christmas Bird Count list here every year since it was inaugurated in 1929-30. Many birds are erratic and come and go over the years like the evening grosbeak, siskins, redpolls and other finches, but the cardinals are constant friends. Like chickadees, they can be trained to take seeds from the open palm of a friendly human.

To insure the presence of the redbirds during their breeding season in summer, plant shrubs, vines and trees that will offer them both protection and nesting sites. Plants that attract them are autumn olive, hackberry, dogwood, evergreen, cotoneaster, firethorn, multiflora roses, other berried shrubs and trumpet vines. Leaving deadheads in the floral garden border will attract them in winter. Cosmos, marigolds, bachelor buttons and other members of the daisy family offer them food. Sunflowers are among their choice foods and they vie with the goldfinches in getting them.

Cardinals are seldom seen on the ground and prefer the height of bushes and low branches of trees. One observer comments on the male as being "an aristocrat, a shining example of self-conscious superiority." One has this feeling when he alights on the feeding tray and will not allow his little mate to eat until he finishes. In the spring, however, he is full of gallantry and even offers her a seed now and then from the tray.

Most female birds do not sing, but the cardinal is an outstanding exception. She has a lovely soft voice, even more musical than his. "Good cheer, cheer, come here, here, my dear, dear." This is the coaxing invitation she hears from him in the spring when nesting time is near. Often they choose a situation close to the house where they have fed during the winter, and sometimes they build so near it is possible to watch the incubation, hatching, feeding and fledging of the youngsters.

They are devoted parents and their family life is exemplary. It is not uncommon for one pair to raise two broods and occasionally even three. When youngsters appear late in September as they did this past autumn, they were undoubtedly the results of a third brood. Since they are non-migratory, they can survive as long as food and shelter are available.

Whether or not you are a bird-feeder enthusiast, may you have many happy glimpses of the Christmas Bird as the winter holiday season comes and goes.

## HOLIDAY TREES

Today trees are as much a part of the Christmas celebration as the star, candle and even the gifts.

This has not always been true, however, for the tree being brought indoors and decorated is a comparatively recent adjunct to the Christmas festival.

It is not, however, a modern part of the celebration of the winter holidays. Even in ancient Egyptian times, during the winter solstice rites, green date palms were brought inside as symbolical of life triumphant over death.

Similarly trees were brought inside by Romans at Saturnalia and were trimmed with trinkets and small masks of Bacchus. The Roman poet, Virgil, wrote of trimming trees with swinging toys.

In Northern Europe, the Druids trimmed trees with golden apples honoring Odin for the favors he conferred upon them through the variety of fruits they had.

In fact, it was because of these early heathen rites connected with trees at the winter holidays that the early Christians refused to allow their use at the celebration of the birthday of Jesus.

The origin of the Christmas tree as a Christian symbol is shrouded in doubt. One of the two more common traditions has it that Winfried, a missionary from England to the Continent, arrived in Germany just in time to see a youth being offered as a sacrifice at the Thunder Oak. The story is unfolded by Henry VanDyke in his "First Christmas Tree" and tells how the young man's life was saved and the evergreen tree replaced the heathen's oak.

The more familiar story is that Martin Luther, coming from church service on Christmas Eve, saw a beautiful fir tree bedecked with snow and frost under the starlit sky. He was so impressed with it that he wanted to share the beauty with his family, so he cut it down, took it home and placed lighted candles upon it to represent the starry sky above the manger at Bethlehem.

Since both of these stories place the origin of the first Christmas tree in

Germany, it is not surprising that it came to England and America through the German immigrants.

In 1829 a German, Princess Lieven, had a holiday party for her children in London and used a tree. It was not until 1841 when Prince Albert, consort of Queen Victoria, set up a tree for the children in Windsor Castle, that the custom really caught on in England.

Tradition says that the homesick Hessians fighting in the Revolutionary War were celebrating around a Christmas tree while Washington's forces were suffering at Valley Forge.

The popularity of the Christmas tree in the United States is usually attributed to August Imgard of Wooster, Ohio, although Charles Follen set one at his home in Cambridge in 1832. It was Imgard's tree, in 1847, that really introduced the custom of the tree to middle America and within a few years the idea was accepted throughout the midwest. From there it went both East and West, so that by 1891, President Benjamin Harrison set up a tree in the White House, played Santa Claus for his grandchildren and mentioned the custom as old-fashioned.

On the West Coast, Christmas Tree Lane was established at Altadena, and the General Grant Sequoia was named the Nation's Christmas Tree.

Now, annually, a tree is lighted on the lawn at the White House in a nationwide ceremony.

The majority of homes now have Christmas trees. Michigan is nicknamed The Christmas Tree State, because of the tremendous annual harvest of evergreens here. Muskegon Heights since 1965, when Lois Lenski wrote of our own Christmas tree farming here, is "the Christmas Tree Town" to her readers around the world.

Christmas trees may be of many kinds — fir, pine, spruce or even juniper and cedar. Firs are favorites because they are especially aromatic, retain their needles, are shapely and are easy to handle. Spruces are popular, and red pines are favorites with some because of their shapeliness and sturdy needles which make decorating them easy. Each kind has its own devotees. Be it fir, spruce or pine it will find its place of honor and be beautified for the celebration of the Christ Child's birth.

After the Twelve Days of Christmas, perhaps it can move outside and become a bird feeder for the rest of the winter. "O Christmas Tree, O Christmas Tree, how sturdy God hath made thee."

# DISCARDED CHRISTMAS TREES

Discarded holiday trees should present no problem for the bird lover. Few devices for winter offer better opportunity for shelter and food than do these Christmas trees when they are cared for out of doors.

Having chosen a suitable placement for the tree, where it is reasonably protected from severe winds and storms which would disturb it, one may attach many kinds of food to it.

Festooning the branches with strings of peanuts, cranberries, popcorn and suet makes a very popular feeding station. Additional food scraps and bones may also be tied to the tree.

One of the satisfactory types of winter food which can be served from the tree is a mixture poured over its branches and needles when hot and allowed to cool and harden. This has been used with great success, not only in this country but in Europe, where it is a favorite method. Quantities of dry feed such as cracked corn, cereals, millet, hemp, meat scraps, nuts, seeds and dried berries are added to suet which is melted over a slow fire. After the suet is melted, the dry ingredients are stirred in and the whole is then brought to a boil. After the mixture is removed from the stove, it is cooled slightly and poured over the entire tree. When hardened, this provides an excellent source of winter feeding for native birds of both the seed-eating and insectivorous types. The seeds imbedded in the suet offer exercise and a natural diet for the seekers.

Extra shelter may be provided during the winter months by tying several discarded trees together and arranging them as wigwams. These are especially attractive to ground birds such as juncos, quail, pheasants, longspurs and snow buntings.

# HOLIDAY GIFTS TO BIRDS

Christmas giving, it is pretty generally agreed, should not be confined to one's kinsfolk and closest friends. In times like these, when so many of our unknown neighbors are needy, our bounty must overflow the boundaries of our immediate acquaintance.

It may require a little sacrifice to bring a measure of Christmas cheer to our hardpressed human neighbors, but it can cost us practically nothing at all to distribute largesse to our lesser brothers, the winter birds.

They will be glad for the crumbs from the table, or for the scraps of suet trimmed from a roast before it is put into the oven. A simple pan of water, warmed up to the temperature of good, hot coffee so that it will not freeze so quickly, will be high wassail for them.

Birds will accept your gifts gratefully even if they are only tossed out on the ground or the crusted surface of frozen snow. It is better, though, to provide some kind of feeding tray, preferably in some corner with shelter from the wind, and as far as possible out of the reach of prowling cats. Food on such a tray will not be wasted through scattering or by burial in loose snow.

Suet is especially prized by birds. It is one of the best of fuel-foods, to keep their small bodies warm against the cold to which they are always exposed, even on relatively good winter days.

This should be secured in some way to prevent a whole lump from being carried off and monopolized by one greedy individual. Squirrels are fond of suet, too, and will steal the birds' supply if they get a chance. Many persons make a kind of suet pudding by melting the suet, adding raisins, cracked grain and other things that birds like, and pouring the mixture into a half coconut shell or some other container to harden. Hung on a wire, this is difficult for squirrels to get at, and no bird can get more than a fair beakful at a time.

A much simpler suet-holder can be made of an old-fashioned wire soap-dish. This can be hinged against a tree trunk with a couple of staples or bent-over nails, with another bent nail on the other side left free to turn as a latch. Birds are able to peck out the suet through the meshes, but squirrels find the cage completely inaccessible.

DON'T FORGET THE LITTLE BEASTS

Since the early snows have come, have you noticed that there are neighbors you were unaware of? They leave their calling cards in their tracks. Squirrels, rabbits, opossum and mice are among those that have visited me during the last few days and nights.

When winter comes, many of our mammals, or "beasts" as our British cousins call them to distinguish them from other animals, have a most difficult time. A very few, such as one of the bats, migrate. A larger group, a traditional seven, sleep much of the winter away and the others try hard to eke out an existence during the long cold months of winter.

Food put out for the beasts will help them through the winter. Mine like carrots, celery tops, apples, corn, lettuce and table scraps. It is important to feed them in a different place from where one entertains birds. My front dooryard is "for the birds," the dune-bordered back for the beasts. A brush shelter will help to protect them and is a good place to establish a feeding ground.

The sleepers are the smart ones, for they curl up in a comfortable den or hollow and forget about the cold. Just as with humans, there are sound and light sleepers and the restless ones often wake up and fare forth looking for a snack between naps.

The bats which do not migrate are among the very heavy sleepers and only a heightening of the temperature will raise them. Even handling does not interrupt their slumber. There are eight species of bats in Michigan.

Bears are fairly heavy sleepers, and it is usually during the hibernation period that the cubs are born. They are blind and almost hairless and from six to eight inches long.

The jumping mice, of which there are two kinds in Michigan, the meadow and woodland jumpers, are great sleepy heads. They go to bed early and lie abed until late. Both are characterized by their long tails and large, strong hind feet. They are climbers and can leap five or six feet, many times their own length.

Completing the quartet of sleepy heads is the woodchuck or groundhog. He is a sound sleeper and don't let anyone tell you he comes out in Michigan on Feb. 2. Don't expect your favorite woodchuck out until late March, if it is unseasonably warm, or April.

The chipmunk, along with the flying squirrel and spermophile (gopher), is a light sleeper. On a warm, sunny winter day he may scoot out to search about and replenish his winter food supply, just as we humans watch for a good day to make a grocery run. Two fairly warm, sunny days in February are sure to bring these little sprites out of their burrows to do some early spring housecleaning.

Raccoons and skunks are also light sleepers. They leave their tell-tale tracks about on moonlit winter nights. They welcome handouts, along with the opossum, who does not know about hibernation and forages all winter. Often opossum pay the price of frozen ears and a frosted tail. There is something about an opossum more than most other beasts that arouses my pity. Few humans like them, except as a "main dish" with sweet potatoes. But they appeal to me, perhaps because they're surely "the low man on the totem pole."

If you are fortunate enough to live in a rural section, your visitors may include mink, weasels, and even a fox or badger. Deer become venturesome in winter and their tracks are sometimes close to human habitations and barnyards.

The muskrats and beaver are in their lodges and literally eat themselves out of house and home during the winter, so that in the spring the roof is apt to cave in at the least provocation.

Many squirrels patronize bird-feeding stations, much to the disgust of some hosts. Perhaps with a little encouragement they can be lured to another spot about the yard where their cousin beasts are feasting. At least it is worth issuing the invitation. I find the squirrels eat in my backyard by day and the possum and rabbits by night — at least that is what the tracks tell me.

## MISTLETOE AND HOLLY

Holly, beloved by old and young alike, has come down to this generation as a Christmas gift from Merrie England.

In England there can scarcely be found a time when it was not a part of the holiday season's decoration.

The exact origin of the holly for holiday use is lost in the darkness of antiquity but one of the early names by which it was known was "holt" or "Holy" tree which later came to have the familiar variation we now know as "holly."

In both the Old and the New World many legends and charms have attached themselves to this tree. With its sharp glossy green leaves and brilliant red berries, it has become an important part in the world's Christmas celebration.

Holly is not confined to the Old World alone but is found throughout many states of America's South and West. In these parts the holly becomes a handsome, well shaped tree upwards of twenty feet tall, symmetrical and well-proportioned. The flowers are inconspicuous and to the less observant the flowering season in May is not even noted. It is when the brilliant red berries appear that the tree really comes into its own.

Our native holly, also called winterberry or black alder, is a food plant of wild game and is eaten by a variety of bird species also. It is a lover of moist places and wet swamps and the finest shrubs are found in almost inaccessible places.

Associated with the holly as a part of the Christmas celebration for unknown ages is the mistletoe. A very different plant from the holly this lives parasitically upon a variety of trees and shrubs. It is widely distributed throughout the world and is found in the southern and western states of America.

Like the holly, mistletoe has rather inconspicuous flowers and is best known for its waxy white berries which are beloved by birds. In fact, birds are the means of its distribution. After they eat the berries the seeds which adhere to their beaks are wiped off on the twigs and branches of trees, thus giving the mistletoe an opportunity to establish itself on a new host. Among American trees which are most subject to the mistletoe are apples, hawthorns, sycamore, lime, locust, poplar and oak.

Few plants have gathered as many traditions about themselves as has the mistletoe. It comes to us from ancient Druid times when it was used in their ceremonials. It was their custom to keep green things indoors as a refuge for the spirits of the wood, driven out by the severe cold and snow. Because of its association in these pagan ceremonies it was long forbidden in the English and Roman church.

If found growing in an oak tree and cut with a golden sword and the recital of certain incantations, Druids bestowed the mistletoe upon people for charms and it was to cure all diseases and to protect in numerous ways.

In Germany folklore claimed that to carry a sprig of mistletoe into an old house would waken the ghosts, and they would appear.

The name comes from the old Saxon "mistl-tan" which means "different twig," because this plant was different than the one on which it grew.

From the Norsemen comes the custom of kissing under the mistletoe. In an old legend the mistletoe promised never to do harm as long as it did not touch the ground. So it became the custom to hang it high up in the houses and to kiss one another under it, symbolizing happiness, safety and good fortune.

Mistletoe and holly, age-old symbols of the holiday season, have joined with such other plants as the evergreen trees, pine, fir and spruce and the brilliant tropical poinsettia to give the decorative background for the Christmas celebration.

APPRECIATE THE FRIENDLY SPARROWS

"April in December," is what we had last Sunday.

I felt it, but I was sure of it when I saw earthworms on the sidewalk, the street and the church parking lot. The mild weather had deceived them and they had come above ground, crawling about in the moisture and venturing far beyond their "diggings." Now they were stranded and could not find their way home.

These marooned worms were becoming the tasty prey of numerous house sparrows, who now had no competition from the robins that have already migrated. They were having a belated thanksgiving feast and they were chirping their thanks as they called others of their friends and relatives to the meal.

Few birds are as ingenious as these house sparrows. It is these qualities which have tended to make them one of the more successful species in America — and the world.

They have an interesting history here in the United States. They have only been here 130 years and were deliberately brought to New York City to rid that area of cankerworms and other insect pests. With the large population there, most of the native birds of marsh, field and woodland had left and insects had become a plague to green foliage everywhere.

Eight pairs were imported from England in 1850, but it was so late in the year when they were liberated they did not have time to adjust to the new land and died. Then, $200 was raised by the citizens. In 1852 Mr. Nicholas Pike, director of the Brooklyn Institute, was enroute to Portugal as consul-general. He was given the money and commissioned to stop in England and make arrangements for a consignment of sparrows to be shipped from Liverpool.

On their arrival here, half of them (50) were released at once and the others were wintered over in the tower of Greenwood Cemetery, Brooklyn. A caretaker was hired to look after them. In the spring they were set free. To the delight of all they accepted their new homeland and built nests and hatched the first clutches of "American House Sparrows."

Cities across the country, where the native birds had deserted, ordered and received shipments of sparrows from abroad. They prospered, not only in cities, but spread out into the rural section and followed the new railroads westward. By 1899 these little immigrants were living in 35 of the 38 states that made up the United States and five territories.

They were called English sparrows, because of their origin, but this is a misnomer, for they are natives of the Mediterranean lands and are not "sparrows," but rather weaver-birds. They are quite unrelated to our native sparrows, which belong to the finch and bunting family.

224

By the turn of the century, opinions differed on these small brown birds and in the farmlands they were injurious. Bounties were placed on them and sparrow-kills were not uncommon. However, they survived all this and are an important part of our avifauna after 130 years. They are the predominant species in many of the heavily populated cities and share that honor with pigeons (rock doves), another foreign bird.

I hear many birders who maintain winter feeding stations for birds complain about the sparrows and their abundance. My answer is usually, "What's wrong with them? They're birds, aren't they — and they get hungry?" The complainer always has a host of answers — usually none is complimentary.

This fellow is a very interesting bird and really deserves a bit of study on the part of the bird-watcher. For the most part they are the only bird that uses their nest as a "home."

Most others consider it only a nursery, but house sparrows use theirs the year around and shelter in it in winter. Sparrows build unsightly nests of whatever is at hand, grass blades, strips of bark, paper, cellophane, string, thread, kleenex, plant down and feathers.

Untidy and unkempt as it may be on the outside, this bird home is the epitome of neatness and comfort in the inner room, which is lined with the softest of materials — one I found had 1,200 feathers.

Sparrows need this cozy nest because they have been known to breed during every month of the year. In fact last Saturday, a warm, sunny day, I was awakened by the spring-song of house sparrows from the hillside cottonwood tree. The sun appealed to them, but their normal breeding season is March through August. Their language is quite complex in that they have a large variety of calls.

If you are a birder and like to feed them in winter, do not be dismayed if house sparrows are your guests. Observe them carefully and learn all you can about them.

Children are alert observers and can be taught to record what they see with care and precision.

Don't overlook the sparrow guests at your feeder, for in the winter remember the old adage, "Constant friends are few," and be glad for their sprightly presence.

# THREE NEW SPECIES

The age of exploration and discovery is not gone as some would have us think. Young people, especially, sometimes think there is nothing left to be found, that all has been revealed.

However, this past year through the efforts of the Michigan Natural Features Inventory, three new species — two plants and one animal have been discovered. All of these were found in the Upper Peninsula.

Larry Master, zoologist working with the Michigan Natural Features Inventory, caught a smoky shrew in a pitfall trap on Sugar Island in Chippewa County. This little animal has six other relatives living in Michigan. They are little known by other than biologists because of their small size, secretive manners and nocturnal habits. They are the smallest of the state's mammals and are bloodthirsty little creatures, fierce and relentless in their pursuit of prey. Because of their small size, their carnivorous diet is mostly insects, although they have been known to kill a mouse twice their size.

The established Michigan shrews are: the masked, the saddle-backed, the water, the pigmy, the least and the short-tailed. Here the short-tailed is the most common and is sometimes called the mole-shrew because of its mole-like appearance, larger size and burrowing habit.

The newly-found smoky shrew is important among other reasons because it is the first terrestrial mammal to be discovered in Michigan in more than 60 years.

The two plants, a sedge and a coltsfoot, were both found by Don Henson of Manistique, also working for the MNFI and the U.S. Forest Service. Both were found in the Hiawatha National Forest. Both have relatives in the state. The newly-found coltsfoot is related to the sweet coltsfoot, which grows in swamps and wetlands with cream-colored flowers and palmate leaves. The new form named sagittatus, has arrow-shaped foliage. Both are members of the daisy family, Composites.

The third new species, a Carex, a sedge, is one of many of these plants found in the state. Here in duneland there are several of which three are common: the shore, the mat-forming and the slender. Sedges, as a group, can be distinguished from two other groups of plants by their triangular stems. Grasses and rushes are sometimes confused with them but rushes have round, unjointed stems and grasses have round, jointed stems, not triangular as in the Carex species.

There is a lovely, dainty little sedge, only a few inches tall, which is one of the early spring flowers to blossom. Often before even the hepaticas are flowering this tiny golden tufted plant will invite the bees.

There is a great thrill in finding new species in an area and always there will be the excitement of discovery, seeing a species for the first time.

## 50 YEARS SEES CHANGES IN BIRD WORLD

Stray robins, which often remain in Michigan throughout the winter, have been joined this year, because of unusual weather, by a number of other regular summer residents.

Red-headed woodpeckers, bluebirds, a mourning dove and a catbird have been reported in this region during the past week.

For the past few years, especially when the season has produced an abundance of beechnuts, red-headed woodpeckers have been seen here more and more frequently. This week they have been observed on Ransom Street, in Lakeside and at Port Sherman. These birds are very beneficial and should be encouraged to remain in the winter because at that season they feed to a great extent upon the eggs and larvae of obnoxious insect pests.

Bluebirds and robins frequently remain in and near the city for the entire year. Usually birds which do this are males and can be distinguished by their bright plumage.

For the past three years a robin has been observed at Port Sherman during the last week of the year. Birds find acceptable shelter in this region and enjoy the houses and food provided for them by residents.

Among the summer residents which have been loath to leave Muskegon this winter is a mourning dove. The bird has been seen near McGraft Park and is always alone. As a rule, these doves winter in the southern and gulf states and some of them go as far south as Panama.

Since this bird has remained here as late as January, without a doubt it will make an attempt to stay all winter and will have a difficult time when heavy snow comes. Residents near the park may help it through the winter by putting out feed.

Most unusual of the late bird residents of Muskegon is a catbird which has been seen repeatedly during the past few weeks. Catbirds generally leave this vicinity between October 10 and October 20 for their southern homes. They winter in the extreme southern states, in the Bahamas, Cuba, through Mexico into Panama.

These birds are lovers of thickets, underbrush and brushy woods. They often nest in tangles of grapevines, woodbine and similar climbers. They also like evergreens, so it is not surprising this remaining catbird should have chosen to spend Christmas in Port Sherman, for there it finds thickets, brambles and a scattering of evergreens.

Although the catbird is fond of insects and eats many in summer, its winter larder consists of a great variety of berries and other fruits.

With the protection afforded in this sheltered place, the pioneer catbird may successfully winter out and be sleek and spry in spite of the northern winter when its kin returns from the southland the latter part of April.

Now, birders, do not rush out to Port Sherman to see a catbird for your early 1983 list nor to McGraft Park for the dove. As far as I know they are not there, for the above was written and appeared in the *Muskegon Chronicle* on the Woods and Water and Wilds page edited by Ben East under the date January 2, 1932 — 51 years ago. My by-line then was Mrs. Paul A. Elliott, for that was before the days of women's lib.

Yes, in 50 years times have changed. Mourning doves, instead of being a rarity, now remain and patronize feeders by the scores — some say "hundreds." One rural resident had 62 feeding with his chickens last winter. Even in the city they visit lunch counters and for the past five winters I have had from two to 11 regulars at a feeder.

The catbird, which was such a treat in 1932, although not on the Christmas bird count this year, is frequently listed and is not an uncommon visitor at food stations.

Perhaps the status of the red-headed woodpecker has changed most of any of these birds mentioned in the last half century. Where at one time it was the most common of the area woodpeckers, it is now at a low ebb and not one was seen on the recent bird count. Its place seems to be taken by the red-bellied woodpecker, a southern form which is extending its range northwards. Each year more of these are reported here, both summer and winter.

Robins and bluebirds had a most difficult time last April when the late blizzard victimized so many of these new arrivals. Hundreds of both species died. However, it is gratifying to know that after this past breeding season they seem to have compensated for the misfortune. The robins raised several broods instead of the usual one or two, and the bluebirds successfully raised larger broods from increased clutches.

Final report from the area's Annual Christmas Bird Count showed 42 species of birds here and 7,666 individuals, including an addition of 2,000 (est.) common mergansers and a mixed flock of 300 gulls.

# ACKNOWLEDGEMENTS

Dana Printing Corporation, Muskegon, Michigan

E. Genevieve Gillette Nature Center, P.J. Hoffmaster State Park, Muskegon, Michigan

Frank Hannum

The Muskegon Chronicle

Muskegon County Museum

S.D. Warren Co., Muskegon, Michigan

# INDEX

231

# INDEX

233

# INDEX

# INDEX

# INDEX

# INDEX

# INDEX

# INDEX

# INDEX

# INDEX

244